Aidan Smith is the author of four previous books: *Heartfelt*, about a Hibby (himself) who turns Jambo; *Union Jock*, the same trick at international level played out across Hadrian's Wall; *Persevered*, how Hibs stopped Hibsing it and finally won the Scottish Cup; and *Bring Me the Sports Jacket of Arthur Montford*, a celebration of what makes Scottish football special. As a journalist he's won nine times at the Scottish Press Awards. He lives in Edinburgh with his wife and four children.

HIBS AT 150

DOWN THE SLOPE WITH FOOTBALL'S GREAT PIONEERS

AIDAN SMITH

For Sadie

First published in 2025 by
Arena, an imprint of
Birlinn Ltd
West Newington House
10 Newington Road
Edinburgh
EH9 1QS

www.birlinn.co.uk

ISBN 978 1 91375 925 4

British Library Cataloguing in Publication Data
A catalogue record for this book is available from the British Library.

Typeset by Initial Typesetting Services, Edinburgh

Printed and bound by MBM Print SCS Ltd, Glasgow

CONTENTS

ACKNOWLEDGEMENTS

WHILE THE bulk of this book draws on my own experiences as a Hibs supporter – and rather less as a match-day reporter in the Easter Road press box where I would be told off for the occasional partisan yelp – I am grateful to the authors of Hibs histories going back beyond my fandom, including John Campbell, Alan Lugton, John R. Mackay and Tom Wright. A big shout out, too, to the purple prose-smiths of that press box from a more lyrical era of sportswriting whose work is preserved in the British Newspaper Archive.

At Birlinn, thanks to Paul Smith and Andrew Simmons for their advice, encouragement and the belief I could climb that sloping pitch and reach 150 chapters, and to Ian Greensill for his usual masterful copyediting.

Most of all, thanks to my team at home: wife Lucy and the children, Archie, Stella, Sadie and Hector, for cheering from the sidelines even when I got stuck on 97 chapters and there seemed nothing more to say about Hibs. On holiday in France in the summer, passing through Paris, passing the umpteenth kid in the colours of the newly crowned champions of Europe, Hec quipped from the back of the car: 'We know a team who were made 150 years ago. PSG were only made last Tuesday.'

INTRODUCTION

ON CHRISTMAS Day 1875, Hibernian played their very first game of association football. Remarkably, they've made it to the sesquicentennial. 'Put that in your pipe and smoke it!' as we used to say, back in those nicotine-clogged days before the Clean Air Act. Put sesquicentennial in the title of this book? Well, I thought about it. The reaction, I'm sure, would have been: 'Ah, how very Hibs.'

I say remarkably because along the way, while on the – cliché alert – journey, there have been bumps in the road as well as a slope on the pitch. In 1891 they went kaput and a century later it almost happened again. But they're still around, entertaining fans like me, occasionally exciting, sometimes enraging, invariably ageing.

How, though, in marking those 150 years, to best describe the club to the unknowing? What to include as essential in the starter pack for those from Bogotá and Basildon who can't stop replaying clips of 'Sunshine on Leith' on YouTube and X and are curious about what else the Hibees might have going for them?

I've tried to come up with a few things which could enlighten. Great teams, great players, great triumphs. Also, because this isn't a hagiography or even a Hibby-ography, great humiliations, great disasters, great moments of unintentional comedy.

But I feel I've only scratched the surface. There's this super-gizmo called the Large Hadron Collider which smashes subatomic particles into each other and from the resulting nuclear debris might be able to unlock some of the mysteries of the universe. Yes, fine, whoopee, but could it answer this question: 'Why are Hibs *Hibs*?' I reckon that would jigger the mechanics, reducing the LHC to a wheezing, clanking heap.

This is not a Hibby-ography and nor is it a complete century-and-a-half narrative. There are books out there which tell the whole story or major on key chunks of it and they do their jobs well. My father, among other things, was a playwright. His best-loved play properly got going when the central character was accused of peddling 'too selective a view of history'. By all means, accuse me of this. Perhaps I've missed the moment when you and Hibs properly got going, your most cherished era. Sorry about that.

Me and Hibs properly got going in 1967. At first, even-handedly, I saw as much of Hearts as I did the Hibees, with 'lift-overs' at both places. Then Dad asked if I wanted to choose. Would it be green or maroon? A few factors influenced my decision – among them the alluring length of Peter Marinello's hair and the unalluring pong of Gorgie's breweries – but colour definitely came into it.

In Sunday school: 'There is a green hill far away . . .' On TV variety shows, Tom Jones: 'It's good to touch the green, green grass of home . . .' Meaning it most sincerely, Hughie Green. From America, escape-the-rat-race sitcom *Green Acres*. Frankenstein. Green Shield Stamps. On tins of peas: the Jolly Green Giant. John Buchan's *Greenmantle*. In comic books: Green Lantern, The Incredible Hulk. Cluedo's murderous minister the Reverend Green. For a boy in the late 1960s there was plenty of green around, much more than there was maroon.

This is personal and there's quite a lot in the book about my early fandom. That phase ran from Easter Road initiation to the last game in the old 18-team First Division. I was, as my O-grade and Higher results will bear out, hopelessly devoted.

Jotters were nicked from school to record Hibs' progress with a multi-shaded jumbo pen in the kind of obsessional spidery-scrawl detail that would have triggered intervention by an educational psychologist, if there had been any of them around. But hopefully he or she would have concluded: 'Regardless, this boy is having the time of his life with new discoveries and excitements every week.' I entered the world of work bang on the start of the Premier League. Both life and football got more serious after that. That must have been when I learned what 'cynical' meant, possibly not being able to spell it before.

The Premier League was Hibs-driven. Lots of things in football have been Hibs-initiated and Hibs-inspired and they're all here, along with others presented for the first time as further evidence, and to seal the deal, of what the old song says: 'There's not a team like the Edinburgh Hibees . . .'

Yes, I make grand claims. Yes, I occasionally get a bit carried away. Sesquicentennials, I find, have a habit of doing that. Pretentious, *moi*? *Un fan* de 'Eebernians', as Franck Sauzée would say? *Mais oui!* Now maybe this is a futile hope, given how tribal the game is now and how turnabouts are gone for good, but I'd like to think that fans of other clubs could get something from all of this. Dumbarton supporters are directed to chapters 11 and 20. Rangers supporters can have a chuckle at our expense in chapters 18 and 19 (but must be prepared to laugh at themselves as well). Jambos: you turn up a lot.

I began the book as Hibs were deep in the mire of their worst run of results for 40 years with yet another manager – and this time a Scottish Cup godhead in 'Sir' David Gray – seemingly set for the chop. Over and above that, football generally had been boring me for a while. At elite level: always overhyped, invariably underwhelming. At Scottish level: mandatory four-Old-Firm-games chokehold, vain efforts to catch up with the elites with inferior technology and passing rondos which come to a quick and dismal end.

But delving into the history of my club – disappearing down rabbit holes to resurface much later with flickering goals from long-lost Muirton and folkloric Cathkin and newspaper reportage in urgent yet poetic language that modern accounts have lost – some of the old excitements have returned. And out on the pitch the team's form has improved to such an extent that, as I write, Hibs are venturing out across the continent again, 70 years after they pioneered European football. I may have to get my kids to nick more jotters and find that jumbo pen . . .

1

FOUL DENS OF VICE AND DISEASE UNPARALLELED IN INFAMY

THEY COULD have concentrated on being a debating society. Majored on the activities of the choral union. Thrown themselves into the drama club or the minstrel troupe or the accordion band. Or simply hung around the smoking room most of the time, occasionally rousing themselves for a game of skittles, dominoes or draughts. But oh no. The Catholic Young Men's Society of St Patrick's Church in Edinburgh just had to go and play football, become Hibs and for 150 years drive successive generations to distraction, despair and – just every once in a while, let's not get too carried away – delirium.

Edward Hannan was a priest from Limerick who came to Scotland's capital for a holiday, peered at the suppurating slums of the area of the Old Town known as Little Ireland and declared: 'There's work to be done here.' So he stayed and in 1865 opened a branch of the CYMS in the Cowgate offering a wide range of improving pastimes for young men of the Irish immigrant population who'd had such difficulty integrating while trying to survive some of the worst living conditions in Europe.

Before long, new and bigger premises were needed. These would be St Mary's Street Halls. Edinburgh's lord provost laid the foundation stone, expressing the fond hope for a fillip to the fortunes of a community blighted by 'foul dens of vice and disease unparalleled in infamy and disgust'. And St Mary's would become Hibs HQ, just as soon as Michael Whelahan came up with the spiffing idea for association football as a means of Little Ireland planting its own foundation stone for acceptance by the wider city.

Whelahan's flight to Edinburgh from Ireland had been more desperate: eviction, journey by foot from Glasgow, the death of a baby on the way. A member of the CYMS, and aged 21 in 1875, Whelahan happened by the Meadows in the spring of that year and was dazzled by what he saw. Rudimentary, near prehistoric football. Multiple games going off simultaneously. Random team sizes and pitch dimensions. Balls whizzing hither and yon. Slightly comical attire. Continuing into semi-darkness. Long-winded arguments and much-winded personnel. Charge and barge. Indeed, it was not unlike the football played on this expanse of green 150 years later by Edinburgh's undergraduate community.

Whelahan relayed his excitement back to Canon Hannan. Football might not be able to wholly eradicate vice and disease and infamy and disgust. Indeed it has never got rid of the latter two in all this time and could be said to require, and benefit from, albeit to satisfy our perverted cravings, regular dousings of both. But football could at least provide the Irish émigrés with a purpose, a means of expression and a role in Edinburgh life.

Whelahan would be the first captain. (And a century later, his great, great, great grandnephew Pat Stanton would fulfil the role most splendidly.) He also came up with the name – Hibernians, from Hibernia, which was what the Romans called Ireland. Everything was set fair for the first game. Except . . . 'the Association was formed for Scotchmen'. The curt response from the SFA to Hibs' application to join was hammered home with the warning to existing member clubs not to fraternise with the ragamuffin outfit. Thankfully, the players of the other Edinburgh teams were much more welcoming. They petitioned the beaks who eventually relented and on Christmas Day the Hibees, amid much nervous excitement over how the upcoming hour and a bit would pan out, never mind the next 150 years, made their entrance in the world.

2

FIRST DAY AT 'EEBERNIANS': SAUZÉE BROUGHT FINE WINE

UP UNTIL 1999, a Hibs fan's favourite Frenchman would have emerged from a five-way face-off involving the boy Baudelaire, the boy Renoir, Monet, Camus and Jean-Paul Sartre.

No, I'm kidding. The actual aspirants were Jacques Cousteau, Inspector Clouseau, the director of cinematography on the *Emmanuelle* films and the two metal-masked dudes out of Daft Punk.

Then on 20 February of that year, in a moment which surely deserved an addendum in at least a few of the histories being readied for the end of the millennium, an ageing French football aristocrat strode on to the pitch at Brockville.

Now, with the ground having a Gallic-sounding name, pronounced with the correct second-syllable inflection, this 33-cap Les Bleus redoubtable could very well have still been in his native land, in a semi-obscure rustic outpost, perhaps for an early rounds cup tie or an exhibition match. This might have been Brockville-sur-la-mer or Baroque-ville, *mais non*?

Plain old Falkirk, nowhere else. Franck Gaston Henri Sauzée, no one else. Champions League winner, serious continental soccer royalty. Tied equal with George Best, the most implausible, preposterous debut in Hibee history and, way out on its own, the most *merveilleux*. The fans probably thought they'd overdone the Cointreau, the Pernod, the Kronenbourg and yes, the absinthe, witnessing the first of many back heels from the midfield, and if they couldn't quite believe it, then neither could Sauzée's new team-mates at, as he would say, 'Eebernians'.

'This was *Brockville*,' said Stuart Lovell, reminding himself. 'Freezing cold dressing room. Condensation gushing down the walls. I'm sorry, but an absolute dump. And yet sitting next to me was Franck bloody Sauzée . . .'

'Surreal,' added Stevie Crawford, possibly unaware of the French origins of a term these days overused by sportsmen but in this instance completely justified. 'We thought him signing for us was a wind-up. Hibs at the time, don't forget, had been relegated. Training was the usual, any available patch of green, and we were like: "He's not coming to this." Then suddenly there he was and he'd brought along a smashing case of wine. Plastic glasses were found and he invited us to toast the day. He said: "I'm here with you my friends and I want us to do well." That was pure class, pure Franck class, which was how he was all of the time.'

Along with the wine, Sauzée had a range of passes to be savoured. 'He saw everything before it happened,' added Crawford, which rather makes you wonder, after Brockville, what advance notice of Boghead had been like in the mind. But amid such modest surroundings the fans saw no need to qualify their approval. They nicknamed him 'Le God'. With his dainty feet and a shot like the classic Napoleonic 12-pounder cannon, he led Hibs back to the big time, to cup finals and Europe. He is enshrined in Leith legend, not least for being part of a select band including wartime guest right-half Matt Busby who never lost an Edinburgh derby – and for two goals against Hearts which brought his disciples to orgasm without the need for any heavy petting from Jane Birkin, Françoise Hardy or Brigitte Bardot.

The first came in the Millennium Derby and just as memorable as the ferocity of the strike was his celebratory yomp the length of Tynecastle to cavort with the exploding away end.

The second at Easter Road cost him his front teeth. How did he hang in the air for so long? How did he stay laser-focused on the ball's flight when he must have known that collision with the back of a thick Jambo skull was inevitable? Because he's Le God. Famously, Willie Henderson's contact lens was retrieved from the pitch by Tommy Gemmell. Every Hibby hopes Sauzée's gnashers are still in the Dunbar End penalty box, undisturbed by seeder or mower, mementoes of a wonderful, 22 month-long *acte de théâtre.*[*]

* Does not include his short, unhappy stint as manager, though he never lost a derby then either.

3

TARZAN, CARMEN, BILLY THE KID, SEX MAGICK

IT WASN'T just about Hibs in 1875. Blackburn Rovers were formed, Birmingham City too. And the first game of college football – gridiron – was staged in America along with the first game of indoor ice hockey in Canada. D.W. Griffith, a towering figure in early Hollywood, was born, along with Carl Jung, a towering figure in psychology. Oh and Aleister Crowley, a towering figure in sex magick where there's a ritual called eroto-comatose lucidity: lots of arousal, bags of stimulation but stopping well short of actual orgasm. Hmm, how very Hibs.

Maurice 'Bolero' Ravel arrived in the world in 1875, as did boxing's 'great white hope' James J. Jeffries who would almost masochistically absorb incredible punishment (Hibs-esque) then contrive a stunning triumph (not so much). Then there were these men of letters, creators of men of action: John Buchan and the two Edgars, Wallace and Rice Burroughs.

Also that year, the telephone was invented. Because in early fandom I soaked up everything about Hibs, memorising entire match programmes like I was in the dentist's waiting room about to undergo root canal treatment and that was all there was to read, or I was a hostage chained to a radiator in some terrorist hellhole and that was all there was to read, I will probably end up quietly mouthing over and over the number to call the stadium, unfailingly printed on page two, during my deathbed delirium: 'Abbeyhill 2159 . . . Abbeyhill 2159 . . .'

Another important invention: milk chocolate. The opera *Carmen* was composed, and also 'I'll Take You Home Again, Kathleen'. The largest locust swarm ever recorded turned the sky black over the Rocky Mountains, Billy the Kid was arrested for the first time (for stealing a basket of laundry) and Captain Matthew Webb became the first person to swim the English Channel.

Then there was Jeanne Calment, born in Arles, France in 1875, the oldest person who ever lived, seeing out of *la porte* 20 of her country's presidents. She died on 4 August 1997, aged 122. Scotland's back pages that day were all about a Hibs victory over Celtic, inspired by Chic Charnley.

Books published included *A Gentleman's Guide to Etiquette* which advised: 'If you have travelled do not be constantly speaking of your journeyings. Nothing is more tiresome than a man who commences phrases with 'When I was in Paris . . .' or 'In Italy I saw . . .' Wise words, although there are exceptions, such as your team being European Cup trailblazers (ch. 57) or the important evangelical work of a tour of Brazil to, ahem, educate the natives about flair-filled futebol (ch. 81).

Among the notable deaths was that of Georges Bizet, the Carmen guy, who went to his grave with the critics' condemnation of his masterwork still ringing in his ears. A performance on the day of his funeral, however, had them all singing his praises. Opera, then, can be said to be not unlike football, with both provoking fickle reactions (cheer today, gone tomorrow). Also, are Hibs not the most operatic of football clubs? And Hans Christian Andersen died, prompting great mourning among lovers of fairy tales, the more morbid and grisly the better, much like a Scottish Cup quest lasting a whole 114 years.

Then there was the Public Health Act. By UK government decree there had to be proper sewage systems, basic jobby-wheeching. The law came into force in 1875, which was also when waste wizard Joseph Bazalgette completed his tunneling to future-proof London against a repeat of the Great Stink. So: a historic year for shite . . .

4

UNIQUELY GREEN AND WHITE, IN SUBBUTEO AND EVERYWHERE

EDINBURGH'S LITTLE Ireland had gathered to dance and sing and commemorate a famous son. The work of Daniel O'Connell, founding father of the modern Irish state, was done and his life was long over. But on the centenary of his birth, Hibs were just beginning with the official unveiling of club colours – white shirts with green trim.

O'Connell had been a huge figure, the champion of Catholic emancipation, whose oratory was of such passion that it brought tears to the eyes of a parliamentary reporter called Charles Dickens. The shirt spoke much more quietly of Ireland, doubtless because of the discrimination and sectarianism suffered in the Cowgate, with just a small harp on the breast.

The next version, taking the club through the remainder of the 1870s, saw more green. This was a hooped jersey, very much on trend in football back then, also for bathing, which enhanced a strapping chest and complemented the tumescent moustaches of the Victorian era.

The game was firmly in its knickerbocker years when knees were not permitted to be seen. It was a chaste time, but with no paparazzi there was zero threat of upbockering, the forerunner to upskirting, or of a gentleman displaying side-knee, preceding side-boob, and the snaps turning up in a scandal sheet.

Then, new century, new freedom. Out and proud and all green. The shade was bottle, changing to the emerald we know and love in the 1930s. And, shortly before the Second World War, following Arsenal and just in time for the dashing, debonair Gordon Smith, the white sleeves made their debut.

The collar – white – stayed rugby-style for the next 20 years. The permissive society hastened much unbuttoning, not just of social mores but football shirts. Along came the V-neck, ideally worn with the quiff popularised by Tony Curtis and all those wild and dangerous rock 'n' rollers.

It was back to round collars for my all-time favourite. You never forget your first replica, this one purchased with paper-round wages from the Thornton's sports emporium in Edinburgh's Hanover Street. With neck and cuffs ringed in green – the vital flourishes – I attempted to dribble like Peter Marinello and defy gravity while waiting on a cross like Peter Cormack, even though that Mitre Mouldmaster, assuming the winger had succeeded in getting it airborne, was bound to hurt.

Turnbull's Tornadoes kept the jersey classic, though mixed it up for Europe and all-green forays into Albania and old Yugoslavia. Then came regular tinkering, necessary from the marketing perspective but wholly unnecessary from the aesthetic one. There have been tight fits and baggy styles. Branding down the arms and bands across the chest. White body/green arms reversals. Ajax knock-offs, shirts for a beach holiday, striped sleeves from a clown show and those designs, since banished from memory, which were worn when performances resembled clown shows.

All told, something like 50 shades of green but fundamentally the colour has been constant which in the footballscape makes Hibs special. There are hundreds of red teams out there and thousands of blue teams. In the classic version of Subbuteo, the teensy plastic figurines referenced as No. 119 and sporting blue tops, white shorts and white socks could be Everton, Leicester City, Ipswich Town, Millwall, Chesterfield, Rochdale, Gillingham, Halifax Town, Queen of the South or Cowdenbeath. But No. 45 could only be Hibs.

5

THREE PARTS HARRY HOUDINI, ONE PART KIM KARDASHIAN

EVERY NOW and again a great escapologist will descend upon Edinburgh, render the populace open-mouthed and quaking with wonder at his uncanny ability to make a mockery of assorted attempts at capture – and then he'll disappear. Aware that the city could not keep hold of him, literally and in every sense, the people are sad to see him leave, but happy to have known him for a while.

From 1904 when he first performed at the Gaiety Theatre in Leith until 1920 and his final appearance uptown at the Empire, that man was Harry Houdini. In all, the capital witnessed 50 show-stopping demonstrations of unshackling, extrication and tight spot-dodging.

From 8 August 2015 to almost the same day three years later, that man was John McGinn. He played 136 games for Hibs, scoring 18 goals. The number of times he emerged from a midfield ambush with the ball miraculously still at his feet is not recorded, but admirers know it to be huge.

America has the Kardashian clan and Scottish football has the McGinns. Stephen, Paul and John all had spells at Easter Road with John's the most dazzling. I don't think Kim Kardashian, the skincare tyrantess at the head of the late-stage capitalist nightmares, will mind me saying that to a not inconsiderable degree, her bahookie has been her fortune. Ditto McGinn.

Our game has produced some notable arses. When John Greig's opponents moved in for a tackle, the Rangers captain would adopt the gait of music hall comedian Max Wall and the poor saps were bounced into the Ibrox enclosure. Kenny Dalglish scored many of his goals for Celtic, Liverpool and Scotland by starting out facing the wrong way then swivelling through 180 degrees, his bum acting as a force shield.

McGinn at Hibs was all-action and all-forward motion when other midfielders were crab-like. He was like the academy boy who skived or just plain ignored the instruction about passing laterally as a means of retaining possession (and sustaining a career). He retained it by charging towards goal and if ever he was halted, and there were times when it seemed he deliberately dallied for fun and mischief, then with the ball safe and under control he'd hunker into the sumo wrestler's address position. There would be some vain attempt at dispossessing him before he'd continue on his merry, marauding way.

Film-maker Werner Herzog described Wayne Rooney as 'half-bison, half-viper'. McGinn was all bison and beyond a game's standard admission, tickets could have been sold for his amazing feats. Roll up, roll up! Gasp at the gluteus maximus which can never be fastened, fettered or foiled!

Houdini was variously billed as the Master Mystifier, the Handcuffs King and the 'justly famous self-liberator', escapologist not being a term used during his pomp. He cheerfully accepted challenges from sceptics and those determined to disprove his indestructibility and in 1913 the Edinburgh City Police Department dreamt up the 'Insane Restraint Bag' only for Houdini to leave the leather and canvas contraption in bits on the floor.

McGinn's greatest showstopper came on Hibs' greatest day, the 2016 Scottish Cup final. Early in the game he found himself surrounded. This was Rangers' Insane Restraint Bag involving almost half their team. Hampden held its breath. The outcome would be psychologically crucial to one of these teams. Then, from the thicket of thrusting limbs, a head appeared. Meatball-shaped as McGinn himself would admit.

Now, there's an act of Edinburgh escapology which predated Houdini and topped his stunts for being real. In 1861 an Old Town building collapsed with disastrous loss of life, but rescuers were encouraged to keep digging by the cries of a boy buried in the rubble: 'Heave awa', lads, I'm no' deid yet!' At Hampden the stupendous McGinn scrambling free with ball still tethered as Hibs justly famous self-liberator sent a similar message to his team-mates, inspiring them to victory.

6

THE JOY OF SIX–SIX: SCOTLAND'S GREATEST-EVER LEAGUE GAME

IT'S THE most exclusive of clubs. More select than a black card bolthole for the super-rich, with the conversation more rarefied than a cluster of the world's greatest intellectuals debating epoch-making ideas. Applying for membership, seconders hold no sway. The key number here is six. No actually, it's 12. Have you ever taken part in a 6–6 draw? That's what will get you over to the other side of the velvet rope.

Hibs are part of this elite. Derek Riordan and Anthony Stokes reuniting need only nod to each other in airport terminals and dodgy pubs to confirm their extreme privilege, though maybe the correct greeting is 12 nods, which might be more appropriate for the special bond between them but could get a bit tedious in performance.

It was on 5 May 2010 that the Hibees journeyed through to Motherwell for an outcome that would be phantasmagorical. Is this the first time that Motherwell and phantasmagorical have appeared together in the same sentence? I reckon so. The league game had been brought forward 24 hours from the general election called by Prime Minister Gordon Brown. That was just as well for the politicians. Perhaps the fixture, due to be broadcast live on Sky, didn't seem like an absolute must-see. But if it had gone ahead on polling day and you thought you'd have a quick look on TV before popping out to cast your vote, you might never have left the sofa. For the 1964 election Labour were so worried about the pull of a smelly, toothless rag-and-bone man that they had transmission of *Steptoe and Son* shifted. Forty-five years later the turnout threat would have been Colin Nish, Hibs' hat-trick beanpole.

In the race for the last available European place, the match – on a pitch resembling waste-ground scrub – was expected to be tense, tight, unspectacular and most likely decided by a solitary goal. Just past the half-hour mark, five had been scored. It was 4–1 to Hibs and later it would be 6–2. I don't know the personality of Motherwell and how the course of this game typifies it. I do know the personality of Hibs and just think: that's us, a Hibsian set-up, script and conclusion. And as the goals kept coming, pubs showing Manchester City vs Tottenham Hotspur in other rooms found punters deserting these teams' Champions League qualification scrap for the Fir Park orgy.

Guinness World Records confirm 6–6 as the highest score draw in football. It was achieved twice previously – in 1999 in Belgium by Racing Genk and Westerlo and the following year in Argentina by Gimnasia y Esgrima de La Plata and Club Atletico Colón. But the goals came easy in the former with five penalties awarded and four red cards, while in the latter there were two penalties and an own goal. So even though they drew on the night, Hibs and Motherwell won with election as joint life presidents of this most special of clubs. And if there is any quibble from the other members, then the trump card is Motherwell's 93rd minute equaliser, an outrageous volley by Lukas Jutkiewicz from a laughable angle.

The best-ever Scottish Premiership goal? Some go further and rate the contest our best-ever. On its tenth anniversary, as we locked down for Covid-19 and wondered where the next game of football was going to come from, it was reshown on TV almost as an urgent salve to the country's crumbling mental health.

Regular screenings should become a thing. And what about a book? I've got the perfect title: *The Joy of Six-Six*. The bearded man and the bangled woman from the original 1970s shagger manual could, through different copulating positions, interpret the goals for sensuous pencil illustrations. Regarding degree of difficulty, Jutkiewicz's would be the equivalent of the one known as 'The Piledriver'. Meanwhile the strike from Riordan who also bisected the posts from way out wide might rate as challenging as the 'The Side Saddle', perhaps even 'The Standing 69'.

7

THE WORLD'S THIRD OLDEST CUP IS HIBS' FOR EVER

THAT VERY first derby at the Meadows finished 1–0 to Hearts. And so began the grand municipal beef . . . After Nottingham Forest–Notts County it is the oldest, continuously played, full and frank exchange of views, football-wise, in the world. And the rivalry really took off for the citizenry early in 1878. On other pages I think about some of the Hibees from history, with the benefit of a time machine, that I'd love to see play. The specific games I'd be programming into the temporal distortion engine would all be from this two-month period, all Hibs vs Hearts and indeed all the same tie.

This was the Edinburgh Football Association Cup, the world's third oldest behind the Scottish Cup and the FA Cup, a first final for both clubs and surely another record: an incredible five matches would be required to settle matters. The final in its various iterations would career round the city like some comic-strip melee. You know: a dust cloud of protruding arms and legs, lurching between locations including Mayfield, Merchiston and Powburn, suggesting a nimby reaction from disgruntled local residents but exciting – and over-exciting – the still-evolving species known as the football follower.

Hibs finished the first match the stronger, also the first replay, confident they could win in extra-time, but the Hearts captain vetoed the additional half-hour. There had been fighting between the fans, so next time, admission was increased to try and price out the unruly element. But Irish navvies desperate to see the Hibees staged a break-in. They were denounced from the pulpit and in an effort to cool tempers the third replay was delayed. More suspenseful than a penny dreadful, the contest which began in the dead of winter was concluded with cherry blossom covering the ground. Hearts had the final say with a hotly disputed goal as their skipper was chased off the pitch and down the road by some badass Hibbies.

Their favourites would gain revenge the following season. And the next and the one after that. Three in a row and Hibs got to keep the cup, despite a last-gasp protest from Hearts that it was a local competition for local players and their opponents had fielded an outsider.

The niggle and needle were certainly enjoyed by local people. The crowds got bigger and more boisterous. Hibs moved around – from the Meadows to Powderhall to Mayfield and then Hibernian Park, a hefty clearance from what had yet to become Easter Road – and Hearts disbanded for a while. But with the Scottish League not yet begun, there was a lustful appetite for a regular fixture of the two teams slugging it out for city supremacy, so the cup was immediately replaced by the East of Scotland Shield.

Other sides from in and around Edinburgh participated, and occasionally won it, but this soon became a private affair and by the time I was hanging about the terraces (both grounds – see ch. 148) I loved the Shield. When we could only count on two derbies every year here was another. When neither club was winning anything, here was have-and-hold silverware. It didn't matter that it was never paraded; that's for this generation. Every kid gets a prize now. Every 6 Nations rugby game comes with a trophy attached. We just wanted, at the fag-end of each season, in the promise of a hot summer to come, to watch in our Simon shirts as Hibs and Hearts crashed into each other for a special offer bonus 90 minutes.

The Shield is still a thing but nowadays just for the youth sides. Who to blame for its downgrading? The Champions League, every single act of Gianni Infantino, football's gigantism. But size isn't everything, you know.

8

BOBBY JOHNSTONE, BOBBY COMBE, BOBBY SMITH, BOBBY'S BOOKSHOP

THE GENTLE descent of the street called Easter Road begins at a kilt shop. Hiring the plaid – trad or zazzily modern and bound to have hoary clan chiefs birling in their graves – is not essential. To the right is an old fire station, bright red doors, Toytownish, Trumptonesque ('Pugh, Pugh, Barney McGrew . . .') and to the left an imposing Gothic kirk. London Road Parish Church predated Hibs' arrival by three years, which makes you wonder how many silent prayers were amassed ('Pew, pew, Allan McGraw* . . .'), and how heavy hung the hope, before 2016 when the blessed Scottish Cup was finally won. Its work done in its Church of Scotland incarnation, the doors closed a few months later and now the born-again congregate here under the banner of Christian Revivalism. (Not to be confused with the 'happy clappers' among the Hibs support, a term of non-endearment for the insanely optimistic who point-blank refuse to adopt the default disposition of epic go-on-impress-us grumpiness.)

Easter Road, the street, used to be soot-caked and forlorn. It's still soot-caked but the shop names beneath the tenements

* 1960s striker, nicknamed 'Quick Draw' when Westerns were still popular, featured in my first Hibs game, suffered for the cause through pain-killing jabs to help the team overcome semi-final strife, hirpled through later years, stood – as best he could – for Scottish Parliament.

read bold and optimistic now: Happy Bean, Écosse Éclair, Dazzelustrous. Further along: House of Lilith, Little Fitzroy, Cute But Deadly. These are obviously not ironmongers or haberdashers but nor are they charity shops. There's vibrant young enterprise here – swagger with a bit of boho. And check out the graffiti on the wall over there: 'Bagdad Bovver Boys vs Bengazi Uzi Krew.' Well, are you going to be the brave schmuck who points out the missing aitches?

A Hibs supporter – he might be a schoolboy or someone who's never been able to kick the habit in adulthood of racing buses down this thoroughfare – will tell you: 'It is fitting, and at least to us perfectly apposite, that the local service is the No. 1.'* The object of the race, of course, at least for adults, is to speed-walk to the next junction before the bus arrives, thereby guaranteeing a win in the upcoming game.

Easter Road's sense of self, the belief that it's no ordinary street, was further evident in the name chosen for its cinema. The Picturedrome opened in 1912, a year Hibs began with a 5–0 thrashing of Rangers. Scribes of the day hailed that result 'one of the greatest surprises known to Scottish football' though Rangers would conclude the season as champions. Hibs, back in their box, were back in 13th.

In 1912, D.W. Griffith was the pre-eminent name in movie-making but coming up fast on the outside, sirens wailing dementedly and tyres screeching, was Mack Sennett and his Keystone Cops. The Picturedrome is long gone, but if you look up at the rooftops, the curlicues from its grand frontage are still visible.

Now, I sense that some of you are yet to be convinced of Easter Road, present or past, as anything resembling exotic. Will Bobby's Bookshop do this? It should. The branch here was like the others in Edinburgh and a comics cornucopia

* The 1 service also calls in on bandit country (Gorgie).

(*Commando*, DC and, before they killed the film-going experience, Marvel). While boys thrilled to vapour trails and splatter, girls coveted scraps of cloud-dwelling cherubs who these days would probably be fat-shamed. I bought my copies of *Mad* from this stupendous emporium, the mag's baby-steps satire, all-American, enabling one-upmanship on schoolmates who'd never heard of Spiro Agnew, or who vainly speculated about him possibly having invented Spirograph. So, while Bobby Johnstone, Bobby Combe and Bobby Smith were all revered at Easter Road, the stadium, Bobby at his Bookshop just around the corner was supplying fun and occasional edification. At least my generation was reading something . . .

So anyway, where is that stadium? After The Edinburgh Honey Company turn right into Albion Road, a few hundred yards, bear left for Albion Place and . . . hunkered next to more tenements it looks faintly ridiculous: an out-of-proportion interloper, far too big for the space and as it looms large, strangely reminiscent of . . . this'll probably sound odd: the giant tabby cat squatting on the GPO Tower in *The Goodies*.

9

JOIN THE HAPPY CROWD BEHIND THE GREEN DOOR

EYES ADJUSTED, let's take a closer look, a voyage round my ground . . . Like Easter Road the street, Easter Road the stadium has a kirk, actually two as its closest neighbours, and similarly they've become surplus to Church of Scotland requirements. But they stay put, jammed together as in a defensive wall facing a free kick, and their continued presence in body if not in spirituals is a good thing. It's important that the club, in their surroundings at least, have constants while players, managers, owners, systems and shirt designs blithely come and go.

Behind the kirks, St Mungo and Lockhart Memorial, is what used to be Norton Park, both a primary and a secondary school. Just imagine the amount of daydreaming that went on during lessons, with playtimes devoted to collecting players' autographs.

It was harsh learning at Norton Park with former pupil chatrooms remembering days when entire classes were lined up for the belt. Almost without exception the kids were moulded for industry, but Alex Cropley was one who went from classroom to changing room across the way. The school and the churches have been repurposed: a charity hub, a conference centre and what the website terms 'green benefits', something Cropley and Turnbull's Tornadoes delivered in a different way just about every week.

These buildings are not going anywhere and neither is the

graveyard across from the club shop, but after moving past what is now called the Famous Five Stand, newish housing pushes us southwards. These dwellings might be coveted by fans but sadly cannot have a view of the park although at times when those green benefits have been beyond Hibs, this must count as a blessing. The same could be said for the flats on the corner of Albion Place. Before the Famous Five Stand went up, the pitch lay out in front of them. And in 2025, ground redevelopment not always being matched by team redevelopment, the gable end issues this directive in big, dramatic lettering: 'Sack the board!'

Continue south and you could easily end up in Lochend Park with its pond, a tranquil spot in spite of the erect dorsal fins, red bellies and psycho grimaces of the sticklebacks. As well as fishes here there used to be loaves. Nearby is the site of the old Smith's Bakery which offered warm walls for kids' wintertime huddles and the sweet aroma of freshly baked bread 24 hours a day, all year round.

We've strayed too far, we'll miss kick-off. Heading back to the stadium up the other side, another former factory, also much loved, is discernible in fading paint on a red-brick wall: 'James Dunbar'. This was the lemonade works which brewed Kola with a K, repelled the advances of Coca-Cola because it regarded the latter as inferior pop, and lives on in the ground. If you're of a certain age, the away fans' stand will always be the 'Dunbar End'.

Nowadays, painters and sculptors exhibit in the premises and as the stands loom into view once more, there is art of a kind on every lamp post and utility box, which have become the canvases of visiting fans. Black-clad junior emissaries from Borussia Dortmund in Germany, Marseilles in France, Burgos in Spain and some skinheads from Italy's Termoli have left stickers as calling cards which form into mosaics. The Hibby response includes 'HFC' in olde script as the letters appeared on the shirts of the 1902 Scottish Cup-winning team. Also this: 'Kensell sells his farts in jars.'*

Now we're back where we started, the north end which honours the club's most famous sons, and the words of the eminent philosopher Shakin' Stevens come to mind: 'All I want to do is join the happy crowd behind the green door.'

But maybe not this green door, some feet below the image of Willie Ormond, for it reads: 'Keep out – danger of death.'

* Ben Kensell, the unloved CEO who left at the beginning of the sesquicentennial just as Hibs posted a £7.2 million loss.

10

HE DROPPED DEPTH CHARGES IN WW2 AND CONTINUED IN PEACETIME

HUGH McILVANNEY'S 1997 documentary *The Football Men* is acclaimed for telling the story of the coal town colossi of the game – Matt Busby, Bill Shankly and Jock Stein. It's terrific but I probably prefer *Bring Your Own Ball* screened 24 years previously and for two reasons. One, I'm biased – it was made by my father who was able to interview the triumvirate when they were still alive. Two, his film featured another great manager who emerged from Scottish mining stock – Eddie Turnbull.

The Football Men borrowed footage from *Bring Your Own Ball* so the year after Dad died, I heard his voice from beyond the grave enquiring of each of his subjects: 'Are you a disciplinarian?'

A bold question – fluffy in-house TV at clubs has allowed coaches to expect softballs now – but can I say, Faither, that in 1973 it was possibly superfluous? Parents were disciplinarians, so were schoolteachers and certainly football managers, not least Turnbull, and while I wish I could have seen him play for Hibs, it was thrilling to watch the team he managed and, later, fascinating to collect my own sound bites about his working practices.

'He enlightened everyone,' John Blackley told me. Alex Cropley said: 'No disrespect to the guys that came before him but they were simply playing at it.' Des Bremner: 'A visionary.' Roy Barry: 'The best coach I ever had.' And this from Ally MacLeod who already seemed to possess sufficient football intelligence: 'I properly learned about the game from him.'

Alex Edwards was managed by both Turnbull and Stein. Who was best? 'Eddie – he was a genius.' Turnbull answered to Ned, although Edwards, who coined many of the Easter Road nicknames, had another one for the boss. 'Remember *Wacky Races*? And Dick Dastardly's dug and how it shoogled its shoulders when it laughed? To me Eddie was Muttley although obviously I never called him that to his face.'

Before the Famous Five – 202 goals in 487 games – he was Able Seaman Turnbull on the Atlantic Convoys during the Second World War. Journeys from Greenock to Murmansk were fraught with danger from Luftwaffe bombers and mountainous seas.

Aboard HMS *Bulldog*, Turnbull dropped the depth charges, which might fit as a description of his management style. Before underperforming Hibs for him, there was underperforming Aberdeen. 'He came to sort us out,' remembered Martin Buchan. 'The club had been a holiday camp for older players from the Central Belt. In just two months he got rid of 17. One guy was sent away from training because he couldn't take a corner. When he came out of the shower, Eddie was waiting for him. "The secretary's got your wages," he said. "I don't want to see you again."'

But those he liked and, who bought into his ideas, loved him. They included Arthur Graham, Davie Robb ('Very hard but very fair; I always called him Mr Turnbull'), Bobby Clark ('Ahead of his time, he had us high-pressing before the world knew about that') and Ernie McGarr ('Rugby gave him the idea for overlapping full-backs and we goalies went outfield in practice matches with the order: "Play starts with you so learn everyone's role"').

Stevie Murray admired his psychology: 'Joe Harper and Jim Forrest both wanted to be centre-forward and wouldn't pass to each other. He moved Jim out to the wing because he was fast but gave him the No. 9 shirt so he'd think he was centre-forward. I was devastated when Eddie left us for Hibs.'

So was Buchan who owed his career to Turnbull: 'He walked us through situations in games until everything became second nature. Average players won Under-23 caps just through what they learned from him. When I left Aberdeen I could have gone to any team in the world and played in any system, thanks to the master.'

And then there was Harper, who emerged from the manager's office with a black eye after failing to adequately explain why he'd been drunk in charge of a snow plough and would later follow Turnbull to Easter Road. He said: 'I'd like to think I was the son he never had.'

Maybe none of the Hibees inherited by Turnbull went quite as far as that. Maybe in Leith, admiration came with a quibble about man management or lack thereof. Maybe that was the world starting to change with official recognition of 'feelings', for at the moment the Tornadoes began to reflect on the Ned experience, bosses were expected to be as adept at an arm round the shoulder as a boot up the arse. But maybe, too, Turnbull's frustration was greater at Hibs because this team could, and should, have been the best in the land.

11

HIBS ACCUSED OF CHEATING, PRIVATE DETECTIVE TRIES TO PROVE IT

FOR A while, not quite 114 years although it felt like that long, many in Scottish football and nearly all Jambos were obsessed with 1902. They knew who sat on the British throne (Edward VII). The identity of the great and goateed Wild West soldier-showman still going strong (Buffalo Bill). The year's whizzo inventions (vacuum cleaner, air conditioning, brassiere). The bloody conflict finally brought to a close (Boer War). This was the sort of stuff which was Wiki-sourced and flung at Hibs for lamentably failing to hoist the Scottish Cup in all that time. Until, after 114 years, they finally did.

But the club's earlier triumph, the one on 12 February 1887, is the better story. Not just for being Hibs' first in the competition, what would now be called a statement win, and the first time the trophy had been prized from the Wild West of Scotland, but a sensational sub-plot straight out of the ripsnorting adventures of Sherlock Holmes who made his debut in print that same year.

Hibs overcame five teams to reach the final including the sadly gone Durhamstown Rangers, Mossend Swifts and Third Lanark, back then still bearing the proud initials RV for Rifle Volunteers. There were some impressive scores, including six against Durhamstown, seven against Queen of the South Wanderers and another five put past the hapless custodian of some mob called Heart of Midlothian. Then in the semi-final they defeated Vale of Leven with Willie Groves (see ch. 28) notching his eighth and ninth goals of the competition.

Not so fast, said Vale, and not so legal either. They alleged skulduggery, lodging a complaint of professionalism against Hibs in what was still the amateur era for the Scottish game. And what Hibees historian Alan Lugton called 'one of the most celebrated, controversial and bitter cases ever heard by the SFA' began just two days before the final.

That's proper stress, something which wouldn't be countenanced by teams now. So close to a grand showpiece, they would want their only angst to concern haircut options and whether the big cardboard sign advertising telly transmission was being held the right way up.

The hearing was adjourned, resuming right after the victory over Dumbarton, when Hibs' accusers produced what they hoped would be their trump card – the findings of a private detective.

Perhaps this gumshoe had been motivated to join this relatively new profession by Allan Pinkerton who'd set sail from Glasgow for America to found the sleuths agency bearing his name. In 1887, what would have been the extent of the Dumbarton man's skill set? And the extent of his disguise? It's probably as well that *A Study in Scarlet* didn't ignite the Holmes phenomenon in time for his skulking around the mean streets of Leith, for appropriating Holmes's deerstalker, cape, violin and intravenous drugging would probably have blown his cover.

As it was, Hibs did rumble him and hurriedly moved training away from Easter Road.

Vale attempted to prove that the so-called Corinthians of Leith were in fact avaricious sybarites. From the agent's shadowing of Groves – how many clubs have ever had a private eye on their tail? – they alleged the ace goal-grabber was paid quadruple his wages as a stonemason for 'broken time' before going out and hammering the Hibees' opponents. Team-mate

Jerry Reynolds was supposed to have earned £1 a week from the club. And what about those breakfasts served to the team each morning in Little Ireland? This was, Vale asserted, payment in bacon and eggs and damn near the equivalent of corpulent Roman emperors roaring: 'Peel us grapes!'

Dumbarton's route to the final hadn't exactly been spotless. They survived protests of rough play, a park deemed too slippery so that tie, having been lost, was declared null and void and opponents conceding another match when they'd been unable to afford the travel costs.

In the end, on a highly dramatic casting vote, Hibs were allowed to keep the cup and the gumshoe presumably went back to trying to catch adulterous wives in flagrante in Alexandria, Balloch and Bonkhill – sorry, Bonhill.

12

THE BAD GIRLS WHO LIKED BAD BOYS, EVEN THE GOOD GIRLS WHO LIKED BAD BOYS

WHAT, YOU can't come? You've got to work so you're going to miss the game? Sorry about that, Dad. (Inside, though, I'm ecstatic.) Would I, heading to Easter Road solo for the very first time, turn up in the usual place? The same safe, spammy, sappy, speccy, Sunday schooly spot on the main terracing, the halfway line signifying even-handedness and where fine play and – jolly good show – goals scored by the opposition are applauded with a spirit of generosity? Would I hell.

This was the big breakout moment. The chance as a Hibby to, as we say these days, speak my truth. Yell it in a not-yet-broken voice. Walk round to the north end of the ground. Yes, the section bounded by Albion Place. Yes, behind the goals at the bottom of the slope. Yes, the Cowshed.

Here was where the bad boys hung out, also the bad girls who liked bad boys and even the good girls who liked bad boys. No one was a member of the Tufty Club. I knew this from the interval changeover when Hibs fans and the away support crossed at halfway. Maybe hard to believe in view of the aggro which came to football a bit later, but this was a solemn procedure which passed off quietly with just a few tough stares.

The Cowshed was Hibs' property. Where, because of the roof amplifying them, songs could be sung the loudest. Nevertheless, supporters were prepared to share it. So really it wasn't just the big jessies on halfway who were fair-minded.

On this night, though, there were no away fans. The opposition were Lokomotive Leipzig in the Inter-Cities Fairs Cup with the Berlin Wall severely restricting travel out of East Germany. So Hibbies could remain in the Cowshed for the whole match. It was too frighteningly exciting an opportunity for this sheltered middle-class boy to miss.

I loved it, even if I lurked on the edges. The brutalist pillars (very East German), the pre-Health & Safety blackness, the attempted surging and swaying in mimicry of Liverpool's Kop – and the rudeness. Pity the poor perambulating woman police officer. Every time her patrolling neared the enclosure she was assailed with a chant of 'Get it up you while you're young!'

The Euro tie in 1968 was four days after Hibs had lost 6–1 at Rangers including a crushing hat-trick from the Cowshed's old idol, Colin Stein, on his Ibrox debut. But his replacement, Joe McBride, would immediately endear himself to his new support by thumping three goals of his own.

Pre-Cowshed, three sides of the stadium were open to the elements. In old photographs, when jam-packed, this was spectacular. But on much quieter days, and severely drookit ones, those little Lowryesque clusters of folk huddling on the concrete steps look utterly desperate.

But here was shelter. Here, when the bad yins started wearing faux-Crombie overcoats from boot-boy boutique Cowan Tailoring, was wool-mix warmth. Here was community. Here was a vague sense of emboldenment, even if after that game, enraptured by the victory, I was relieved to be able to scamper home to my Ovaltine, Winceyette pyjamas and night light. And, the very next game, to be back at halfway with Dad.

13

GREAT TOURISTS, UNPERTURBED BY DARK SKIES OR DARK-SKINNED OPPONENTS

WHAT IS Hibs' strange and mystical power? It's more than being in the right place at the right time, which is what strikers say about their craft. Could they in fact be 11 Zeligs?

In Woody Allen's mockumentary *Zelig*, the eponymous hero is the 'human chameleon' who amazes with his ability to assume the physical appearance of those around him, becoming something of a freak show. And his weird gift enables him to sneak into shot as momentous history plays out.

The first European Cup in 1955/56 was momentous football history but Hibs didn't enter via the back door sporting joke shop beards. They were invited.

The visionary behind the tournament was Gabriel Hanot, editor of French football daily *L'Equipe*, who was stirred into action by English triumphalism. Boastful Wolves acclaiming themselves as 'champions of the world' after a couple of friendly wins at home over foreign opposition caused Hanot to choke on his croissant. '*Anglais typique*!' So he devised a means by which the premier *chiens*, within the continent at least, could be officially recognised.

Now, admittedly Hibs' involvement in the inaugural competition seems odd. The previous season Aberdeen had claimed their first-ever league title. A glance at the final table with the Hibees back in fifth might give the impression they'd somehow Zeliged the Dons, possibly by adopting the north-east greeting

'Fit like?', claiming to have left wallets at home or at the very least waving a knock-off copy of the championship flag fluttering over Pittodrie.

But Aberdeen were unenthusiastic about what was christened the European Champions Cup. In this they weren't alone in British football. Parochialism and a lack of vision abounded. English champs Chelsea snubbed the tournament under pressure from FA blazer Alan Hardaker who snorted that the competition would be teeming with 'too many wogs and dagoes'.

Aberdeen failed to see the light in another way. The tournament would mostly be played at night, a problem for clubs suspicious of floodlights. It would be five years after Hibs had got themselves illuminated (see ch. 29) that the Dons would lose the fear and agree to play them after dark.

In any event the first edition of the tournament would differ from all those which came after. As a one-off, to capture the football public's imagination, the teams didn't need to have won their leagues but definitely had to be progressive Europhiles who played exciting football and were pro-floodlights.

Hibs' credentials were impeccable. The Famous Five's reputation for swashbuckling attack went worldwide, while Aberdeen's title had been built on a dourly strong defence. Hibs were great tourists unperturbed by dark skies or dark-skinned opponents and gladly took up the offer of a place.

This wouldn't be the last time they leapt from an unprepossessing fifth spot domestically and straight into Europe, though there was an element of fortune about their admission to the Inter-Cities Fairs Cup of 1967–68, as if some *Zelig*-style shape-shiftiness had indeed been involved.

Clyde in every meaningful respect had earned entry by virtue of finishing third – an achievement matched by the similar-sized Dunfermline Athletic and St Johnstone in later seasons before league reconstruction effectively shut the door on these little guys. But the Inter-Cities didn't permit more than one club per city so second-placed Rangers represented Glasgow, the Bully Wee stayed at home – and the Hibees dug out their passports once more.

It was as slick and seamless an entrance as Woody Allen in the film appearing from nowhere as a kilted Scotsman, Hibs only succumbing to eventual tournament winners Leeds United after fiendish deployment of the new four-step rule for goalies.

14

CHOOSE THE BELTER AGAINST ST MIRREN, CHOOSE THE BOMB VS KILMARNOCK

I SUPPOSE nowadays it would be called his resting bitch face but in the noughties we knew this as Deek's reaction to not being played in for a shot at goal. Never mind the strike's high degree of difficulty, that the risk involved in failing to execute would prompt some lesser frontmen to demand a flight to Venezuela, a suitcase stuffed with used notes and a new identity. Derek Riordan spied optimum opportunity and the potential for yet another screamer.

It's true that his scowl could darken the sky as if all the camouflage tarpaulins in the Army & Navy Store on Leith Walk had been stitched together and thrown over the stadium. Here's Lewis Stevenson on his Hibs debut as Riordan's flunkey/fluffer: 'I had a sore head at the end of the game from all his moaning when I didn't pass to him quickly enough or accurately enough.' But it's also true that one of Deek's goals could bring all the light rushing back. 'A top player, a fantastic finisher,' confirmed Stevenson.

Choose just about any of the goals against Hearts, even the late consolations. Choose the belter against St Mirren. Choose the bomb vs Kilmarnock. Choose the time he bazooka-ed Rangers. Choose a fucking big television, leisure wear and matching luggage. No thanks. Just give me more of the wee skinny guy who doesn't look like anything lurking on the left and about to slink inside . . .

How did he hit the ball so hard with that shilpit physique and those scrawny legs? Technique. He didn't need to be the strongest, just to know how to make the perfect connection, and in so doing, firing the ball into a whole other dimension.

The circumstances of his development in Edinburgh's West Granton scheme were somewhat less than ideal: blasted heaths strewn with broken glass and dogshit. Generation 5G, the snowflake prospects indulged with impeccable, kissed astro bounces, would faint at the sight of Deek's municipal parks. Gen 4G would stage a walk-off, the 3G lot as well.

By the time he left youth football he'd amassed 75,417 goals including 63 in one match. Something of that order, anyway. Often he'd decide to only use his weaker foot, whichever one that was, because after breaking through at Hibs in 2001 then embarking on the officially recognised haul of 104 goals in 260 games, no one could tell.

The circumstances of his career between two spells at Easter Road and later were somewhat less than ideal. The most gifted of Tony Mowbray's kids, everyone agreed, he moved to Celtic where manager Gordon Strachan hailed him as the club's best finisher but hardly played him.

Did Riordan indulge in too many haircuts? Did he accumulate too many nightclub bans? Did he surround himself with unwise counsel? And did he fail to make the most of his sublime talent? Perhaps. Steven Fletcher was Riordan's understudy for a while although would eventually shoot past him. But despite keeping elite company in England's Premier League for many years, Fletch remains in awe of his old torn-faced team-mate.

Some goals are vastly overrated. In 2008 for Hibs, John Rankin scored one from distance which deceived the Celtic goalkeeper. The swerve on the ball seemed unplanned but the player was able to dine out on what he immediately christened 'the squiggler'. Well, it didn't top those Deek wobblers.

Fletcher sometimes wondered if Riordan was moving the ball with a concealed remote control and loved the innovation. He told me: 'The top scorers when I was down south were Robin van Persie, Carlos Tevez, Didier Drogba and Luis Suárez. Amazing players, but could they wobble the ball like Deek? I don't think so. Everyone tries to move it in the air now but for me he was a proper pioneer.'

15

SIX OLD PENNIES AND LADIES ARE FREE TO SEE THE CHAMPS OF THE WORLD

I SMITE the leather, you smite the leather, we all smite the leather! And no matter the funny language, which was how kicking the ball used to be described, Hibs smited sufficiently to become – wait for it – world champions. Or rather Hibernians did, this being how the club were described in 1887, the year of the first Scottish Cup triumph and the challenge which came right after – the 'Association Football Championship of the World Decider'.

The Intercontinental Cup, Racing Club intimidation and Celtic retaliation, Yogi Hughes scudding and Tam Gemmell slugging, may be Scotland's most vividly recalled and indeed most notorious involvement in these global face-offs for the right to nominate yourselves the absolute best across the seven oceans. But it wasn't the first.

Eighty years before, when football was admittedly on a smaller scale and not yet developed worldwide, and leagues didn't exist anywhere, beaks in Scotland and England collaborated on the idea for a one-off game between the top smiters from each country.

Hibs were eminently suitable candidates following their success against Dumbarton, but strangely the English did not put forward their FA Cup holders Aston Villa, instead Preston North End who were beaten semi-finalists.

Hibbies understandably gloss over such finicky detail. Also

that the match, on 13 August, took place at Easter Road. Also that when the contest was repeated the following year there was a trophy, Renton won it, and this is the achievement commemorated in the Scottish Football Museum rather than their own. Also that Hibs' success didn't seem to have been greeted with much hullabaloo.

In 1887 hullabaloo was probably considered bad manners. And this was the era of Britain reckoning it pretty much ruled the world therefore another honour of that sort was no big deal. So all of this might explain why the 2–1 victory was written up in the *Glasgow Herald* next to similar-sized reports on pigeon flying, aquatics and a flower show. *The Scotsman* allowed itself to get a bit more excited in its intro: 'The celebrated English professionals opened their season in a most disastrous manner.'

Edinburgh, though, seemed to have been sold on the concept of a global tiebreaker with 'as large an assemblage as has perhaps ever visited Easter Road', requiring the erection of a new grandstand. Admission was six old pennies; free for ladies.

The match was 'fast and furious and somewhat rough' while the *Herald* rated it 'hard-fought and very interesting'. Our captain, James McGhee, smited 'a grand shot which passed through the bottom goal, out of the visiting custodian's reach', while the decisive 'swift and low' second from James McLaren prompted 'good and long-continued cheering'.

Champs of the whole planet. Some may scoff, except what does America call its baseball showdown but the World Series? Maybe we gave the US the idea. In which case, go Hibernians!

16

THE *GOODFELLAS* BAR SCENE: WITH HIBS AS 11 WAITERS, HEARTS AS 11 JOE PESCIS

A FEW years ago, writing a piece on a just-published book about the world's greatest football derbies, I tried to get the author to admit he'd blundered by not including Hibs vs Hearts. Really, what was I thinking? This was 2003, which began with the Hibees chucking away a 4–2 lead in Gorgie added time. The previous trip way out west, the Mark de Vries game when Hearts' big Dutchman ran amok, was still pungent in the memory, like a giant muscly chunk of rotting Gouda. There's loyalty to the fixture and then there's idiocy.

Had I forgotten that my first Edinburgh derbies as the 1960s turned into the 1970s were nearly all drab 0–0 draws including a run of four in a row on New Year's Day? Had I also forgotten that even at their brilliant best the Famous Five frequently lost the contest for city supremacy with Hearts' Terrible Trio?

Like all derbies, I suppose, the Edinburgh one is sensational when you're winning, rather less so when you're not. In 2004-05 Tony Mowbray's Hibees played sexy, exuberant football but Jambos would pop an asterisk next to that season. In three contests it was like the bar scene in *Goodfellas* with the Hibs kids as 11 waiters and the hard men of Tynecastle as 11 Joe Pescis demanding the little squirts dance before shooting them. Every time with four bullets.

Lazy pundits and Old Firm groupies can be sniffy about Hibs vs Hearts, insisting it's a slight difference of opinion in a zinc bucket next to the full-on punch-up in a nuclear reactor that is Celtic vs Rangers.

This is probably true if you rate derbies by the political censure they provoke or the cancelled police leave they demand. But here's another system of measurement: how many Polish experimental theatre companies or avant-garde Belgian dance troupes – or indeed Ladyboys of Bangkok – ever wander down to Ibrox or Parkhead in search of a game? There's far more chance of that when a capital clash coincides with the Edinburgh Festival in full swing. Dadaists who appreciate the absurd and the nonsensical should find plenty to enjoy.

Of course silky play is generally not available – bad news for an often quite 'La De Da' team such as Hibs. In space no one can hear you scream. In an Edinburgh derby the ball is yelling, 'Would someone please stop firing me into the stratosphere and just make a bloody pass!' But the players don't listen or fail to hear or are simply paralysed. In the derby, competent footballers can suddenly find themselves unable to perform the most basic of tasks, like lacing up their boots. Once, half the Hibs team emerged from the dressing room, took a wrong turning and walked into a cupboard where they remained. Some will know the game as the 2012 Scottish Cup final whereas I know it as the worst day of my life.

When Sky poured big money into Scottish football at the end of the last century, clubs spent it on loads of foreign imports. A handful have written themselves into derby history while far too many amid the increasing number of loan players have passed though the fixture leaving no trace.

Previously Hibs v Hearts, the westside frenemies, was a local shop for local people. All the combatants 'got' the rivalry and if they weren't hardcore fans themselves they grew up from folk down the street who were. And if they weren't that then they stayed long enough to become indoctrinated.

Drew Busby (Hearts) once told me: 'There was a derby where I took out Arthur Duncan and Des Bremner in a single movement. They were carried off and I was sent off. Then at the mouth of the tunnel [Hibs coach] John Lambie took a swing at me. We all made up later.'

Which chimed with this from Jackie McNamara (Hibs): 'There was a derby when I came face to face with a seething Jambo who'd jumped the wall. I'd just slide-tackled Jimmy Bone, continued into George Cowie and from there set up Paul Kane for a goal. Do you think that might have provoked him?'

Some of these guys are inextricably linked. Kane played in a juvenile team run by Hibee John Hughes's dad and was then coached by Jambo Gary Mackay's dad. John Robertson's dad died when the future Tynecastle goal demon was 14 and thereafter was driven to training and games by Keith Wright's dad, a grand gesture by a Hibee family which would cost them later through Robbo's 27 derby strikes (see ch. 116), with gratitude for the haul being passed to Keith's mum from her patrons as bar stewardess at Craigmillar Hearts Supporters' Club. And Hughes's cousin is Allan Preston (Hearts).

Some of these guys couldn't control their derby emotions. 'I was always too hyped up, never played my best in the games and I reckon mad Hibbies like Paul Kane and Gordon Hunter would say the same,' Mackay admitted. To which Robertson added: 'Gary was a lunatic the whole week beforehand, and hyperventilating so much he was given placebos to try and calm him down.' It didn't work. He was sent off against the rivals three times.

And some of these guys are still living the derbies, Kane refusing to drive along Gorgie Road, having never done it, and detouring through Pumpherston if necessary, while Robertson is always winding up his Hibs besties. Said Wright: 'He'll sign off texts: "See you on the 27th." I'll go: "But Robbo, we're meeting on the 24th." "Ach, sorry. Don't know why the number 27 sticks in my mind. Any ideas?"

'And invariably his messages will come at 12.55. Five to one, in other words. Apparently that's quite a significant scoreline for some folk in the city . . .'

17

'IF WE PASSED SIDEWAYS THREE TIMES, EDDIE TURNBULL HAULED US OFF'

PASS PASS pass pass pass pass pass pass pass pass pass pass pass pass pass pass pass pass pass pass pass pass pass pass pass pass pass pass pass pass pass pass pass pass pass pass pass and – wait for it – pass. Full-back to full-back, a little private, safe game. Then suddenly the pair of them involve a centre-back and, what, we're supposed to think this is exciting, sexy even, like a vanilla couple inviting a third person into the bedroom?

It's still pass pass pass, tedium tedium tedium, but wait, the goalie's just got in on the act. Come on, stop it, guys, you're actually killing me. And who's this *now*? The 'CDM'? Is that like a CEO? He sounds important, and because the central defensive midfielder inhabits a slightly more advanced position, I suppose technically the ball is moving marginally forward, but not so you'd really notice. The four of them – woohoo, dangerous – have formed a circle, the passing going interminably round and round. Honestly, were any of the nine circles of hell in Dante's Inferno quite so diabolical?

Does this even qualify as football?

What it does, though, in the modern way, is qualify as 'passes completed'. Entire careers can be built on shuffling the ball back and forth, a distance of just a few yards, well inside the defensive half, no proper threat, no problem.

Meanwhile in windowless rooms, peely-wally from being hunched over laptops, stats minions in club sweats will log the whole bloody lot. And successfully transferring the ball to a team-mate and doing it repeatedly, even though this is the easiest, most straightforward thing, can get a robo-player a 70 per cent rating and very often higher than that.

Why has football become so mechanised and standardised? How did this start? Do we blame Pep Guardiola? Under his watchful – nay, obsessional – eye, the possession game can be beautiful. Viz, Barcelona's tiki-taka, although its best expression, with the highest degree of difficulty, was further up the park where Xavi and Andrés Iniesta worked their beautiful and devastating magic.

Now Manchester City have some progressive footballers, no doubt about that, and maybe they've been the best at playing out from the back – the very back and the footsure keeper – and bringing play to meaningful conclusions. But at peak Pep everyone copied him or tried – in his touchline casuals and his tactics. And just as these coaches will have gone shopping for Stone Island and come back with River Island – chavvy, not to be confused with Xavi – they haven't always had the quality of player to make the system work in a way which isn't stodgy and stultifying and likely to result in either someone getting horribly caught in possession or – bored, even more bored than us – thrashing the ball anywhere.

So who can stop all the pointless passing? Maybe he doesn't exist right now but there was a man once: bold of thought, independent of mind, messianic about style, relaxed about doing his dinger. His name was Eddie Turnbull.

'We weren't allowed to pass the ball sideways,' Jim Herriot told me. And the Tornadoes goalkeeper confirmed the rule even applied to training. 'The matches we played among ourselves obviously weren't high intensity. Ned might have been using them for a potential scenario, working out how we should counter a specific threat. But he was absolutely adamant: if the ball went sideways three times the session would be stopped. That happened on a few occasions and then it didn't. Sideways was a crime against football. We got the message.'

18

THE PASS OF THE MILLENNIUM: SO WHAT IF WE LOST 6–1?

. . . MEANWHILE, IN other news about passing, it was 11 August 2019 and the 40th minute at Ibrox when Scott Allan collected the ball in the Rangers half, a few yards beyond the centre circle. What happened next was very Hibs. *Very Hibs.* There used to be Sunday colour mag advertisements with the tagline 'Very Sanderson'. Thinking man's crumpet like Diana Rigg would be draped seductively over sofas and beds, showing off the deluxe furnishings. There was a snob appeal to the ads, that they could only be properly appreciated by a certain kind of aesthete. So it was with Allan's pass that day.

Looking the other way, he arrowed it right through the middle of the Rangers defence. Four of their guys were left with their shorts round their ankles, along with the following:

Tina Turner, Gordon Ramsay, King Billy, King Billy's white charger, Frank 'Ol' Bluenose' Sinatra,* Lex McLean, Queen Elizabeth II, Terry Hurlock, Hurlock lookalike Leo Sayer (if he'd been in Slayer), the unknown composer of 'God Save the King', Willie 'The Deedle' Waddell, Don 'Rhino' Kichenbrand, George 'Corky' Young, Korky the Cat, Marti Pellow, Alastair Burnet, Jim White, Brian 'Why are you so great?' Laudrup,

* Sinatra performed at Ibrox in 1990, his last-ever UK show, mercifully resisting the temptation to sign off: 'I did it my way by the way . . .'

Gazza, Bazza Boozegate, The Two Andy Gorams, The One Andy Cameron, Ginger Spice, Buffalo Bill,[*] Helen Baxendale,[**] Clive Anderson, the gastronome who dreamed up the Loyalburger, the culinarian behind the Jock Wallace Memorial Monkey Steak,[***] Donald Findlay, Sean Connery, all the Orangemen in *Just Another Saturday*, all the Scottish meeja types who are closet Rangers fans, Monster Munch's orange beastie,[****] Lulu, Jim Davidson, Reverend Ian Paisley, Pastor Jack Glass and a hologram of Scott who followed, followed the boys in royal blue in his youth.

The pass bisected all of them, it was the pass of the millennium. No, more than that: *the assist*. For a goal resulted from this pass of passes. And what was the final score again? Rangers 6, Hibs 1.

For this – for their eulogising, fetishising, canonising of the pass – Hibs fans were subjected to plenty of merry abuse. They weren't just consoling themselves with it; all supporters after a gruesome afternoon in Govan will do this, pounce on the teensiest crumb of comfort. No, it was the genuine, unshakable belief that the pass – The Pass – trumped everything.

* One of the giants of the American Old West brought his travelling show to Glasgow in 1891, basing himself in Dennistoun not far from Ibrox, which is enough for Rangers fans to claim him as a celebrity supporter.

** 'Who do you love?' John Hannah asks Baxendale in the romcom *Truth or Dare*, to which she replies: 'Hamilton Accies.' Hannah snorts: 'Ach, you've always been a Rangers fan.'

*** The snack of choice for Wallace the squaddie when stationed on the Malay peninsula during the 1950s, and as he was engaged in fierce jungle warfare there really wasn't much alternative.

**** Monster Munch was the favourite wheat-based nibble of Kris Boyd. 'My body is my temple and I've always loved the sheer scale of Angkor Wat,' the player might have affirmed, tipping the Boydy Mass Index to the supreme irritation of Ibrox manager Paul Le Guen.

The result? Didn't matter. Disillusionment with the state of the country? Not important. Deap-seated personal unhappiness? And your point is, caller? Because here was great beauty, the ultimate expression, football as art. And did the faithful cringe or feel even the tiniest bit embarrassed when social media jokers among the teasing mob freeze-framed Allan in the act of delivering his rapier swish and submitted the image to – *mon Dieu!* – the Louvre? Not a bit. In fact, this only encouraged Hibbies to luxuriate in The Pass even more.

How far had it travelled? Estimates varied from 40 yards to halfway back along the M8. How the heck had he managed to thread it directly into the quivering heart of the Rangers box? Fearless Thai cave rescuers, or daring Chilean mine collapse squads, would have gasped at Allan's selected route. There simply seemed no way through.

And how beautiful was the player who mined this diamond from the rubble of the game? Allan must go down as the biggest Hibee man crush, provoking homoerotic tingles in hulking Leith stevedores with the merest wisp of hair falling over his pretty face. His manager in 2019 was Paul Heckingbottom who on another day, responding to fan displeasure at having cut short the floppy-fringed, dimple-cheeked pin-up's contribution, sarcastically quipped: 'I didn't know it was a criminal offence around here to substitute Scott Allan.' Heckingbottom was sacked soon after.

19

CUSTARD PIE MALARKEY, STEPLADDER MISHAP, RUNAWAY BEDS AND PIANOS

THEN . . . IN another game at Ibrox, another demonstration of piercing precision, another dubious claim to fame. And something else which, try as Hibs might over the next 150 years, they will probably never manage to repeat.

On 30 March 2024, Nectarios Triantis lined up a free kick in the Hibees' half, struck it with extreme prejudice like he wanted to clear the Copland Road stand at the other end of the ground, but only succeeded in smashing the ball into the face of Joe Newell who'd been a few feet up ahead but made the mistake of turning round, possibly to caution his team-mate a split second too late: 'Try not to do anything risible.'

Newell was knocked out, which might in itself have qualified as a uniquely ludicrous moment, but it wasn't over. The ball had been struck with such force, that rebounding back the other way and past Triantis, it scudded the phizog of Will Fish who promptly joined Newell prostrate on the turf.

Street football urchins still playing in darkness under sparking lights would view the events at Ibrox as the nearest equivalent to the freak, never seen and surely mythical 'double kerbie': striking one pavement edge then bouncing across to the other.

And black-and-white movie comedy titans Charlie Chaplin and Buster Keaton, and Laurel and Hardy and the Marx Brothers, would reflect on whole careers devoted to carefully and minutely assembled chaos, of custard pie malarkey and stepladder mishap and runaway beds and pianos, and reluctantly concede: 'That beats us for slapstick, oh yes siree.'

Football bloopers tapes – once a solid Christmas stocking filler – have had their appeal dulled by social media pouncing immediately on every calamity. Hibs' Three Stooges, though, will never get boring. If a zany comic strip about a hopeless football team was to lose two players in this manner, it would not be credible. Which makes the real thing all the more bogglingly bonkers.

The poleaxed pair didn't seem to be faking it, which has become an issue amid football's new concern over head injuries because players quickly realised they didn't actually need to have been decapitated to get games halted and waste time. We might wonder, when Newell and Fish came round, if there was agreement between them that they should stay down, rather than face the jeers of an unsympathetic Ibrox, and who knows, maybe this was done in shrill female falsettos like that of Stan Laurel singing 'The Trail of the Lonesome Pine' in *Way Out West*, right after having been bashed on the head with a mallet.

With checks that neither player had been left as cross-eyed as Ben Turpin still ongoing, the incident was already rebounding round the world and the world couldn't stop laughing. The manager, Nick Montgomery, ensured even more hilarity by demonstrating a level of deranged upbeatness which suggested he might have been a third casualty of Triantis's unguided missile. 'It's great that this has gone viral, for whatever reason,' he said. 'Any publicity is good publicity. The club are being 'liked' worldwide and obviously we'd want that to happen because of our goals and our successes. But there are probably people somewhere on the planet who had never heard of Hibs before and are now following us.'

To all the nutters, masochists, perverts, sad sacks, absurdists and doomed romantics out there, a big Hibees welcome.

20

IT'S TIME TO SAY SORRY TO DUNDEE, AND DUMBARTON

APOLOGIES ARE having a moment. Or at least the demanding of them. In far-off lands, King Charles will endure three-and-a-half-hour welcome ceremonies of native custom and alarming dance, with a canopy of three and a half banana leaves offering zero protection from the baking heat, and for this there's no gratitude. Just: will he say sorry for some colonial unpleasantness, three and a half centuries ago?

Politicians get it constantly. 'Are you going to apologise, Minister?' demand the doorstepping hack pack. 'What for *now*?' 'Oh, we dunno, turning up five minutes late for your weekly surgery last month? That'll do . . .'

But maybe, given that Hibs are big and grown up and 150, it's time to show some contrition. Proper regret, not what's become known as the non-apology apology, Boris Johnson's snivelling, sleekit 'Sorry, but, uh, not really . . .' And the reason why we should? Those songs.

'We are Hibernian FC, we hate Jam Tarts and we hate Dundee . . .'

Obviously a disinclination towards the capital rivals is understandable and indeed compulsory, but what have Dundee ever done to us? There is no history of ill-feeling or grudge. For Hibs the city by the Tay is not most associated with jute, jam, journalism . . . and jinx.

Dundee have never stopped us winning the league. It might

have been different on the last day of the 1947–48 season if the Famous Five had still required a point from Dens Park, but Rangers crumbled just before then so the trip became a pleasant spring excursion up the coast. And in 1951–52 it was a victory over Dundee which clinched the title again.

In the Scottish Cup Dundee have never beaten Hibs with a miles-offside last-minute goal. The most memorable tie was in 1974: a tremendous 3–3 draw at Easter Road (Alan Gordon hat-trick), Dundee winning the replay, combined attendance 60,000, no complaints.

It is Hearts who have cause to stick pins in an effigy or a Robertson's marmalade mascot with Dundee having effectively relegated the Jambos during the Covid interruptus season with the most controversial vote since Cliff Richard lost the Eurovision Song Contest to Spain's 'La La La' as General Franco was accused of rigging the outcome.

And then there was the 1985–86 season when Hearts chucked away the title at Dens Park (see ch. 122). Hibs have a lot to thank Dundee for, yet poor show, we denigrate them in song for the sake of a cheap rhyme.

And what about Dumbarton? Why take their name in vain? In 2015–16 with Hibs and Rangers in the Championship missing their time-honoured foes, they had to make do with each other. It was a fair old ding-dong. Rangers manager Mark Warburton wound up Easter Road by refusing to ever mention Hibs by name. Meanwhile the Ibrox hordes sang of their man's 'magic hat' and he steered the club to the title.

But when Hibs beat Rangers to the Scottish Cup, the fans came up with their own version of the chant:

'Warburton's a fanny, he wears a fanny's hat. Works against Dumbarton and other shite like that . . .'

Okay, so maybe the critical response to that lyric would not be of the order of: 'Thank you, Noël Coward!' Perhaps for sly, sardonic wit it's some way short of Donald Fagen and Walter

Becker's Steely Dan *oeuvre* (and how I love using that term, being a swotty student of the *New Musical Express* when the mag was peak pretentious). It's still pretty funny, I think, but hard on Dumbarton, by no means the worst team in the division that season, mucking up John McGinn's debut and mugging Hibs again later in the campaign. We've never had any issue with them. They were the team we beat to lift the Scottish Cup for the first time in 1887. So soz, sons and all.

21

FIRST TO WEAR THE GREEN

WE COULDA been contenders. We coulda lived in a place called Paradise. We coulda had as our No. 1 celebrity fan an octogenarian, blonde-on-blonde (-on-blonde), gravel-gargling, couldn't-keep-it-in-the-breeks,couldn't-be-dissuaded-from-leopard-skin-breeks, never-with-wallet, never-without-volumising spray, model train-shunting, knighted, tonight's-the-knighted rock superstar.

Yes! Rod Stewart! Why didn't he implore *us* to loosen off that pretty French gown? Spread *our* wings so he could drive his OO gauge Chicagoan through *our* love tunnel? Why's he not a Hibby, especially considering his dad idolised Gordon Smith, hanging an action shot of the great man on the wall at home, and how come it's Celtic he arranges life and touring around, gets all teary-eyed in the stands about?

It's complicated, as they say in romcoms. Hibs, as we know, began life in 1875, the first club founded in Scotland by Irish immigrants. In 1887 they won the Scottish Cup and Glasgow's Irish were impressed, all the more so when having feted the victors in a church before the journey back east, they were urged: follow our lead. Hibs were happy to help Celtic get started with games and guest players. And then . . . murder polis! You've nicked half our team! No, we haven't, football's still amateur, contracts don't exist, we simply offered the guys, admittedly your top men, a few florins and half crowns and they came right across.

Hibs, having done all the hard work, suffered 'Scotchmen only' rejection, persevered, endured more setbacks but ultimately they made it easier for the next Irish roots team to come along. Whereupon the next Irish roots team to come along simply sailed straight through.

'We are sailing, we are SAIL-ING! . . .' Yes, Rod, we hear you, and we know how things panned out. Celtic embraced professionalism, Hibs saw the treasurer abscond with the funds, temporarily going out of business. Hibs threw away the green and white hoops, Celtic retrieved them from the smelly kit box and made them world famous.

Celtic are a global brand. Invited to play glamour friendlies all over the world, they can plant flags and sell shirts in virgin territories ripe for a soppily romantic origin story, though perhaps the actual beginnings are skimmed over, along with the Wayne Biggins years.

And in America everyone wants to be Irish and they'll try and trace their own origin stories all the way back to the old country's Horetown or, just along the raggedy County Wexford road, Bastardstown. And it's not just the ordinary folks of Bastardstown, Ohio who do this but politicians and actors too.

Hibbies must sup their Bovril peevishly and watch as the Celtic family grows, and grows. When an actress like Jennifer Love Hewitt (not her only appearance in this book) informs a US chat show host that, yes, she's a Celtic fan, we might want to yell at the telly: 'Really? And are you going to tell us that in your dreamboat-obsessed teens you had a poster of Pat McCluskey on your bedroom wall?' But there's no getting away from it, Celtic are huge, and they win everything.

Did we miss a trick? Are we jealous? In October 1888 when Celtic came to Leith for what was supposed to be a friendly, Hibs-supporting navvies shouted 'Judas!' at their former players for swapping sides and invaded the pitch. These days the cry will more than likely be: 'We're the first to wear the green!'

But really, good luck to Celtic who, with the advantage of a bigger heartland didn't have to keep nicking Hibees and so were always going to outstrip us. Yes, they were sleekit at the outset and lacked some grace, but there's never been a Politeness & Decorum Cup or a Selfless Shield in football (though a Moral High Ground Bowl or a Shy Retiring Founders Quaich would definitely have our name on it).

Would we want to be them? Not for me. Relentless success must surely get boring. Could my Celtic friends distinguish one Scottish Cup from another on the honours roll call and remember who they beat in which final? No, I'm happy to have won once in 123 years and counting, honest. And in 2016 we had a lovely big parade, something denied Celtic because of the local difficulty with Rangers and the fear of Glasgow blowing up. We'll always have 2016 and if I may paraphrase Rod the Mod: it's in my heart, it's in my soul, it'll be my breath should I grow old.

22

GOTHENBURG? FERGIE? YOU'RE WELCOME, ABERDEEN

JUST THINK: the Swedish city of Gothenburg would mean Volvo and Björn from Abba and . . . actually that might be more or less it. Nothing resembling a fantastic European triumph, anyway. Alex Ferguson's sacking by St Mirren could have been the last anyone heard of him. No New Firm, no globe-swallowing Manchester United, no old-school socialist homilies for New Labour, no racehorses, no elasticated concept of time, no hairdryer, no knighthood.

There would have been no trace of these guys: Wee Gordon Strachan, Big Doug Rougvie, little, round Joey Harper, snake-hipped Charlie Cooke, Zoltan Varga, Graham Leggat, Jock Hutton, Steve Archibald, Jimmy Smith, Henning Boel, 'Tubby' Ogston, 'Bumper' Graham or Willie Miller holding up all those cups with one mighty, macho paw. At least not in the red of Aberdeen FC.

None of the local colour: swooping, pie-crazy seagulls, scrapping casuals, 'Stand Free', self-deprecating ditties about sheep. And all because – get this – there would have been no Dandy Dons if it wasn't for Hibs.

In 1902 Hibs had the league flag and the Scottish Cup but didn't really know what to do with their prizes. Where to display them when they didn't feel properly at home anywhere? Nomads, the club wondered after their difficult early years if they were truly welcome in Edinburgh. And, tired of this rootless existence, they contemplated a new life in the north-east.

It's difficult to grasp this now. How the Hibees might have just skedaddled, their story ending abruptly in the capital and restarting in Aberdeen. All the highs and lows, comedy and tragedy, coagulating into a maddening obsession, an open-ended box set, for an entirely different audience. A century-plus of Hibs that at first some might have followed keenly if wistfully from a distance of 128 miles, but before long the ties would loosen – passing them to the next generation becoming a near-futile act – and eventually there would be no one left alive back where the club used to belong who remembered them.

But the Granite City had no interest in this simpering, slushy – and as would be obvious later – very Hibsy melodrama and no intention of letting it play out. Here, hearts were obviously carved from granite, too.

Three senior clubs operated in the city at that time – Orion, Victoria United and the team calling themselves Aberdeen. There had been an idea to merge, producing an outfit capable of competing in the top flight of Scottish football which Hibs occupied, but within the city this had been met with some resistance. Each club was a separate entity. Each fancied they could win parochial competitions such as the Rhodesia Cup. Each viewed the others as rivals.

Then suddenly, stomping over the moors, came these marauders from the south. Pittodrie had staged a Scotland international and for Hibs the former police horse dunghill seemed an attractive option for relocation.

Now, it's a bit of a stretch for Hibbies to visualise their club as big shots, being this arrogant and presumptuous. But 'the Hibernian question', as it was called, finally registered with those opposed to amalgamation, prompting them to wake up to the threat. Like the Spartans and the Athenians putting aside their enmity to fend off the Persian invasion, the three Aberdeen teams joined forces. They did not erect a wall or conscript local fishermen and instead in 1903 formed themselves into the club* that exists today.

* And the name of that club? What about 'Abdn'? Removing the vowels might have been trendy and edgy back then, too, and maybe there wouldn't have been any ridicule. Didn't happen to the football team. Can't speak for any of the finance houses.

23

INVOKING THE SPIRIT OF MUNGO PARK, WITHOUT THE SPEAR-CHUCKING NATIVES

IT'S 1909 and Celtic have achieved Scottish football's first double and Rangers have gone an entire season winning every match. So our game is properly established, right? All the big boys present and correct, and the two biggest already up to their tricks and their tyranny? Not quite, for here come Dundee United, with a little help from Hibs, the missionaries-cum-business start-up experts from Leith who, venturing along the Tay this time, might have been attempting to invoke the spirit of Mungo Park and his exploration of the Niger, though without being waylaid by territorial hippos, spear-chucking natives and dangerous rapids.

Aberdeen had been formed out of mild panic and Celtic's emergence was highly controversial. By comparison, the arrival of Dundee United might have been drama-free, but again Hibs' inspiration had been crucial.

As with Edinburgh, Ireland's Great Famine had brought an influx of migrants to the city of Dundee, initially those drawn by its textile and linen factories, and by the 1850s nearly a fifth of the population was Irish-born. These people needed a football team to follow and the first to take their lead from Hibs were Dundee Harp in 1879. They disbanded before the century's end and other Catholic clubs were just as short-lived, but in the spring of 1909 local bicycle trader Pat Reilly and some Irish business chums founded a team they hoped would last – Dundee Hibernian.

This was United's original name. They also took their colours from Easter Road. It was only polite, therefore, to say nothing of a sound move commercially and also motivationally, to have Hibs as special guests at their inauguration on 18 August.

'Wearin' o' the green,' was the headline on the *Dundee Courier*'s report. 'An epoch in the football history of Dundee was entered upon last night, when the new Irish senior combination, the Hibs, had a house-warming.'

A crowd of 7,000 rolled up for the 'gala match' at Tannadice, renamed from Clepington Park, purchased when yet another Dundonian side had gone bust, taking all but the grass with them.

The local Irish community worked tirelessly to have the ground ready. A new pavilion was erected, turnstiles in the nick of time, with music on the afternoon provided by a band from the Mars Training Ship moored in the Tay as a refuge for destitute boys.

Lord Provost Sir James Urquhart performed the ceremonial kick-off – a 'very neat pass', added the dispatch. The *Courier* declared the match 'interesting'. The Provost went further, calling it 'very interesting and altogether instructive', complimenting the home side on the manner in which they'd 'comported' themselves – especially given they were 'pitted against a team of the calibre of the Edinburgh Hibs'. He hoped the newcomers would 'enjoy many years of prosperity in the game'.

The match finished 1–1, Hibs' goal from half-back John O'Hara earning him maybe the most unusual individual prize in the club's 150 years – a top-of-the-range two-wheeler from Reilly's bike shop.

The Provost hoped the bike would carry the player to 'many scenes of future victories'. What became of it, no one knows. What became of Dundee Hibernian was that they held on to their name for 14 years, were forced to drop out of the Scottish League, almost went to the wall, attempted to resume as Dundee

City only for Dundee to pull rank, eventually agreeing to drop 'Hibernian' in favour of 'United' to broaden the club's appeal.

They dropped the green shirts, too, but peak prosperity would come in the 1980s with a league championship and sensational European nights. Later, United would claim Scotland's best run-on song – 'Love is in the Air' by Australia's Glasgow-born ex-sheet metal worker John Paul Young.

24

WERE HIBS, MISSING THE JOKE, FIRST TO GO WOKE?

IS THERE a perky little Beatles connection for Hibs? Where is the Fab Four/Famous Five interface? Stuart Sutcliffe, the fifth Beatle, was born in Edinburgh. The teenaged John Lennon loved his summer holidays in the capital, hanging out with favourite cousins, and when old enough to bus it up from Liverpool by himself amusing the coach driver sufficiently with his skiffley routine to be gifted a mouth organ from St Andrew Square lost property – the very moothie, so legend has it, later played on 'Love Me Do'.

It's 'Cry Baby Cry' which features the only Scottish reference in the entire, glorious *oeuvre*. A namecheck for the 'Duchess of Kirkcaldy', then, if not the Prince of Wingers.

But George Harrison wrote 'Taxman'. And in 2012 the song was played in a gently provocative manner over the Easter Road public address. This act cost a man his job.

At the time Hearts were bankrupt with HM Revenue & Customs threatening liquidation. Willie Docherty, Hibs' stadium announcer, thought he'd have some fun with this and, after all, what's a rivalry for if not Simon Wiesenthal Center-level interrogation of their every move and especially every misfortune, throwing up the opportunity for wind-ups – be they large, small or here, a £450,000 bill for unpaid tax?

The Hibee hierarchy didn't see it that way and when, in the build-up to a game against Dundee United, the unfortunate DJ spun Harrison's wail over the Beatles having to hand over 90 per cent of their earnings to Harold Wilson's government, the club sacked Docherty for a 'breach of conduct'.

Were Hearts stung by Hibs' teasing? Someone who wasn't was Docherty's opposite number at Tynecastle, Scott Wilson. Knowing the pair were good friends I looked up Wilson, since retired from his gig, in the hope he could put me in touch with Docherty but the latter had passed away just a few weeks before. 'Willie was a great announcer and I chuckled as loud as any Hibby when I heard he'd played "Taxman" that day,' Wilson said. 'If the roles had been reversed I'd like to think I'd have had his wit and done the same thing. He shouldn't have been sacked. Humourless Hibs!'

It seems as if Hearts allowed Wilson more leeway when spinning platters. Either that or they missed his subliminal messaging. When the perma-tanned Jimmy Calderwood brought one of his teams to Tynecastle, Wilson would reach for REM's 'Orange Crush'. After Hibs' Leigh Griffiths felt the firm tap of store security on his shoulder as he tried to exit his local Tesco, the song was 'Shoplifters of the World Unite' by the Smiths.

Wilson added: 'The average football-goer is a hairy-arsed, 37-year-old male who might not have picked up on these wee jokes. Maybe the troglodytes would, when Celtic visited, have wanted me to play "Gypsys, Tramps & Thieves", but that would have been disrespectful.

'I remember, though, Rangers being at Tynecastle in the wake of the SFA vowing to clamp down on sectarian chanting and their fans defiantly belting out the complete horrible songbook for 90 long minutes. At the final whistle, after the usual housekeeping messages, I signed off: "Wherever you're headed, be it home or back to the 17th century, thank you very much for your attendance and have a safe journey."'

Hearts may have been broke but concerning Docherty did Hibs have to be quite so woke? That said, 2012 was long before the world started to find offence in absolutely everything. So sadistically – I'm Hibs therefore I am – the unfortunate incident has to be claimed as yet another first for our club.

25

HOMBURG HAT, FROCKED COAT, STRIPED TROUSERS . . . A CIRCUS SHOWMAN

ON 17 JUNE 1939, Willie McCartney sent a letter to each of his 28 players: 'I trust your holidays have been well enjoyed. Training for the new season commences on Monday 24 July at 10 a.m. Will you please be forward early so that no time will be lost in getting down to work.'

The letter was published in the *Sunday Post* which predicted a bright future for the young team. 'I don't think there is a more ambitious club in the country at the moment than Hibernians,' declared the author of the piece. 'It's a great and glorious adventure, this Easter Road experiment with youth.'

The adventure was stalled by the Second World War causing the abandonment of the league after just five matches. But this wasn't a new challenge for the manager – he'd had to rebuild Hearts when they were decimated by the First World War. McCartney wasn't quite able to bring success to Tynecastle and so was determined to be 'forward early' in his endeavours in Leith, hence the reason that on one notable Sunday in 1941 he pointed his car in the direction of Arbroath and its Seaforth Hotel.

Sixteen-year-old Gordon Smith believed he'd joined Hearts, the team he supported from afar in Montrose. After all, the *Sunday Express* said so. But he went to meet McCartney anyway and found him most persuasive. The Hearts deal was conditional on a trial; Hibs would dispense with any audition and,

£10 signing-on fee in his pocket, put him straight into the team – against the Jam Tarts. The rest is history.

A big man with a big laugh, McCartney always made an impression, always stood out. Not difficult amid the hodden grey of wartime, but his favoured garb is worth detailing: 'Homburg hat, carnation, frocked coat, striped trousers – he looked like a circus showman.' The description was Lawrie Reilly's, next of the Famous Five to join, and then came a further key signing, with the *Sunday Post* almost orgasmic, if that's conceivable, after a goalscoring debut: 'Manager McCartney has produced another one out of his hat. Meet flaxen-haired Eddie Turnbull, a boy with personality plus . . . the most thrustful, intelligent attacker in this galaxy of forward talent . . . if this is by way of a rhapsody, it must be excused.'

In January 1948, Hibs were bidding for a first title in 45 years when, during a Scottish Cup tie at Albion Rovers' Cliftonhill, McCartney suffered a heart attack in the boardroom. He was rushed back home to Edinburgh where the players followed, hoping he might make a recovery, but he died later that night. Determined to hoist the league flag in his memory, his charges went on a brilliant ten-game winning run.

In 1952, a few months after the team that McCartney built had claimed their third championship, Hibs were invited down to Arsenal for a friendly. In his preview of the match, the *Daily Mirror*'s Ross Hall paid fulsome tribute: 'I can visualise Willie in his fruity bass baritone, booming out as Hibs take the field: "What fun I had signing him, and him, and him, and him."

'Easter Road, before he dropped his considerable bulk into the managerial chair, advertised poverty.' And from 'barren wastes' he fashioned one of the most exciting teams in all football. 'The walls were painted, the floors re-covered and fresh young faces made their appearance.' Only Tommy Younger from the side which lined up at Highbury came after him. Only Willie Ormond cost more than 'a few shillings'.

Hall continued to imagine Leith's dandyesque alchemist looking down on the challenge match: 'He'll crack a joke, and the thunder of his unheard laughter will go echoing through the corridors to be lost in the vastness of the unknown from whence there had come earlier the shades of the great . . . the great Willie McCartney!'

26

DON'T OTHER TEAMS 'HIBS IT' TOO?

IT'S ANOTHER claim to fame. Or notification of our notoriety. No team can lose like Hibs. That is, no team can Hibs it like Hibs. Is that true, though? We may have a way of cocking up that's defined and dictionary-ratified, but don't other teams do something similar? Lose when they should win? Lose when winning in the game and seemingly serene? Lose because in the closing minutes knees turn to jelly and brains to blancmange?

Apparently not. There may be 50 ways to leave your lover. There may be an indeterminate number of things to do in Denver when you're potted heid. But Hibsing it is right out there on its own, an exclusive club for an exclusive experience and private pain. Total number of members: one.

Peak Hibsing it came in 2016 when Alan Stubbs's side were desperately striving for a return to the Premiership while maintaining interest in both cups all the way to conclusion. But the term wasn't properly understood. Every setback was described as the team having snatched defeat from the jaws of victory. No matter the opposition's efforts and rightful claims to have been better on the day, yet more Hibee calamity and collapse was what swung the result and ultimately this was the story.

There was a feeding frenzy. Erudite observer or yappy social media wind-up merchant, the phrase was irresistible. 2016 was a fractious year of Leave vs Remain but it seemed that Hibsing it was being referenced even more times than Brexit.

The long-suffering faithful bristled. Hang on, if this is our thing – and we like when things are specific and special to us – then don't dilute the essence. Don't cloud real, proper, verifiable Hibsing it. Indeed, when there's an opportunity to insist without fear of contradiction that we've Hibsed it, don't, you know, Hibs it.

Perhaps the first instance was way back in 1890 when the club took absolutely no interest in the formation of the Scottish League, neglecting to send a representative to the inaugural meeting. So the membership of ten included Vale of Leven, Cowlairs, Abercorn – and Hearts – but not Hibs.

In the 1947 Scottish Cup final, much fancied, they scored first against Aberdeen – after just 35 seconds – but ended up losing. In 1950, they went to Fir Park, demolished Motherwell 6–2 and eagerly looked forward to the next match – the League Cup final against the same side a week later. Result: Hibees 0, Well 3.

Two years later, while regularly trouncing top English teams in friendlies, Hibs were selected for a live TV first. Fans crammed on to pavements outside electrical stores, some possibly experiencing television for the first time, maybe a few nervously wondering if the medium might steal their souls. The images beamed up from Highbury may have been fuzzy but the scoreline was clear-cut: 7–1 to Arsenal.

Also in the Famous Five era, also receiving the big build-up, Easter Road's first-ever floodlit match would end in defeat, as would the game in front of the stadium's all-time highest attendance. But that team won a few games as well. No one accused them of Hibsing it.

So then what? The world went tabloid, dealing in extremes. Black or white. Death or glory (preferably death). It keeps happening. OMG. Who's to blame? Hell to pay. Perspective – in politics as well, in everything – was replaced by shrieking. And Hibs, with their fanciful notions and absurd dreams and yes, increasingly horrible history, weren't allowed to lose any more significant games.

And on 21 May 2016 we didn't.

27

'I BOUGHT THAT SHEEPSKIN COAT FOR EASTER ROAD IN WINTER'

RUNNING THE gauntlet of the hodden grey mass. Engaging with your public, whether you like it or not, on a long, steep, completely exposed climb up one of the biggest terracings in the land. Then, still conspicuous, the ascent of a ladder to reach the gantry. It's constructed from scaffolding poles, planks of wood thrown down for the flooring, tarpaulin sheets lashed together for the walls. Who works here? Or rather: who can possibly work here when their job is to theorise, extemporise, intellectualise and lyricise? About football? What's more, Scottish football? Yes, this is an actual job, or it was – a highly specialised position, highly situated.

Archie Macpherson created the role for himself, and when the occasion demanded, when Easter Road was the game of the day, he'd be right up there on the cloud line, like Christ the Redeemer in a sheepskin three-quarter-length coat with a microphone jammed against his chapped lips, describing the action for *Sportscene* while the seagulls impersonated Stuka bombers.

The most inhospitable, unforgiving vantage point in football commentary? 'Well, the views were worth it,' laughed Macpherson when we spoke, shortly after his 90th birthday. 'There was the Firth of Forth over my shoulder and across to the left Arthur's Seat.' Mountain and sea. Or to be precise, an extinct volcano and an inlet keeping Fife at a safe distance. John

Ford with the benefit of VistaVision couldn't have improved on it. 'Wonderful!' confirmed our guide.

Down the years the camera position has moved from one side of the pitch to the other and nowadays is snugly situated at the back of the West Stand, no chance of runny noses forming icicles, but Macpherson achieved a full service record on the old roofless East Terrace, and the sheepskin served too.

'That bloody coat,' he said. 'I have to tell you I bought it specifically to cope with Easter Road. One time there, in the deep midwinter, snow falling snow on snow, my director Bill Malcolm made a snowman and stuck the coat on it, together with my hat and scarf. Sam Leitch on *Grandstand* said: "And now over to Archie . . ." Instead the nationwide audience got Frosty.' Rightly, the coat now has pride of place in the Scottish Football Museum.

Macpherson added: 'It was at Hibs, for the one and only time in my career, that the merest shred of sympathy was extended towards me. High winds blew the tarpaulin right off. It was terrifying. The gantry was shoogling and swaying and I feared it might come down. We carried on – we always did. But in my earpiece, from back in the warmth of the outside broadcast van, I could heard Liz Rennie, a lovely lady who commanded me with a stopwatch, whispering: "Poor Archie."'

But was Easter Road actually the worst? Our man thought for a bit and remembered Hampden: miserable view, anaemic floodlights and, on one fateful night, a nervous trainee cameraman who kept fumbling cases of film, conspiring in a Rangers–Kilmarnock ten-goal thriller appearing in highlights form as a 1–1 draw. 'Years later, on a flight to the States, the stewardess said: "Sir, would you like to go up to first class – there's a gentleman offering you a drink." It was the rookie lensman, who went on to become a famous movie-maker, who directed *Gregory's Girl*. Bill Forsyth and I had a chuckle about that dire night on our champagne ride.'

Then Macpherson remembered Rugby Park: 'The commentator had to shin up a pillar then traverse a chasm to reach the gantry over the heads of the crowd. That was too much for poor old George Davidson with his war injury. But, no, Easter Road wasn't the worst. Hibs supplied an urn so we had tea to warm us and the fans weren't too antagonistic – they were there to see good football. My son became a Hibby, also my grandson – Dr Stuart Macpherson of Darwin College, Cambridge, and you can't get better than that in physics – who's an absolute fanatic.

'Eddie Turnbull was irascible. Once, when an interview was halted by the clanking of hammers, he marched up to the maintenance crew and shouted at them in language that would get you thrown out of a brothel. Another time, when I couldn't tell him how much he was going to be paid for his wise words, he turned on his heel with a snarl – "Ach, fuck off!" But the Tornadoes were a swashbuckling team. Rain, snow or typhoon, when I was down to cover Hibs I was always expectant, always excited.'

28

'NONE MORE FASCINATING IN A FOOTBALL ARENA'

FOOTBALL'S GONE mad. Everyone says this all the time now and it's to do with the money. How much is spent. How much is wasted. How many sacked managers clubs can be simultaneously compensating at any one time. How much players earn per minute. How much super-agents pocket in cream-offs.

How much that 'celebrity chef'* forked out to get on to the pitch at the 2022 World Cup final and grab the trophy for his 'famous salt-sprinkling gesture'. And, though he's given up the gig, the memory endures: how excited Jim White used to be on transfer deadline day and, how if you watched Sky's rolling coverage for too long, his trademark bright yellow tie took on the power of the sun, causing permanent damage to the retinas.

But maybe it's always been like this. And maybe way back in 1893 when Willie 'Darlin' Groves became the world's first £100 footballer, there was much choking over the mutton stew and the collective gasps scared the horses pulling the streetcars.

Groves's career was one of many firsts. A first league title for Aston Villa. Triumph with West Bromwich Albion in the first

* Salt Bae, whose London restaurant has been described as 'ludicrous' by food critic Jay Rayner and where prices peaked at £1,450 for the signature gold-covered steak.

FA Cup final played with goal nets. The first Celtic goal in the inaugural Old Firm match. But before all of that he was Hibs' first superstar.

In 1887, first game at inside-forward, aged 16, he scored a Scottish Cup hat-trick. Groves was rapid with a diabolical dribble and a rocket shot, although accounts vary on what he looked like on the pitch. He was 'stocky and powerful' or perhaps 'dainty and timid'. There was no dispute, however, over the handsome features borne out by old photos, like those of a matinee idol, although Groves predated the movies. Little wonder Hibs fans conferred that nickname on their pomaded prodigy.

Darlin' became the team's lucky cup charm, scoring all the way to the final and after another goal against Dumbarton the trophy was theirs for the first time. As the world came to know, this wouldn't be a happy Hibee habit, and the tenuous cup connection very nearly didn't begin there (see ch. 11).

Teenaged he may have been but Groves, whose Scotland debut quickly followed, was already developing a keen sense of his own worth. He quickly moved to Celtic then just as quickly followed the money to England's professional set-up and WBA where he shared a dressing room with Jack Reynolds. 'I'm Darlin',' he might have ventured. 'What do they call you?' 'Baldy,' would have been Reynolds' reply.

Villa were powerless to stop the pair in that FA Cup final so decided to tap them up. There were fines – and the order to pay Albion the record sum for Groves. The next time the two clubs met and fearing crowd trouble, stronger fencing was installed. Although the fee – half the average house price – didn't seem to put our man off his game, a contractual dispute would force him home to Hibs. He helped his old club reach the 1896 Scottish Cup final against Hearts, played at St Bernard's Logie Green, and the only time the showpiece has been moved out of Glasgow.

There was a sad end: Groves was struck down by tuberculosis and died aged just 39 and penniless. 'No more fascinating player ever appeared in a football arena,' read one obituary. 'A sort of Romeo figure in the sport . . . tall, sinewy and graceful on the ball, his work was beautifully close, deceptive and artful.' What a darlin'.

29

IT WAS AS IF THE H BOMB HAD BEEN DROPPED ON ARTHUR'S SEAT

CLICHÉ ALERT No. 347: A game described as being 'one for the ages'. No. 348: 'Iconic'. No 349: 'Under the lights'. Of course it is, the match is happening *at night*! *In darkness*! 'Under the lights' infers significance, prestige and for goodness sakes glamour. Inviting a sense of wonder, when all evening kick-offs, right down the leagues and involving much thud and blunder, require artificial illumination. 'Under the lights' is superfluous, the function of floodlights self-evident. And honestly – broad-beamed, high-intensity – they've been a thing in football for a while now.

From that you might assume the only legitimate response to a telly commentator blarting about an '*iconic*' game that's '*one for the ages*' and is taking place '*under the lights*' would be in the spirit of *Wacky Races*' Dick Dastardly: 'Aagh, aagh and triple aagh!' But wait, I know of a match deserving all of this drool: Hibs 5, Napoli 0.

The Hibees were 4–1 down from the first leg of their Inter-Cities Fairs Cup tie in 1967 and presumed to be out. But at Easter Road Bobby Duncan struck a wonder goal to ignite the club's greatest-ever comeback. 'Every time I see Bobby and the chat gets round to that game the yardage gets longer and longer,' Pat Stanton told me. 'I'm sure next time he'll be saying he hit it from way back at Smith's Bakery.' (See ch. 9.)

Stanton scored, too. A photograph of his header is the game's defining image, and for two reasons. The first is that the Napoli goalkeeper, performing a star jump in a vain effort to save, is the great Dino Zoff. Three years later for Italy in the Azteca Stadium, after Carlos Alberto roared on to Pelé's supercool set-up in the World Cup final, he might have screamed to himself: 'Okay, Goal of the Century, but *por favor, Dio*! Don't let Brazil get to five like Hibs!'

The second reason is the glow. In the photo, looking back towards the Dunbar End, it's as if the lemonade factory is on fire or the H bomb has been dropped on Arthur's Seat or the aliens have landed their spaceship.

It could be about the photography; it could be to do with the floodlights themselves and the liquidy shimmer – the equivalent of vinyl LP warmth – which comes from them being fixed to tall pylons rather than stand roofs which is the norm now. In other words: it's an analogue thing. Most of the pylons have gone from football grounds. At the age I was when darkness fell, figuratively, on Zoff and Napoli, they didn't really work for Subbuteo, getting in the way as we crawled across the carpet, flicking fingers poised and alert, but glimpsing the towers for real from a car or train window, the snuggly reassurance of towns with teams, never ever got dull.

And in Scotland the very first pylons to go up were at Easter Road. Hibs on a European tour in 1950 were initially nervous of floodlit football – thinking already plugged-in friendly hosts Young Boys of Bern would have an unfair advantage – but very quickly entranced. 'This is the future,' they reasoned, 'let there be light.' And on 18 October 1954, when Hearts were invited across the city for a friendly to christen the system, there was.

30

'GLORY, GLORY TO THE HIBEES' IS THE A-SIDE AND IT PRESAGED RAP

WHAT, YOU think fans are petty and provincial? Flashback to the school common room where we'd argue about anything and everything. The scariest film, the funniest sitcom, the sexiest girl, the droniest teacher, the zestiest crisps, the optimum width for Oxford bags, music (of course) and football (obviously). We should have joined the debating society only it was full of dweebs.

And sometimes, when we'd exhausted everything else, it would be football *and* music, such as which was the A-side of the great inter-city run-on-song twofer – 'The Boys in Maroon' or 'Glory, Glory to the Hibees'?

Honestly we did this. It seemed to matter. We were told the single was a joint A, like 'Strawberry Fields'/'Penny Lane', the Beatles' most fabulous 45, but with nothing written on the label to suggest ranking, reckoned this to be just mimsy diplomacy. No and no again: one song had to be the virile lead and the other the fluffer.

Both were sung by the hoary Scottish entertainer Hector Nicol and recorded in 1958, the year of the UK's first proper rock 'n' roll platter when Cliff Richard urged the populace to 'move it and a-groove it'. Nicol, though, must have decided this kind of subversion and danger would quickly blow itself out, for he opted for prolonging the heedrum-hodrum tradition. This is most pronounced on 'Glory, Glory' when he hollers the names of the Famous Five – 'Smith! Johnstone! Reilly! Turnbull! Ormond!' – accidentally inventing rap. It seemed at that moment that his sporran must have exploded. One-nil to us, Hibbies reckoned.

It's true that Hearts were crowned league champs in 1958 and that for Hibs who finished ninth there was the consolation of coming out on top in a Scottish Cup derby classic, although they would go on to lose the final to Clyde.

But 'The Boys in Maroon' is in waltz time. 'Glory Glory' is much the more rousing tune, being ripped off by Nicol from 'The Battle Hymn of the Republic' from the American Civil War. After Hibs' reworking, Manchester United and Tottenham Hotspur fell in behind and adopted it.

Whom did Nicol support? Not Hibs or Hearts – or Dundee or Dundee United or Morton whom he also sang about – but St Mirren whom he strangely didn't. YouTube burbles with clips of his bawdy stand-up from swingin' Falkirk and downtown Larkhall. Sample gag: after a visit to the gents and a sneak peek into the neighbouring urinal: 'Ginormous, like Kojak in a turtleneck sweater.' Then from nowhere, or maybe from the Tartan Arms, Bannockburn, he was the dying hard man in *Just a Boys' Game*, the magnificent Peter McDougall Play for Today, a haggis supper western where with his last breath Nicol's character tells the grandson anxious for rapprochement: 'Ah wis never fond o' you . . .'

He died in 1985 and so cannot confirm the song hierarchy and Jeffrey's Audio House in Edinburgh's Tollcross where the rival ditties were recorded is long gone. Gorgie supremacists are in no doubt theirs is the A-side and those owning copies of the disc do their best to obliterate the choon they don't want to hear, using paint, industrial adhesive tape or gouges with an old school compass, courtesy of Edinburgh Corporation Education Department.

But there's an intriguing line in 'The Boys in Maroon': 'Though we sometimes go down we can aye come back up.'

Hearts when Nicol sang it had never been relegated, so what did he mean? Maybe this was a doomy prophecy akin to Black Sabbath's backwards warnings about an impending new world order under the totalitarian rule of headless bats.

It took a while but the Jambos did eventually plunge through the trapdoor and perhaps subliminally that was Nicol – forced to choose – tipping his gaudy tartan bunnet at Hibs. One more time, then, from the top: 'There is a bonnie fitba team at Easter Road they play . . .'

31

ALL HIS BRAINS WERE IN HIS HEID

THE MATCH programme introducing Alan Gordon to Hibs fans in 1972 made mention, before getting round to goal feats, of his MA in Economics from Edinburgh University and his ongoing traineeship as a chartered accountant. How many exasperated fathers that February afternoon will have drawn the biog to the attention of their football-daft sons in the vain hope it might have encouraged the boys to devote more time to their school studies? I know mine did.

Letters after your name are rare in football. They'll prompt teasing, maybe derision and possibly even suspicion, concerning the risk your larger-than-standard brain could be distracted mid-match by a random intellectual consideration, causing you to miss a hurtling cross, the proper function of the head.

I don't remember Gordon not headering the ball. In fact, it's just about all headers in the memory: slight neck twist for the subtlest of skiffs not disturbing the blond hair, solid gold easy action.

Or . . . front-on with the forehead, straight and forwards and straightforward. These were meatier headers, demonstrating he wasn't above meat-and-potatoes goals. The real McCoys for the more prosaic centre-forwards of the period, Gordon would revert to this no-nonsense method to beat the real Peter McCloy.

If the ball struck Ibrox's infuriatingly square posts, there was little chance of an in-off, but he scored one via the Parkhead crossbar and, same end the following season, there was a stupendous diving header. When The Who played Celtic's stadium a couple of summers later, I dragged my best friends – one Hearts, the other Rangers – to the spot where Gordon had taken flight and we recreated the goal with a plastic polka dot brought along for this very purpose.

Head or foot, I don't think he ever scored an ugly goal. He saw no reason to be crash-bang-wallop although there was at least one hard-to-please journalist who expounded the hypothesis that he was 'too languid, too soft'. I remember this fellow's match preview, and my teenage enragement. What a clown! And the score later that day? Airdrie 0, Alan Gordon 4.

He wasn't – and this was also written – 'too smart' for football, even though his hard-to-please manager Eddie Turnbull famously growled: 'The trouble with you Gordon is that all yer brains are in yer heid!' But my favourite story about him comes from his youth when he was almost certainly 'too football' for George Heriot's School.

The august Edinburgh academy was rugby all the way so must have taken a dim view of the 17-year-old preferring the plebian sphere, never mind that he was already a Hearts starlet, never mind that he was already driving his own car, and parking up next to the teachers.

The Jam Tarts were bound for Inter Milan away in the Inter-Cities Fairs Cup and Gordon, though not likely to play in the San Siro, had been named in the squad for what would be valuable experience. 'I obviously needed the headmaster's permission to miss a few lessons,' he told me. 'But Heriot's would be proud, you might think? No, as it turned out. The heidie was so ignorant about football that he seemed to think I was Billy Liar, a fantasist who was making the whole thing up. 'Gordon, this simply will not do,' he said. 'If I were to grant this request I'd have a queue outside my door all the way down to matron's room. Every ruse for a skive would be more ridiculous than the last. Now be off with you, straight back to class before I find my cane . . .'

32

'THEY'D SHOUT "GET OFF!" AT ME IN THE WARM-UP'

IN MOVIES, 1971 was the year of *Diamonds Are Forever*, *Get Carter*, *Love Story* and *Straw Dogs*. Plenty of 'kiss kiss bang bang'* amongst that lot though astonishingly they would all be beaten to the box-office No. 1 spot by a flick that was more bus bus prang prang. *On the Buses* with Reg Varney, the feature-length version of the ITV sitcom about a municipal omnibus service, was monumentally unfunny. But On the Buses with Benny Brazil? Hilarious.

I met Brazil at his Edinburgh depot between shifts post-football when he was being feted by his fellow drivers as the 'People's Champion', an award for trying to save a passenger's life which had stunned him, being the first time he'd ever won anything. He had a neat line in self-deprecation, having heard all the gags about his modest abilities as a player. As I stumbled over a question concerning them which might have seemed impolite, he helped me out. 'Sometimes on my bus, kids too young to have seen me at Hibs will go: "My dad remembers you." I'll think to myself, oh that's nice, but then they'll add: "Aye, he says you were absolute rubbish!"'

Many clubs have had an Ally Brazil, that being his real name. Someone about whom fans will wonder: 'Christ, how the hell

* How the doyenne of film critics, Pauline Kael, summed up the appeal, and also the limitations, of popular cinema.

does he get a game?' Who doesn't look like a footballer, rather a guy from the crowd who's won a competition to pull on the strip for a day. Who's too skinny, too awkward, too gawky. Who'll fulfil their need for macabre, masochistic comedy when there's nothing much else happening for the team.

When I asked about his relationship with the support, he quipped: 'You mean the two fools who didn't mind me?' The Brazil moniker probably can't have helped, as he seemed the most un-Brazilian footballer imaginable. He played alongside some of the Tornadoes but knew he couldn't compare with them, that he looked capable of being knocked over by the merest, mildest zephyr. 'Skinnier than a butcher's pencil, so I was.' Manager Eddie Turnbull put him on Complan, the food supplement which counters malnutrition. 'Then he made me eat a ton of steak, which I had to bloomin' pay for myself.' None of this worked.

His debut was in 1977. 'Early on, there would be shouts of "Get off!!" That was in the warm-up.' Benny was his nickname, origin obscure, with fans assuming it came from the bobble-hatted odd-job man on *Crossroads*. 'That lad was a bit soft in the head, wasn't he? Maybe we did have something in common.'

Brazil came to Hibs not from the Bash Street Kids 2nd XI but having been rejected by Hearts, the club he supported as a boy. 'I was at the seven-nil game and stayed right to the end. Well, I believe in getting my money's worth.' He finished his career at Forfar Athletic whose manager Henry Hall hailed our man as 'pound for pound' his best signing. 'He actually got me for free!'

Four Hibs bosses post-Turnbull continued to pick him. They called him a 'player's player', which invariably provokes cynicism among supporters, as if they're being sneered at for lacking true football insight. But at Hibs Benny won the crowd over. Finally recognised for his plucky striving, it was almost a slug-to-butterfly transformation and figure of fun to cult favourite, a classic popcorny set-up beloved of the big screen. Kiss kiss bang bang.

33

IT LOOKS GREAT FROM THE TOP OF JOHN LEWIS, A PLANE OVER THE FORTH

IN THE Netflix dramatisation of David Nicholls' *One Day*, the star-crossed lovers endure some awkwardness the day after their introductory non-shag on a climb up Arthur's Seat when they struggle for meaningful conversation. Something is missing and I think I know what it is: Easter Road, nowhere to be seen from the summit, probably photoshopped out of shot so its reconfigured outline wouldn't jar with the romcom's period. But, you know, the stadium might have given them something to talk about.

It looks great from up there. It looks great from the top-floor restaurant in John Lewis. And it looks great from a plane window while in a holding pattern over the Forth awaiting a landing slot. No, it is not the stadium I once knew. After so many years, how could it be? None of the grounds I visited before has stayed the same. If so, they would probably be the same only worse. More rust, more rotting timber, more crumbling concrete, and more irritation from pillars blocking key moments, with there being no blocking of the wind, rain and snow owing to a lack of cover.

But, regarding this slippery concept known as 'progress', we tend to view modernised stadia the same as dreadful competitive parents do children: highly critical of other people's kids while ignoring the same faults in our own and indeed bragging about them whenever possible.

Yes if I'm honest, up close from the outside, this is a

breeze-block colosseum. Remove the branding and it could be just about anywhere. It isn't a bowl – okay, the old ground was only ever three-quarters of one – but four stands not joined together lending a vague air of vulnerability, as if one of them could suddenly be repossessed because of unpaid bills and like a giant telly despite the wails of the bairns, just carted off.

This blandness of design is everywhere in sport. In America, veteran baseball fans burn candles for Ebbets Field and other grand old ballparks long gone, replaced by stadia with mod cons but lacking in character. Ebbets has been immortalised in some of the most acclaimed sportswriting and also Sinatra laments, but at least Easter Road is still Hibs' home. The Brooklyn Dodgers were packed off to Los Angeles.

It's Fester Road to the Jambos. It's Leith San Giro and The MethaDome. But this is where – if all the 90 minutes were added together, taking account of the AWOL seasons in the 1980s, minus dreadful games when I left early but adding extra-times, penalty shoot-outs, victory laps, 'Sunshine on Leith' singalongs, staying behind to dodge Rangers fans, the odd reserve fixture, skiving school for power-cut-enforced weekday matches, etc., etc. – I must have spent close to six whole months of my life.

If you didn't know the old place then the revamped arena will seem just fine. And never mind the architecture and individuality of the stadium in its former guise, that patch of green down there was all that concerned me for my first game, first versus the Old Firm, first derby, first evening kick-off, first continental tie, first pie, first time struck by a flying bottle, first time on my own, first time joining in a chant, first time on the pitch, first time after my father died, first time with my future wife when the guy in the next seat threw up over her new trainers, first time with my eldest son.

And today, right at the end of Hibs' 149th year, on 'football for a fiver' tickets, I'm with my youngest son, just turned seven, for his first game. I've passed an incurable affliction on to his big brother and am nervous about doing the same to Hector and for once almost hoping that he's missing his Minecraft.

We climb the stairs to the top of the West Stand. Different stairs, different fixtures and fittings, different seats with no risk of splinters or passive smoking and no threat either of someone else's piss running down the back of the legs.

The patch of green, though, is unchanged. Hector gazes down at it. What do you think, son?

'Wow!'

34

HIBS IMMORTALISE ADIDAS TRAINERS, SUNAK KILLS THEM OFF

THE NADIR of the Adidas Gazelle – destined to figure high up in the obit of all trainers when it's time for that to be written – happened during campaigning for the 2024 UK general election. Rishi Sunak, the sitting prime minister, was attempting to rock them. Ditto Keir Starmer, the man about to boot him out of No. 10. And so was Nigel Farage.

This clown, this carpetbagger, was all suited up with a formal shirt and tie. Probably the collar had stiffeners in it. There was the suspicion of cufflinks, doubtless monogrammed or bearing a family crest with a Latin inscription of pomposity and boiling-oil-and-moat defiance. In one particularly dispiriting photograph Farage was manspreading with a ridden-up trouser leg revealing a pale, hairless, unathletic calf. And, tragically, Gazelles on his feet.

This was not what the three-stripe sportswear giant envisaged for its low-slung suede shoe after all the retro-marketing and all the fashionista influencing. No self-respecting Gen Z-er was going to be seen dead wearing it. And, in the wake of Gazellegate, did anyone check on the Adidas share price?

Maybe the CEO and the board were casting back minds to happier times for the Gazelle, indeed what surely rates as its apotheosis. In 1994 the Scottish Football Museum opened. Based on the smacked-arse, bed-with-nae-supper attitude of the beaks down the years, and especially when they were so niggardly about important games being shown live on TV, you might have expected a safe, bowdlerised and po-facedly revisionist take on the history of the national sport. But no. Rather than be embarrassed by, say, hooliganism and pretend it had never happened, there's the remnant of a mass pagger in one of the display cases – a single, cast-aside Gazelle.

The trainer is green and belonged to a casual. Presumably after it came off in the kerfuffle, its wearer was forced into an embarrassingly hopalong exit of the scene with only one shod foot. I smile that it has a place among all the cups and bawbees and memorabilia from glorious days. Sticking it on a plinth behind glass demonstrates impish, self-deprecating humour of which Scotland can be justly proud.

Would an FA-approved exhibition do the same in England? Unlikely. The English gave the world 'the English disease'. The flying plastic chairs of Luton Town and the flying plastic chairs of successive international tournaments on the continent. Richard Allen's skinhead books and the thugsploitation movie genre. And let's not forget Heysel. There's not much scope for English football telling a joke against itself among any of that lot.

One thing I'd like to know: with Hampden's Gazelle a permanent exhibit, where's its companion? Has the owner kept the other trainer as a personal memento? Or did he actually lose both and is the second one housed in another case, in an underground gallery, secret stairway behind a bookcase, much like in *The Man From U.N.C.L.E.*, lighting and temperature carefully monitored, having been stolen to order for a mysterious international art collector with outré tastes and only viewable by close associates under the strictest vetting?

After all, this was no ordinary casual. The fellow supported Hibs.

35

SCOTLAND'S GREATEST MUSICIAN WAS BURIED IN HIS HIBS TIE

FOR LONG enough, whenever I heard 'Turnbull's Tornadoes', the song, with the team all clustered round a microphone, tone-deaf squawkers and foghorns safely at the back, I thought to myself: 'John Lennon will sue.' The 1972 official club ditty sounded like a direct steal from 'Happy Xmas (War Is Over)'. The ex-Beatle was going to halt his bed-in, apologising to Yoko: 'We'll give peace a chance later, duck. Right now I've got to see the lawyer. These bloody Hibees are ripping me off.'

And I thought this would be fun. And – just as long as a courtroom barney with one of the most famous people in the world didn't bankrupt the club – exciting. Rock 'n' roll, in fact.

It never happened but no matter. 'Turnbull's Tornadoes' is still a terrific story, or rather the story of the man behind it is. Johnny Keating, as his obits remarked, was 'perhaps the greatest modern musician ever to have come out of Scotland'. He went from Holyrood to Hollywood. From a poorhouse to *Hotel*, the big, sumptuous 1967 movie for which he dreamed up the score. But he wasn't too busy hanging around with square-jawed leading men (Rod Taylor) and sexy Italian It girls (Catherine Spaak) to dash off a ditty for his football heroes. When Keating died he requested he be buried in his Hibs tie.

He was a composer, arranger and conductor. He was probably unique in having hits right across the genres – swing, big band, jazz, rock, pop and classical. All from unpromising beginnings in Edinburgh's Old Town, just like the Hibees.

Thought to be the last person born in his Royal Mile workhouse, his Irish-born father was a street bookmaker. Poor in circumstances he might have been, Keating resolved to make himself rich in musical appreciation. He taught himself accordion, piano and trombone and was on stage with local bands from the age of eight.

Joining Tommy Sampson, 'Scotland's King of Swing', he played the Eldorado Ballroom in Leith and the Fountainbridge Palais. Then, just like the promising footballer at a smaller club, he was cherry-picked by the Ted Heath Band, a gig which showed him America.

He became an arranger-for-hire for pop hits for Adam Faith, Petula Clark, Anthony Newley, Helen Shapiro and a No. 1 for Eden Kane. The *Z-Cars* theme reached No. 5 and that was a parping Keating confection which became Everton's run-on song.

He was an early adopter of the Moog synthesiser for the groovily named Johnny Keating Space Experience. The maestro would swear his musicians to secrecy over the alchemy involved in creating his recordings and high-end hi-fi emporia spun Keating platters to illustrate the wonders of stereophonic sound.

Beatles producer George Martin and Burt Bacharach hailed him as one of the 20th century's great all-rounders and Tony Bennett rated their collaboration on 'The Very Thought of You' as the finest recording of his crooning career.

Keating's music took him all over the world but he would return to Edinburgh to catch up with Hibs whenever he could. The chorus of 'Turnbull's Tornadoes' goes: 'Hibs, Hibs, Hibs for the cup . . .' Sadly he didn't quite see it happen, taking his place in the great recording studio in the sky in 2015, almost a year to the day before Hampden glory.

36

WHAT HAVE WE GOT AGAINST ELVIS?

REGARDING ELVIS Presley, we should not be surprised by anything. That there are so many people who still worship him and love his music. That so many have, um, suspicious minds over his 'death' in 1977 and want to believe he popped up later at Legoland, was an extra in the movie *Home Alone* and even appeared at what would have been his 82nd birthday. Also, that so many are Elvis impersonators. In '77 the total was around 170. By 2010 there were believed to be as many as 400,000. Keep increasing at that rate, claimed the *Daily Mail*, and in a further ten years one in three of us worldwide could be warbling 'Love Me Tender' in white polyester jumpsuits with rhinestone flourishes and a greasy jet black wig resembling a duck taking off from an oil slick.

So, all that said, is it a pretty humdrum, ho-hum thing for a Scottish football team to have had in its ranks at different times two players involved in altercations with Presley mimics?

Now, Scotland is the only part of the UK ever to have been visited by Elvis – the two-hour stopover at Prestwick Airport in March 1960 when he was flying home from Germany after finishing his national service. So might it be the case that we have more ETAs – Elvis tribute acts – per head of population and therefore on any given Saturday night after the football more pub amateur hours and social club talent contests where these mimics are able to channel the spirit and the lip curl if not quite the diabolical, censored hips of the man they revere as The King?

But even if that is true, and taking into account the law of averages as well as the power of coincidence, and taking into account that footballers are persuadable and like to copy each other's behaviour, it does seem – cue dear, old David Coleman, *quite remarkable* – that the incident involving Garry O'Connor was followed by the incident involving Anthony Stokes. Ah but except . . . if you believe the excitable papers, Hibs at one point were top of the league for 'bad boys'. Footballers who did not spend their downtime on macramé.* Who habituated the front pages as well as the back ones.

Besides O'Connor and Stokes, there was Jason Cummings and Leigh Griffiths and Derek Riordan. All strikers, they all scored thundering goals. On their game they were human fireworks. Off the park, in built-up areas, that was more problematic.

Some of the stories, such as Cummings wrestling in just his budgie-smugglers, were high jinks. Not every incident happened at Hibs. Nevertheless, it's probably just as well these guys weren't all at the club at the same time. A quixotic quintet – the Infamous Five – they would have had the redtops portraying them as football's answer to the Rolling Stones. (Though I'd love to have seen them play together, just once.)

Lock up your daughters? Maybe ship your ETAs off to Las Vegas and out of harm's way. It will follow, though, that some Hibbies just can't stop believing. Assuredly they will be Presley fans. For after all, what is 'Glory, Glory to the Hibees' if not a steal from 'The Battle Hymn of the Republic', an Elvis standard?

* Which footballers were ever macramé enthusiasts? There was a sweet old documentary about George Best which showed the future Hibee taking a break from tying full-backs in knots to weave a tea cosy for his landlady. That said, the same doc featured him in a nightclub watching a champagne waterfall – an image which, different poison, brings to mind the Bryan Ferry lyric 'Pale fountains fizzing forth pink gin' when the Roxy Music crooner resembled nothing so much as an Elvis wannabe.

37

OFF TO SEE THE WIZARD

OF THE five men in Scotland's greatest-ever forward line, he might be the one that pub quizzers forget, the Wizard most capable of making himself disappear in a puff of dark blue smoke. He didn't clang with winners' medals like Alan Morton, or possess a colourful nickname ('The Wee Blue Devil'), or swing over the sumptuous crosses for Alex Jackson ('The Gay Cavalier') to score a hat-trick on that momentous day in 1928 when England were humbled 5–1 at Wembley. Strangely, it's Jackson who's had pieces written up describing him as a forgotten man when back in the day he'd been a world superstar, a handsome, charismatic, bar-owning, ciggie-advertising celebrity credited with revolutionising wing play. No, our man was none of these things.

Nor did he score the other two goals in the game – that was Alex James who conspicuously wore the baggiest shorts to hide long johns which themselves were concealing rheumatism and could tell an incredible story about being shipwrecked with Raith Rovers. Nor was he like Hughie Gallacher – rascal, roué, white bowler and spats off the pitch, who made a triumphant return to the national team following a two-month ban for shoving a referee into a bath.

Jackson would die tragically, just after the Second World War in an overturned army truck, and Gallacher more tragically still, a bankrupt alcoholic who at Dead Man's Crossing near his Gateshead home, deliberately walked in front of an express train. But Jimmy Dunn, the fifth member, did not simply make up the numbers. 'I want to emphasise that all our forwards are inherently clever,' insisted captain Jimmy McMullan when invited to dissect the sensational scoreline as hurled tam-o'-shanters darkened the North West London skyline. True, an otherwise authoritative history of Scottish football lists him as 'Tim', but Dunn has never been forgotten – not by Everton and not by Hibs.

Another thing: all our forwards were inherently small, Dunn just 5ft 5ins in his size two boots. Glasgow-born, he joined Hibs in 1920, scoring his first goal in a 5–2 win over Albion Rovers, and from the berth those top-hole Pathé newsreel narrators termed 'right inside', there would be a hundred more in eight seasons at Easter Road. His Hibs side was a fine one: Scotland goalie Willie Harper, Hugh Shaw who'd later manage the Famous Five, Jimmy McColl, another fellow internationalist in Harry Ritchie and 'Darkie' Walker. Dunn had a nickname and inevitably given his red hair it was 'Ginger'.

In the Roaring Twenties these Hibees stormed to successive Scottish Cup finals, only to lose to Celtic (1923) and Airdrie (1924). The same team turned out in both, heart ruling head as Dunn had been bothered by an injury and in the second final he couldn't produce his tanner ba' trickery.

Among the vanquished English was the Evertonian goal monster 'Dixie' Dean. His club asked: 'If we were to sign one of the Wizards, who would you most want manufacturing your bullets?' He replied: 'I liked the little fellow with the ginger hair.' Hibs couldn't turn down a bid of £5,000 and Dunn would help Everton become champs of England's old Second Division, win the First the following year and 12 months after that hoist the FA Cup.

The 1933 final against Manchester City was notable for it being the first time the teams walked out side by side, and the first time shirt numbers were worn. And the first time a wee guy of 5ft 5ins appeared to climb halfway up the Twin Towers to head a glorious third goal for the victors – an act which, according to reports, due to the heaviness of the ball, 'very nearly knocked him cold'.

38

FOOTBALLERS COULDN'T BE EVEN SLIGHTLY RECEDING OR VAGUELY BANDY-LEGGED

PETER WILSON played for Hibs when they would lose seven goals to Airdrie and Clyde and – yikes – eight to Hearts and regularly flirt with relegation. This was in the 1930s when, no matter how grim things were on the park, I find it hard to believe that fans ever turned on the players and got personal. People back then were simply more polite.

Wilson had a fine set of lugs on him. Highly grabbable like the handles of the Scottish Cup, though Hibees of that era had no experience of the sensation. The half-back, a good sort, addressed the elephant in the room, which is not to say his prominent features were anything like elephant-sized, but still: the ears, he quipped, robbed him of a vital yard of pace.

By the 1980s players couldn't be even slightly receding or suspiciously portly or vaguely bandy-legged. Fans – Saturday specialists in ears, nose and throat – would be on to them. 'I got called Popeye and Cyclops,' Alan Sneddon told me. 'And always some wise guy in the crowd – maybe the same guy – would shout: "Watch your blind side!"' The rumour around Easter Road was that the full-back had only one functioning eye. 'A myth,' he laughed. 'I have a condition which causes my right eye to droop, that's all. I can see perfectly well out of it – my left eye, too!'

Generously, Sneddon insisted the taunts never bothered him because if he was being targeted then a team-mate might get an easier ride. And when fans thought about it they probably concluded: of course Snoddy has two eyes. How could he play the game otherwise?

But then in 2004 along came Dean Shiels. A blond-haired buzz bomb in Tony Mowbray's first midfield, fast, bold and fearless. He was a smash hit in a side full of sassy kids and we thought nothing more of his brightness in the box, rapid feet and sharp shooting than this: the Northern Irish lad had talent.

But there was more to Deano, or in one way, less. He was operating with a 50 per cent reduction in vision compared to everyone else on the park. Aged eight there was an accident at home involving a wallpaper scraper. Five operations in five years but doctors couldn't save the sight in his right eye. He was nine when he was picked for his first 11-a-side game so he never knew what it was like to play football without being partially sighted.

Apart from family and his closest pals, Shiels didn't tell anyone. He didn't tell the Manchester United and Arsenal youth teams and he didn't tell Mowbray or anyone else at Hibs. Then in December 2005 – worried about headaches and the eye being increasingly bloodshot – he owned up to his secret. Hibs found him the best specialist who confirmed the eye had long since died and that blood vessels were bursting and increasing the pressure on his skull.

The eye was removed and Shiels came back. Capped for Northern Ireland while at Easter Road he played in England, returned to Scotland to help Kilmarnock lift the League Cup, moved to Rangers and won titles. Then, turning out in the Kincardine Bridge derby for Dunfermline Athletic, the rednecks of Falkirk threw joke-shop eyeballs on to the pitch, this after he'd been taunted about his disability by rival players.

I don't know how he did it. Coped with the abuse – everything.

Shiels scored one of my favourite Hibs goals at Dundee United – a lob in a packed box requiring coolness, bravado and above all precision, and which seemed like a tribute to an old piece of brilliance from his great countryman, vs Pat Jennings and Spurs.

Except George Best was able to use both eyes.

39

TONY BLACKBURN MISPRONOUNCES 'MARINELLO'

THE HAIR on the featured bands is long but not so long that dads will look up from their evening papers, remove tobacco pipes from lips with a forceful *phttttt* and enquire: 'So is that a bloke or a bird?'

Now, this is not a classic edition. Bryan Ferry – a bloke – is not pouting with gold-lidded eyes at the drummer – another bloke – who's cementing the beat in a leopard-skin leotard.

Nor is it an epoch-making edition. David Bowie is not singing of 'some cat' involved in the fabrication of 'hazy cosmic jive', only this cat, guitar slung as low as his musketeer's knee breeches, turns out to be a bloke, just like him, and *they've got their arms round each other*.

But it's Thursday – 5 February 1970 – it's 7.30 p.m. and that means *Top of the Pops*. And even though Jimmy Savile – the scary monster, to quote Bowie again, the super creep – has done his damnedest to ruin memories of a cherished television institution, this is an instalment of great significance for Hibs fans, prompting wee sparra chests to swell with pride.

It's a pretty skew-whiff show, not yet shot in colour and missing the churning roar of theme music 'Whole Lotta Love' which came along later. There's wonky captioning in the Hit Parade rundown – at No. 30 it's *Jackson's Five* – and regular bloopers from host Tony Blackburn who introduces a song from the new movie, Butch Cassidy and the . . . what does he say . . .

Sundowner? Sundial? But it's also fantastically exciting when the girls in the audience dance.

Some of the music around at that time was a challenge for dancing – heavy prog, for example. But this lot are fearless, always reacting to the beat with arm-flailing abandon. There's something feral about them, out of control, as if a spectacular coup of the BBC is a distinct possibility. Just as well, then, that the set designer decided to erect prison bars round the raised platform.

'You could be arrested for some of these movements,' says Blackburn, sweating under the studio lights in a thick polo neck and velvet jacket. Nowadays you could almost be arrested for a comment like that, but really, is it not possible to gaze at this display with admiration if not wonder, at the radical cut of Chelsea Girl hotpants and the unfettered swish of the C&A miniskirt?

Jim Reeves was a chart act in 1970 although mercifully the Wild Women of Wongo are not required to dance to his mawkish mush. Not Mary Hopkin or Roger Whittaker either. But there are stompier and sexier tunes from the long-forgotten Shocking Blue and Candy Choir and you have to ask who is directing the show and could it in fact be Russ 'Faster, Pussycat! Kill! Kill!' Meyer?

Blackburn announces the dancing is going to be judged. Who will do this? Someone is going to have his work cut out, deliberating on these ultravixens' crazy bopping. And, look, here he is now, a personable young man in a snazzy suit, nervous but polite, complimenting Linda on her moves, marvelling at Celia's geometric eyelashes.

Blackburn will mispronounce his name. The clown will make fun of his keelie Leith burr. But this is Peter Marinello, Hibee idol, or that is what he was until just a few days previously . . .

40

SWOONING AND SQUEALING AT EVERY SWERVE AND SWAY

THERE ARE sex symbols and sex objects. Sex bombs and sexpots. Sex idols and sex icons. Sex queens though maybe not too many sex kings. Sex kittens and – don't think we've met – sex bunnies. But was Peter Marinello Scotland's sex winger?

Teenybopper girls in trainer bras pressed themselves against the terrace wall to swoon and squeal at every swerve and sway of his hips. The shirt was worn outside the shorts, fairly radical for 1969 when there were still plenty of collars and ties in the main body of the Easter Road kirk.

Meanwhile, the Cowshed massive, digging the groovy hair, reworked Donovan's 'Mellow Yellow' to serenade their hero: 'They call him Marinello . . .'

Tactics used to be so simple. Some of today's players, who must feel like they're auditioning for *The 39 Steps*' Mr Memory when coaches shove iPads in their faces and unleash torrents of spittle-flecked instruction, will wish they were still straightforward. To Marinello, manager Bob Shankly simply said this: 'Go oot and run rings roon 'em.'

And it was working brilliantly for the exciting young Hibees who'd won at Tynecastle, Parkhead and, after two goals from the pretty-boy pin-up at Ibrox, were topping the league. Hail, the conquering heroes? Not quite. Next home game vs Clyde the crowd was just 8,677. And so Marinello's Hibs came to understand, like other iterations before and since, that Edinburgh can be a small and reserved place. That early-season bursts tend to peter out. And that the most talented will eventually be flogged. So it was Peter, out. Destination: Swingin' London.

Enjoying the adulation and his home city's modest approximation of *la grande vie*, the discotheque-inhabiting 19-year-old should have been excited, yes? Well, he didn't really want to leave Hibs. And the extent to which footballers back then had no say in their destiny is perfectly illustrated by the story Marinello told me about the end of his time at Easter Road: 'Peter Cormack was my lift to the stadium and because he was a brilliant trainer and I wasn't, sometimes when he called round I'd still be in my pyjamas. That morning he couldn't wait any longer so I was standing at the bus stop when Arthur Duncan tooted his horn. "You should be at Partick Thistle," I said. "No," he said, "you're going to Arsenal and I'm your replacement."'

A Gunners director boasted they'd signed a Beatle. Marinello would be the new George Best. His debut was against the old Best's Manchester United and he scored right away. Neither English giant impressed our man overmuch. 'My old Hibees played with so much more flair.'

Unfortunately on the pitch that was almost as good as it got. Off it he advertised milk and was milked dry for promo: modelling fab gear with Lulu, a newspaper column and in addition to *Top of the Pops* he reviewed 45s for *Melody Maker* and raved about Spooky Tooth and Van Der Graaf Generator. '"You'll want to write a book," they said. I said: "But I've only been here ten minutes." Tony Hatch and Jackie Trent came up with songs for me but then they heard me sing.

'Danny La Rue spotted me at his cabaret show, announced my name to the audience and I just belted out of the theatre. There was daft stuff. Me and Alan Ball got drunk and bought a racehorse. When my wife found out she perfectly understandably tipped a plate of spaghetti bolognese over my head. I'd gotten too showbizzy.'

Then his life got too dark with bankruptcy and the involvement of gangsters. And with this most cautionary of tales eventually making a book, and with Wayne Rooney at Man U beginning to turn up on newspaper front pages, Alex Ferguson flung a copy of the Marinello memoir at his player with the instruction: 'This is *not* how to fuckin' do it.'

41

'EVERYTHING TOM CRUISE KNOWS ABOUT HIBS HE LEARNED FROM ME'

TOM DOUGRAY must have been the best referee in the land during the years before and after the First World War. Otherwise he wouldn't have been the man in the middle at ten Scottish Cup finals – a record unlikely to be broken – and these included the Hibs ones of 1923 and 1924.

Pity he couldn't have been more accommodating to us, but then any favours would have been cheating. Better to wait patiently, sort of, and honourably for the club's day in the sun, ensuring 2016 was extra-special for everyone at Hampden including the great-nephew who the official couldn't have known would turn out to be a fine actor and quite possibly football's most authentic celebrity fan.

Admittedly that's a pretty thin field and almost a contradiction in terms. Dougray Scott's man cave, though, is not decorated with images of his sex-bomb co-stars Eva Longoria, Jennifer Connelly and Jennifer Love Hewitt. Instead there are vintage Hibs match programmes.

There's also a Franck Sauzée shirt although perhaps no longer treasured quite so devoutly. 'It was covered in the legend's blood. My mum thought a thorough boil wash was required. Absolute tragedy!'

If Scott cannot jet in for a day to see his team in the flesh because he's on location in Argentina or New Zealand, he'll be furiously fiddling with a laptop to beam pictures into his trailer.

This is the Glenrothes-born hunk who absconded from Kate Winslet's arm at the UK premiere of *Enigma* to watch Hibs on TV at Ibrox – and was warned that a repeat of the stunt stateside would result in the producers 'handing him his ass'.

Whatever Tom Cruise might half-remember about the Hibees comes from Scott and their time together on *Mission: Impossible 2*. 'I told him how the club were founded in 1875 by an Irish priest attempting to instil self-worth into a community suffering much hardship – a wonderful act of kindness.'

The '23 and '24 finals are not Scott's only link to Hibs and indeed Tom Dougray was not the only referee among his ancestry. So were Tom's brothers James and John and from one of them Scott was handed down a whistle made from bone. And there was the other great-uncle who served as a Hibs scout, who took Scott's father Allan to marvel at the Famous Five, the latter in turn introducing his laddie to Turnbull's Tornadoes.

Scott told me: 'My first time at Easter Road, six years old, we lost to Celtic. There was a ceremony to the game like being in church but with this huge noise. I loved it. Then we played Celtic at Parkhead [in 1975] where we hardly ever won, only for the ref to abandon the game because of fog with just a few minutes remaining and us leading two-nil. I could see John Blackley perfectly clearly. He was flicking the Vs at the Jungle as he stormed off.

'I loved watching Hibs with Dad, a mad fan, and I also loved watching him flog fridge-freezers because – this'll sound funny – it's kind of why I'm an actor. Dad had dreams. He was an apprentice at Queen's Park but didn't make the first team. He was a copyboy at the *Scottish Daily Express*. He acted himself with [Glasgow's] Unity Theatre and although he ended up a salesman to feed our family it was a role he was playing, a performance, and just fascinating.'

Scott says if either acting or football had to be excised from his life, it would be the former. If he had to choose between an

Oscar and Hibs winning the title it would be the latter. Acting simply can't compete with the great gamut of emotions offered by football. His actress wife Claire Forlani was sitting next to him at his lowest point (the cup final scudding from Hearts). When there were tears of joy, hoodoo smashed, his eldest son Gabriel could share in them.

Acting can play tormenting tricks on its practitioners. In the detective drama *Crime*, Scott had to adopt the persona of a Hearts supporter. His chief super was played by Ken Stott, a real Jambo, who previously in another cop show, *Rebus*, was required to be a Hibby.

'I'm afraid I used to sing the 7–0 song to Ken every day: 'Who do you think you are kidding, Jim Jefferies, if you think you're No. 1/We are boys from the Leith San Siro/We are the boys who fucked you seven-zero.'

'Actually, I'm not sorry about that at all!'

42

WE DON'T NEED NO STINKIN' BADGES

WAS THAT it? I remember sometime during the 1970–71 season, the feeling of disappointment, if not mild embarrassment. For after Hull City's angry tiger and Charlton Athletic's fiercely gripped sword and even Oxford United's slightly camp bull, there it was in my sweaty palm – the Hibs badge.

I'd convinced my father that the family saloon could do with topping up, even though the tank had been filled the day before and we hadn't been anywhere. The Shell garage was nearer but I'd persuaded him that, as the jingle had it, 'the Esso sign means happy motoring'. It also meant little foil football crests free with a purchase of petrol and maybe this time we'd get lucky.

But . . . a generic castle, a not especially Hibee green wash? Where was the history? Signifiers of the club's origins? And wasn't there a growling beastie we could press into service? I didn't remember noticing the badge previously and wasn't in a tearing hurry to see it again.

Then came new insignia, a clean, modern design and so still not historical, with a ball garlanded by a laurel and topped with a crown. At least the fetid pond backdrop had gone, replaced with white. I had this badge on a watch worn on a thick studded band as if I was medieval cannon fodder, or a Deep Purple roadie.

A republican Hibby might have quibbled at the crown; the Lord Lyon did. Why was his lordship's court, which regulates heraldry, bothering itself with a football club, tiny in the general scheme, when notwithstanding my watch, merchandising in the sport was small scale? It's not as if the offence was a depiction of Pat Stanton scaling the Buckingham Palace ramparts to snaffle 'By appointment . . .' cheese and crackers, glug from a bottle of gifted vintage wine and bounce on the queen's bed.

Stanton, by the way, went through his entire Easter Road career badge-free, as did Gordon Smith. Most club colours, certainly in Scotland, were crest-free, but the next attempt to capture the Hibee essence did appear on the shirt and it remains the most controversial of hallmarks, if not the most risible.

The 'Saturn'. So nicknamed because of the rings, except they weren't encircling a football but what looked like a rugby ball. I didn't get the rugger connotation right away. Being a child of the Space Race, by then with hormones whizzing like meteors, I saw Lieutenant Uhura's breasts. No, Gabrielle Drake's breasts.

Drake was Lieutenant Ellis in *UFO*, Gerry Anderson's spiffing TV show about an impending alien invasion of Earth. The badge looked better suited to all-in-one spacewear, although if you weren't into sci-fi or rugby you might have thought, as others did, of beer bottle labels, and considering the badge came out of the club's wine bar years (see ch. 87) maybe this wasn't accidental. Whatever the inspiration, the design lives on in the Famous Five Stand having been immortalised in the girders.

The current crest at least acknowledges history, both of the club's origins (harp) and Leith as a port (galleon), but it's cluttered. Maybe emblems just don't do it for me. Cue the Mexican bandito in *The Treasure of the Sierra Madre*, delivering the 34th greatest movie quote of all time: 'We don't need no stinkin' badges.'

And after all, Hibs can't be great at *everything*.

43

THE UNPEELING OF THE ONION

A FEW years ago in John Brownlie's house, I watched intently as he rubbed his index fingers together. A magic trick? Sadly not. 'The best right-back in Europe' as of early January 1973 was demonstrating what happened to his 'tib' and 'fib' – tibia and fibula – in the leg break which ended his season.

This was 40 years after the fateful game and more time has passed since our meeting, but I can almost embarrass myself by recalling my hushed, melodramatic questioning, like I was some serviceable character in a South American soap opera, purely there to set up the big reveal.

Note the 'almost'. I'm not remotely self-conscious, for this was major, this was heavy. As those who were present would mourn, the game against East Fife was the day the music died. Brownlie's injury – together with Alex Edwards' long suspension – would render Turnbull's Tornadoes becalmed. Top of the league, they would lose the following week. The following month, out of the Scottish Cup. The month after that, the European Cup Winners' Cup. Tib, fib, Hib.

'Guys like you have never stopped asking me about that day,' he said. 'What could that team have achieved if it hadn't turned out that way? I mean, I don't know what I was thinking about really. I'd hit the ball too far ahead of me . . . [no, John, surely not, when did you ever?] . . . and then I heard a yell. Mickey wanted it passed to him. So maybe if he hadn't shouted I wouldn't have stretched to try and retrieve it.'

Aagh! This was too tragic. Mickey was Edwards. If only he hadn't been being harassed by Nemesis John Love – perpetrator of what the *Leven Mail* admitted were 'three devastating tackles' on the Hibs man – then he might not have been so frustrated and perhaps wouldn't have demanded a pass. (And if he hadn't then seen his mate stretchered off, maybe he'd have recovered his cool.) The club have been responsible for plenty of 'What ifs . . .' down the years, but maybe no one match has provoked more. In their report, *The Scotsman* dubbed East Fife's approach as 'destructive' and reported a shout from the North Stand of 'Nihilists!' Ah, good old Hibs. They breed a better class of doomed romantic, of educated nutter.

Hibs are fond of their firsts, and the faithful very fond of talking them up, but it cannot quite be claimed that Brownlie was the first attacking full-back. By common consent that was Brazil's Nilton Santos who, versus Austria en route to the 1958 World Cup triumph, embarked on a run from deep that had his coach hollering to retreat, until he scored with a casual flick with the outside of the foot.

Santos's free-spiritedness prompted keen and ongoing debate about the changing role of full-backs. In 1961 French football intellectual Gabriel Hanot, a friend to Hibs (see ch. 13), urged teams to properly let them loose and stop sending over men to cover. In response, English football intellectual Brian Glanville stressed full-backs were still defenders and as such 'attacking play is merely the gilt on the gingerbread; it cannot be the gingerbread itself'.

In '61 young John was prototyping that long-legged stride for his school team in the village of Caldercruix, North Lanarkshire, coached by the janitor. Ten years later, aged 19, he was debuting for Scotland against the USSR.

A year after that he was coming off at Airdrie having scored with two rocket shots in a 6–2 win when he spotted the jannie beaming with pride. And a week after that the international team embarked on qualification for the 1974 World Cup with Brownlie, according to the *Daily Record*, the 'inspiration' behind two victories over Denmark.

His nickname of 'Onion' was derived from an unflattering haircut. It is not known if the barber's in Caldercruix also functioned as the local sawmill. But what is certain is that Scotland were going well, Hibs were going well – and the young No. 2 was sensational. 'What a player,' gushed *Sportscene* commentator Alastair Alexander. 'Like Mill Reef and Brigadier Gerard rolled into one.' But then – tib, fib, Hib. 'My leg went hot and after that numb.' He didn't hear the crack but the crowd did. 'My dad said it was pretty loud.'

He didn't blame the East Fife man for the tackle. He insisted Edwards' ban hit the Easter Road challenge harder. He would undoubtedly take issue with *The Scotsman*'s claim that he was 'half the Hibs team'. But while he made a good comeback, the unpeeling of Onion that dark January afternoon caused tears to fall. To Hibbies he really was the Gingerbread Man.

44

BOB CRAMPSEY CALLED US SILKY AND I BLUSHED

TO CONTRADICT Arsène Wenger, not everyone thinks they have the prettiest wife at home. Not every fan values prettiness above all else. Some like brawny, breengey football and are not averse to winning ugly. Indeed if pushed – and they like pushing in a game – wouldn't mind if this was the norm. At Hibs though we like pretty.

In football, in Scottish football, this is the exception rather than the rule, but honestly, I don't think Hibbies feel smugly superior about this. When someone pays us a compliment about how the team play I remember it, am grateful for it, flattered by it, such as: 'Midfield masterclass.' This was in *The Independent*'s match report of the 1991 Skol Cup semi-final. Mickey Weir, Murdo MacLeod, Pat McGinlay and, not forgetting but he sometimes is, Brian Hamilton had orchestrated the victory over Rangers, although the credit in the piece went to Alex Miller, a manager who hid his tactical smarts under a bushel. I remember the name of the journalist – David Livingstone – and still have the cutting, tucked inside the match programme.

'Smooth, silky Hibernian.' I remember these words too. They were uttered 20 years previously by Bob Crampsey. There was no way of recording TV programmes back then but I've stored them in a sacred memory bank.

Why? Well, there was much less punditry in the 1970s compared with now and comment of any kind, particularly learned comment, stood out. One of the few regular slots for this was the Sunday sermon of the *Scotsport* oracle.

The Old Firm, then as now, dominated debate. Therefore Crampsey from his plywood pulpit must have sounded, to the established order, as hysterical as he was heretical to suggest Hibs could be the next Scottish club to triumph in Europe. Who, little old us? Attendances not always reaching five figures? No absolute dead-cert Scotland picks? I'm sure I blushed, like the demure wallflower scrunching her empty dance card who's suddenly invited up for a waltz.

Smooth, silky? Crampsey wasn't dreaming up taglines for chocolate ads. He really did believe that Hibs side, with Pat Stanton and Alan Gordon and Alex Cropley, could win the old Cup Winners' Cup. They didn't of course. It was *pure indulgence* to think that they could. They were *full of eastern promise* but ultimately proved to be the *crumbliest, flakiest* team that a *Fruit and Nut case* could have decided to go all in with.

Of course there have been many iterations of Hibs which have been unsmooth and distinctly non-silky. Just as there have been versions of Everton and West Ham United and Tottenham Hotspur which have fallen short of the ideal – the style charter that isn't written down anywhere but which the supporters, in spirit anyway, carry around with them at all times like an organ donor card. At Hibs it is to be devoutly hoped, given a fair wind, a purist in the dugout and a couple of bold, buccaneering creatives in the middle of the park, that the team will play a certain way. I've always thought it a bit bumptious to call this the Hibs way, but it's definitely cavalier rather than roundhead, inspiration rather than perspiration, playmaker rather than haymaker, panache rather than stramash. And, look, I haven't even mentioned the f-word, for flair. Although there's still time . . .

45

WHEN WE THOUGHT BIG LIKE HITLER

BUILD IT and they will come. Well, maybe. Some grand plans in construction end up being too big, too ambitious, too costly, too heavy, too much about the monstrous egos of dangerous madmen. Hitler had such plans. There was the 'Strength Through Joy' holiday resort which was supposed to keep the workers happy and on-message for world domination. Intended to accommodate 20,000, it was never finished. The same fate befell the Deutsches Stadion, a Roman-style arena for when the Olympics would be usurped by the Aryan Games. Then there was the Volkshalle, modelled on the Pantheon, for public worship of the Führer with room for 180,000 to be rapt at his ranting underneath an 80-foot Nazi eagle.

But that didn't fly either and nor did Saudi Arabia's self-sustaining linear city, the dome which would purify Manhattan, Illinois' mile-high skyscraper, the world's tallest hotel in North Korea and the *Blade Runner*-inspired answer to Tokyo's over-crowding where one million would be housed under a giant pyramid – if only someone could have invented sturdy enough materials for its construction.

And then there was Hibs and their enormo-park. Maybe the ghost of old Adolf would have sneered at the proposed capacity, around half of that of the Volkshalle. But still: 98,000. Who the hell did Hibs think they were?

Actually, at the time the most exciting team in Scotland.

The Famous Five were in their full-on illustrious phase, league champions in three from five seasons. Coming out of war, people craved escapism. Cinemas and dance halls boomed and football, in a charming phrase from the period, was 'the glorious king of games'. And for admirers of Hibs there was no rationing. In 1952–53, which wasn't even one of their title seasons, they scored 93 goals.

In 1946–47, 123,830 watched the Hibees contest their League Cup semi-final with Rangers. In the teams' Scottish Cup semi of that season, the crowd was 143,570. Ibrox groaned at the seams with 102,342 in 1951–52 as these rivals clashed again in the Scottish. The Easter Road record came in the 1950 New Year derby – 65,850.

That will remain Edinburgh's toppermost for ever now, but back in the day Hibs thought it could be beaten. The proposed expansion of the ground involved raising three terraces to the heavens. Bold or bonkers?

Six-figure crowds have only ever been recorded in Glasgow, an in-your-face, fierce, fanatical football city. The capital isn't that, although the eyes can sometimes be bigger than the stomach, e.g. the unfinished Parthenon replica which, when the money ran out, was dubbed 'Edinburgh's Disgrace'.

Standing between its columns on Calton Hill you're presented with a fine view of Easter Road. The ground never got anywhere near 98,000 and, while the chutzpah can make us smile and even be proud, perhaps that was just as well.

For one short decade after the grand plan bit the dust, and when the humbling of Barcelona should still have been vivid in Hibby memories, just 2,942 souls were rattling like the proverbial peas in a drum for a forlorn match against Stirling Albion.

In his novel *Fatherland*, Robert Harris envisaged Germany winning the Second World War and the Volkshalle rising up from the architect's table and dwarfing the rest of Berlin, the new capital of the world. An alternative history of Hibs with a steroid-pumped super-stadium displaying 'House full' signs for a front three of – oh choices, choices - Jarkko Wiss, Eduardo Hurtado and Alan O'Brien might have been stretching credulity somewhat.

46

THE REAL JIM HERRIOT CAME FROM LARKHALL, HOME TO ALSATIANS CALLED REBEL

IN 1972 a floundering literary life suddenly took off for the vet-cum-author who called himself Jim Herriot when his books were jazzed up by a New York publisher in urgent need of a hit. The story thereafter: 60 million copies sold. Also in 1972 the real Jim Herriot was keeping goal for Hibs, a job which may have allowed for the odd moment of leaning on a post and enjoying the attacking verve along with the crowd as, down the far end, Turnbull's Tornadoes required only five months to reach 100 goals.

It's a ripping yarn, the tale of how Alf Wight alighted on a nom de plume for *All Creatures Great and Small.* And even though this was before Herriot joined Hibs, the Leith literati will quote it. Jambos will claim Sir Walter Scott, author of *The Heart of Midlothian*, as one of their own. In the scramble for writerly endorsement, Hibbies could counter with Sir Arthur Conan Doyle. Sherlock Holmes's creator – also a goalkeeper – was born into an Irish family at the top of Leith Walk. Yer actual symmetry: Doyle's masterpiece *The Hound of the Baskervilles* dates from 1902, the year of Hibs' notorious pre-history Scottish Cup triumph. So of course when the trophy was at long last paraded down the Walk once more, Holmes in statue form was among the happy hordes festooned for the day in green and white.

But back to Herriot. In 1969 his heroics for Birmingham City against Manchester United in a thundering FA Cup thwarted George Best, Bobby Charlton and Denis Law. Best in his *News of the World* column wrote that Herriot was 'safer than the Bank of England'. There was always going to be a semi-fictional vet tramping the Yorkshire Dales, but who knows, he might have been christened Blenkinsop or Glasscock or Shufflebottom if Wight hadn't caught the game on TV and been enthralled by our custodian, Scotland's goalie at the time.

'I suppose *All Creatures Great and Small* made me a wee bit more famous than I was,' Herriot told me. 'When I found out about the books I just thought, coincidence: here was a writer chappie with the same name. Then my niece told me she'd spotted in *Reader's Digest* that he'd actually nicked mine.

'Folk I'd never met before would tell me my life tending all those animals in such lovely countryside must be wonderful. I'd sometimes say to them: "Well, I'm the real Jim Herriot. I live in Larkhall and there's only Alsatians here and they're all called Rebel or King. I don't even keep a goldfish but my life is no' too bad."'

'It was great to eventually meet Alf. He told me he needed a pseudonym because the Royal College of Veterinary Surgeons banned vets from any kind of self-promotion. He gave me a first edition of *All Creatures Great and Small* and he got one of my Scotland jerseys. We sent each other Christmas cards every year until he passed away.'

Hibs in their time have employed keepers great and small. Utterly distinctive because of his panda eyes – mud smeared from his goalmouth to dull down glare – Herriot may not have been the best of them but he was far from the worst. His walk to take up position between the posts was a slow, suave saunter which prompted Alex Edwards to nickname him 'Big Bob' after Robert Mitchum, star of no fewer than 31 Westerns. Despite the bandy-legged gait I don't ever remember him being nutmegged.

47

WAS PRINCE PHILIP IN PAT STANTON'S PUB, CHATTING TO JIMMY BOYLE?

I'VE GOT a great idea for a stage play. No, hang on, I'm not getting all poncey (or even more poncey). Pat Stanton's in it. Here's the set-up. Man walks into a bar. Actually, duke walks into a bar. Prince Philip when he was kipping at his Edinburgh but 'n' ben, the Palace of Holyrood House, was a short walk from this establishment, and if there was no carriage driving on Sky Sports 17, he might have been tempted of an evening to saunter down for a swift half.

Then, first man is joined by second man, Jimmy Boyle, the convicted killer turned celebrated sculptor whose Gateway Exchange rehabilitating ex-offenders and drug addicts via art is even closer to the pub.

Then a third man. Directly across the road is the Aghtamar Lake Van Monastery in Exile, simplified for the capital's dine-outers as 'The Armenian Restaurant', although nothing about it was straightforward. The prospective clientele thought they were calling a phone box to make reservations. They were still ranked prospective when the door opened, for if the strange fellow in the Cossack hat took an instant dislike they could be turned away, and if even a few minutes late they were not getting in. Too loud at the banquet tables, too demanding or refusing to join in the folk dances or help wash up and they could yet be turfed out. Before food bores competed to find the most original and eccentric culinary experience, before Gordon

Ramsay became famous for flambé-ing himself over something going wrong in the kitchen, there was Petros Vartynian.

So there you have it: three formidable characters who almost certainly never met at Cairns Bar in Abbeyhill. Still, it's fun to imagine being a fly on the wall or buzzing around the pie warmer for their highly opinionated chatter directly beneath thundering London-bound trains – especially with Stanton as mine host.

He ran the pub when the restaurant was still functioning and the Duke of Edinburgh was still around. For local colour, Cairns might beat other pubs which have had Hibees pulling the pints – there have been plenty of these down the years, and plenty of reminisces worth chasing.

In Shades in Easter Road itself, for instance, how many asked Erich Schaedler if he truly meant his sensational dipping volley way out wide at Partick Thistle in the Scottish Cup in 1972? I wish I'd done that.

A 'To Let' sign hangs over this howff now. It's tough times for the licensed trade and the tradition of footballing publicans has died out, although nearer the stadium the Iona survives and this used to be Cropley's. Alex Cropley (see ch. 89) definitely meant every sensational dipping volley and he also has the distinction of a Sunday amateur team being named after him – Liberton Cropley.

The great transtemporal Hibee pub crawl would stop for two at the Old Eastway Tap. Not that old, it recently had Derek Riordan's name above the door and before him this was Paul Kane's Four In Hand. Jumping further back in time, still on Easter Road, there was ET's where presumably Eddie Turnbull was a bit less gruff than he ever was in the dugout.

Leith Walk used to boast Marinello's, run by Peter of that ilk. A hefty clearance away was Tommy Younger's pub. Down on Leith Links his team-mate Lawrie Reilly was behind the bar at the Bowler's Rest. From the same glistening era Gordon Smith's pub was The Right Wing at Willowbrae except being Gordon it was different – a roadhouse.

Jackie McNamara and Ralph Callachan teamed up for The Sportsman in Musselburgh where legend has it they once had to reprimand Garry O'Connor lighting up a cigar with a £20 note. Their old centre-half George Stewart boldly ventured into Jambo territory with the Chesser Inn. The clincher for Willie Irvine's new contract after going goal crazy was the tenancy of Blithe Spirit uptown in Rose Street.

But the pile of pennies and year's supply of cheese and onion crisps for Most Prolific Pubsman – Jock's Lodge, Corstorphine Inn, Pig & Thistle, Struan to name but a few – must go to Jimmy O'Rourke.

48

THREE HANDLES: THE FIRST DRAFT OF A *TWO RONNIES* GAG

IT'S BEEN kicked around the place. It's been shunted from winter to spring and back again. It's had a dozen different names, passed from sponsor to sponsor like in a children's party game, but no one seems to want to be left holding it for long. And how do you hold it, exactly, the Scottish League Cup? It has three handles, which sounds like the first draft of a *Two Ronnies* gag. The third handle possibly makes it self-conscious, if trophies have feelings, like everyone's staring at it and wondering if this is elephantiasis – especially when sitting alongside the far more storied Scottish Cup, fitted much further back in history with just the classic two.

It has long since lost its entitlement to European competition so a League Cup winners' medal will not speed a footballer through border control. Indeed, in the post-Brexit age, he may be the cause of even longer delays for grumpy holidaymakers as security staff puzzle over the tournament's relevance.

But don't try telling a Hibs fan it's the diddy cup. Especially not one who in 1972 stood on the railway sleeper-and-red blaes steps of Hampden and wondered how the hell the mighty Celtic would ever be toppled. Jock Stein's team could win 6–1 without dominating, and hat-tricking somersaulter Dixie Deans could impersonate Olga Korbut without embarrassment.

That was the Scottish Cup final and then at the end of the year the two teams reconvened. In between Hibs had managed to beat Celtic to win the Drybrough Cup (see ch. 98) although there was creeping unease that Scottish football's supremacists would revert to serious faces for an established prize.

'We knew we could beat them so we just had to be brave,' Alex Edwards told me. Mickey never lacked self-belief. Not at 13 when Stein, to clinch his signature for Dunfermline Athletic, was obliged to stump up £1,000, a TV set, a paint job for the family home in Rosyth and a Ford Classic for when the player had learned to drive. Not when later at the Pars he went on strike. Not when his hot temper resulted in regular disciplinaries where he'd scold the beaks for dozing off. ('It was aye better if your hearing was in the morning, before they'd been for a long lunch.') And not when, after football, he landed a lucrative brewery job ahead of two ex-Hearts men. ('I couldn't resist a fly dig: we'd all stopped playing but wee Mickey was still beating the Jambos.')

Discounting the Drybrough, and I really don't, it had been 70 years since a cup had been smeared with muddy hands from Leith. As well as demonstrate bravery the team would need to live up to the port's motto and persevere. A properly hardcore 11 ties had to be negotiated, with the Hibees hitting five goals at Tannadice, six at Broomfield and disposing of Rangers in the semi in a manner that was becoming routine. Diddy? Not back then, although admittedly these days in the League Cup it seems that teams might be able to reach Hampden simply by answering random quiz questions, and more adroitly than the *Family Fortunes* bozo who, challenged to name a bird with a long neck, ventured: 'Naomi Campbell?' In 2021, for a Celtic final again, just three games were required.

The one game remaining in '72, requiring Hibs to stick their necks out, would see Edwards at his cocky, crafty and tippy-toe tricksiest to lay claim to one of those three handles. But he'd admit that the other two belonged to his captain, for this was the Pat Stanton Final (see ch. 72).

49

'FOLKS, JUST LOOK AT THIS RESULT . . . HIBS 8, RANGERS 1'

IN RAP at the last count, according to America's Revolt TV cable network, experts in the field, there were 33 acts using the appellation Lil. These included Lil Wayne, Lil' Kim, Lil Baby, Lil' Ronnie, Lil Peep, Lil Bibby, Lil Boosie and the only one who gets near my radiogram on account of his soft spot for soft rock, Lil Yachty. It's highly unlikely, no matter the lack of height, that there is ever any display of inferiority complex among them – hip hop's braggadocio simply doesn't permit this. But when I look at photographs of Hibs' Lil Arthur Milne, he seems to be straining every muscle to hold himself up to his full 5ft 4ins and a bit beyond.

Lil guy, huge goal numbers, including a couple in one of the Hibees' biggest, bogglingest victories in a century and a half. 'Yes, folks, just look at this result again,' began a report from the match on 27 September 1941 at Hampden . . . Hibs 8, Rangers 1.

Brechin-born Milne was the centre-forward before, during and after the Second World War. His figures were sensational – 186 games, 106 goals. Yet there was a moment when Liverpool, his loan club, decided they were 'rather afflicted with too many stocky little forwards' and Dundee United, his parent club, no longer seemed to want him, so in 1937 manager Willie McCartney snaffled Milne for Easter Road, unperturbed by recent criticisms of Hibs men being too diminutive.

His career, like those of all footballers, was interrupted by the war, but he was prominent in every effort to keep the game going in its reduced state, providing the occasional 90 minutes of escape from worry. He played alongside wartime guest Matt Busby; in the League Cup which came out of the conflict; in the Summer Cup, another improvised competition in which he netted a Parkhead hat-trick; and in the War Emergency Cup. Players could move around the regional leagues and, having patched things up with Dundee United, helped them to the final of the latter tournament in 1940, won by Rangers.

Milne's revenge would come back in green and white in what has gone down in history as the Gers' heaviest domestic defeat, topping the 7–1 scoreline with which Celtic won the 1957 League Cup. (This was the 'lens cap match', where a cameraman's blunder deprived the telly audience of some of the goals, and the ripple which built into a torrent of Old Firm conspiracy theories.)

The Sunday Post's Jack Harkness was left breathless by the Hibees hammering. 'Ponder over it slowly,' he urged readers, 'lest you fail to grasp its significance. The score suggests a thrashing. And thrashing it was. For if ever a team was whipped upside down and inside out, it was the Rangers. In every art Hibs were masters.'

This was the Southern League, not the suspended full division, but so what? 'The most amazing procession of goals in either Hibernian or Rangers' history,' raved Harkness. 'Clever goals, brilliant goals, cheeky goals. This game had 'em. On they came like the Lord Mayor's show. Milne made it four, and [Bobby] Combe five, six, and seven. And because he's allergic to odd numbers [Gordon] Smith made it eight.'

Milne also helped Hibs to the final of the Victory Cup. Truly in those dark days he served. He'd forgotten his shooting boots in Hibs' most ignominious day in the Scottish

Cup[*] when they were beaten by little Edinburgh City in 1938. In tasting triumph and also the most rotten pie, he was indubitably and incorrigibly a Hibee.

* All right, the worst until 2012.

50

WHEN WE CALLED TYNECASTLE HOME

THE GAME'S gone. Where's the loyalty nowadays? Well, we should have been around a century ago. When Hibs marked the first 50 years of their existence they did it with an eleven the fans could recite in verse, a team as sturdy and dependable as Edinburgh's old tram service (cable-operated for uptown, pioneeringly electric in Leith).

This was the line-up which prevailed in the face of rickets, reinforced toecaps, typhoid, laissez-faire refereeing, rudimentary sanitation, balls like depth charges, a national diet 'insufficient to maintain health' and with the Great Depression coming round the next bend:

Willie Harper, William McGinnigle, William Dornan, Peter Kerr, Willie Miller, Hugh Shaw, Harry Ritchie, Jimmy Dunn, Jimmy McColl, Johnny Halligan, John Walker.

This was the team that took Hibs to two Scottish Cup finals in a row. The next time this happened, in 2012 and 2013, there were only three players who stuck around for the second one. At the end of the 1924–25 season, the four Willies, two Jimmys and the rest could reflect on a job well done, third place in the league being the club's best finish since the championship was won at the start of the century.

The campaign featured a quirk never repeated before or since – when Hibs called Tynecastle 'home'. It was only for a few games on Friday nights while work on the Easter Road grandstand was being completed. Today's harsh bants would view the team having to hole up in Gorgie as yet another disadvantage to be endured beyond the greater risk of infection at a time when the average life expectancy for men was 49. But really, wasn't it a decent gesture from Hearts to refrain from the standard Edinburgh greeting – 'You'll have had your Bovril' – and throw open the door to the strays from across the city?

Kicking off 1925–26, Hibs' closest game to the 50th anniversary was at Parkhead when chaos reigned due to the introduction of a new offside rule. At least that was the excuse for Celtic winning 5–0. But to be fair it didn't take the Hibees long to get the hang of the law change when in the next match every member of the forward line scored against Kilmarnock, eight goals in total.

That was the last time the team were all together. Nine of them would play more than 300 games for Hibs, Kerr reaching 483. Harper was hardly a fly-by-night with his 205 appearances and his transfer to Arsenal would help pay for stadium development. Gunners fans were able to marvel at his mighty goal kicks for what was a world record fee for a goalie of £4,000.

Son of a blacksmith, Scots Guardsman on the Western Front during the Great War, captain of the regimental rugby team and also heavyweight boxing champ, Harper enjoyed an eventful life before Hibs and the same after it.

He was Scotland's goalie and never lost to England. Fancying America's nascent soccer league, he turned out for some splendidly named outfits: Fall River Marksmen, Boston Wonder Workers and New Bedford Whalers. He returned to Arsenal and helped them win their first league title. Then came another green team, Plymouth Argyle, where he was literally in with the bricks. In recognition of his half-century of service as keeper, trainer, groundsman, laundryman and barman, the club's training ground was named after him – Harper's Park. 'Willie's life was wrapped up in keeping out goals,' read the programme notes for his testimonial match against Arsenal. 'That was his grand purpose.'

51

'I REFUSED TO STICK IT UP TO HIBS FOR GETTING RID OF ME'

INDEX FINGER and pinkie, extended like a stag beetle's pincers, a hand sign not seen for 50 years. Thankfully this was Jimmy O'Rourke. As a middle-class boy from Edinburgh's New Town in the early 1970s I occasionally had to venture into the capital's outlying schemes to get a game of Subbuteo. This was when the street gangs rooled OK, ya bass and, negotiating Clermiston, you were fortunate if your only exposure to the unfraternal greeting was from glancing up at the top deck of a corporation bus as it disappeared over the hill.

'The Clerrie Jungle,' confirmed O'Rourke, who grew up on the estate. Similar societies at the time – Crombie-coated, *Clockwork Orange*-apeing, little in common with the Algonquin Round Table – were Young Mental Drylaw and Niddrie Terror. 'I wasn't in the Jungle but my three older brothers might have been. I was much more interested in chasing the lassies,' he chuckled.

Before long O'Rourke was chasing Alan Gordon flick-ons and Alex Edwards dinks and arrowed passes from Alex Cropley as a £35-a-week, thunder-thighed penalty-box plunderer, a Tornado and fans' favourite. 'Everyone knows his name,' went the song although sceptics – the mad fools – did exist. 'I don't like to bum myself up, so this is what Sandy Jardine had to say about me, just after we'd beaten Rangers for the umpteenth time: "That Rourkey, all he can dae is score goals."'

In all, there were 122 for Hibs. It's funny that opponents

were caught unawares because from the terraces one of his brothers used to ring a bell every time O'Rourke was on the ball. This was Michael, 'a master at no' paying for anything', who for England–Scotland games at Wembley would hop on the midnight special for free and at the stadium negate the need for a ticket by offering to carry the pipe band's bass drum. Ironically he became a tax officer but O'Rourke only had one ambition.

When we met he reeled off the Real Madrid team from Hampden's 1960 European Cup fantasia, although that wasn't the first final to excite him. 'The night in 1956 when Hearts came back with the Scottish Cup, my mother took me over the back of Clerrie and down to Corstorphine Road to meet the open-top bus and acclaim the great Alex Young.' So he could have been a Jam Tart? 'Dinnae print that! I went turnabout to Easter Road and Tynecastle; everyone did in those days. I was at Tynie when Eusébio came with Benfica. I saw Standard Liège who had a centre-forward called Bonga Bonga. I probably preferred Tynie because you got a halfpenny more there when you took back the empty beer bottles, but dinnae print that either. Mr [Tommy] Walker [Hearts' manager] had me in his office but I only ever wanted to play for the Hibs and thankfully I got to live the dream.'

Peak Jimmy came in a three-month spell in 1972, the Weeble-shaped goal demon hitting 25 including six hat-tricks. Yet he always thought the rest of the Tornadoes were way more talented than him and, as Edwards told me, fretted most Fridays about being dropped. Eventually he was, to make way for Joe Harper (see ch. 82). 'There was only going to be room for one wee fat barrel,' he laughed. For new club St Johnstone he returned to Easter Road and netted the winner. 'Afterwards all the papers wanted me to denigrate Hibs, stick it up to them for getting rid of me, but I would never have done that. I loved the club too much and still do.'

52

A WAR RELIC, LIKE AIR RAID SIRENS AND SHORTAGES OF NYLON STOCKINGS

WHO ARE some of the great avant-gardists? There's Picasso and Dali and Marcel Duchamp. In music, the Johns, Cage and Coltrane, plus Stockhausen and Frank Zappa and the Velvet Underground. In literature, Beckett, Burroughs and Scotland's own Alexander Trocchi. Oh and Hibs. If the definition of avant-garde is being forward-thinking and innovative, progressive and pioneering, then that's us, yes? And in the spirit of Picasso's *Homage to the Sun*, Dali's *Le Soleil* and Nico warbling 'Who Loves the Sun?', may we present the Summer Cup.

It's not a thing any more but the trophy resides permanently at Easter Road for the club having come up with the original idea. And – wide and squat like a chamber pot – it might well have been designed by our friend, the boy Duchamp, as a companion piece for his famous, scandalous urinal.

In 1941 with the Second World War raging and Winston Churchill urging 'Holidays at Home' to free up the trains for our brave boys, league football was already regionalised. To keep the games coming for the nation's morale, Easter Road chairman Harry Swan proposed a cup competition to run through May and June and Hibs won it in the inaugural year, beating Rangers 3–2 in the Hampden final. The Summer Cup was staged four more times for teams in the Southern League, the Hibees playing in two other finals but losing to the Rangers in '42 – on a coin toss – and Partick Thistle in '45.

When the fighting ended, the tournament stopped and became a war relic like air raid sirens, children being labelled and billeted to the countryside and critical shortages of nylon stockings. But in 1964 it was revived. Grounds were still very much open to the elements and clubs, not yet willing to fork out on roofing, wondered if the often drookit masses might enjoy some football in the sunshine.

This was early in the Jock Stein era, a bit of a misnomer for the stint was all too brief. In programme notes he wrote: 'I'm sure that Hibs won't disappoint their supporters in the new competition.' But the first three matches in the team's group resulted in just one point. 'All looks lost,' admitted the manager, who'd had to rethink his strategy for the tournament. 'The main purpose now is to find a team for next season.'

Then group leaders Hearts rethought their strategy, suddenly upping and leaving for a North American tour. Hibs once again assumed the Zelig role (see ch. 13) to appear in a trick of the light at the business end of the competition, overcoming Kilmarnock in the semi-finals with Stein describing the big crowd at the Easter Road leg as 'a setback to the critics of summer football' as he looked forward to a showdown with Aberdeen.

But life in the Granite City was dramatically put on hold. The Covid pandemic would provoke chilling memories of a typhoid outbreak there 55 years previously when hundreds were quarantined in hospitals, the stricken could only glimpse their families through closed windows, travel was banned and with it football.

The medical officer issuing daily bulletins became a TV personality and wild rumour spread like germs, with Spanish media claiming rotting corpses were piling up in the streets waiting to be thrown into the sea. And all because of a tin of contaminated corned beef.

The final of the Summer Cup was delayed until the start of the following season. By then Aberdeen, the city, was still suffering the stigma of disease so it would have been no surprise if Aberdeen, the team, had been disrupted by all the turmoil. The postponement probably suited Hibs who'd begun the tournament poorly but by the September had found a new star in Peter Cormack (see ch. 112). It was all square after two games when the exciting teenager, who'd hardly figured previously, was pitched into the side for the Pittodrie decider on the back of a hat-trick in the league at Airdrie. Cormack scored again, made Jim Scott's goal and like everyone else admired Willie Hamilton's glorious strike for a 3–1 triumph.

Hibs loved this competition but just about everyone else, lacking the avant-garde vision, seemed to view summer football as incongruous as a Zappa xylophone solo, with normally sturdy pie crusts at risk of melting like Dali clocks. Still, the bedpan is ours for ever.

53

HOW HIBS KILLED THE BEST PANTO GAGS STONE DEAD

DID HIBS save pantomime? Oh no they didn't, you say. Oh yes they did. Kind of . . . In the mid-1990s the grand tradition was dying on its horse's rear end. Grant Stott, who at that moment as a panto performer would have been just above horse's rear ends on the cast lists, remembers when it was David Essex or some other English trouper topping the bill. Productions moved round the UK lock, stock which could mean the set displaying the Cross of St George and a Christopher Biggins-led show at Glasgow's King's Theatre opening with a song in praise of old London town. 'Then in 1995, also at the King's, the *Evening Times* turned up at the stage door and the front page was all about that panto being shut down. The stars were Cannon and Ball and Bobby was running around and shouting: "Tommy, Tommy, you know who they're gonna blame . . . us!"'

Revolution followed. Glasgow started going with Scottish stars and site-specific jokes and Edinburgh's King's, which had been dependent on the same venerable, gnarled randoms, followed suit. Stott's lowly place in any Edinburgh show had been via another hoary panto tradition as a concession to local: the bloke off the radio. He thought he was for the chop but instead, for a capital production of *Jack and the Beanstalk*, was handed a bigger role, the villain of the piece who was facing banishment, and because of his football affiliations this would be to

Tynecastle. 'Half the audience groaned, the other half cheered. I thought to myself: "There's something in this."'

Stott was a latecomer to Hibs. Growing up, older brother John Leslie had Hibee paraphernalia on the walls of their shared bedroom. 'I was determined to be different so my side was plastered with photos of, er, Gary Glitter.' Then, while John was starring on TV, he was a policeman. But pantomime has enabled Stott to climb the beanstalk to a showbiz career, with Edinburgh football and especially Hibs supplying a constant source of gag-worthy material.

He said: 'Hibs never winning the Scottish Cup obviously became a running joke and [co-stars] Allan Stewart and Andy Gray would almost fight over delivering it because there was always a great reaction.' Green and maroon shirts and scarves began appearing in the stalls. In 2008's *Goldilocks and the Three Bears*, Stott portrayed Hearts supremo Vladimir Romanov as a demented circus impresario which wasn't so far from the truth. In 2012 he was thrown in jail, his cell containing a 50-inch telly, which didn't seem such a leap from prison reality, but it was programmed to only show the five Hearts goals from that year's cup final atrocity on a loop. And then in 2016's *Cinderella*, Christmas Eve performance, Hibs loaned him the trophy to parade on stage, killing the best gag stone dead. 'Allan and Andy were raging about that.'

Other jokes have had to be hastily updated, rewritten or junked, such are the erratic and ever-changing fortunes of both teams. Stott is in charge of the football material, moving it on from tired, generic gags such as the one about team brassieres: 'No support, no cups.' In his dressing room before some Saturday evening performances, if there's been a shock result or a managerial sacking, he'll be like a newspaper editor with a full-on deadline sweat. He's also the guy who comes up with the funny songs celebrating improbable iconography such as Edinburgh's out-of-town retail parks and so must be attuned to city life in the round, and attentive regarding all the fads, obsessions and grumps.

At Glasgow's King's the performers can't really touch football without the risk of a riot in the cheap seats, such is the deadly serious nature of the Old Firm rivalry. 'But we can have a laugh about it, such as the routine when I stopped Allan mid-gag because he wasn't being funny. VAR had to adjudicate. The big screen behind us flashed up "Checking for possible humour . . ." then "Still bloomin' checking . . ." before finally: "Penalty to Rangers."'

Edinburgh's pantomime is back to being an Edinburgh show and as much of an institution as the football teams. And as long as this pair continue being classic Hearts and quintessentially Hibs that should continue. 'If they were successful most of the time that would be bad for us,' admitted Stott. 'And though it pains me to say so as a fan, Hibs being Hibs is best for the panto.'

54

THE BRAVE MEN WHO TRIED TO STOP THEM PAINTING THE TOWN MAROON

LAUREL AND Hardy's *The Music Box* must be the greatest 29 minutes and 16 seconds to come out of black-and-white, between-the-wars, two-reel Hollywood and I never need much excuse to drop it into discussion. Usually with a thud, like Stan and Ollie allowing the piano to tumble down the long flight of stairs, *again*, but maybe this time my referencing the flick isn't quite so clunky or contrived.

The comedians' eternal struggle sounds not dissimilar to the push-me–pull-you of local government politics as it involved two Edinburgh councillors near the end of the last century. One of them supported Hearts, the other Hibs. And pianos figured, an undisclosed number of them.

Both Eric Milligan, the Jambo, and David Begg, the Hibby, did much good work on behalf of the capital. Begg was Milligan's protégé and they were on the same page most of the time, just not regarding football.

Begg told me: 'When Wallace Mercer tried to take over Hibs, Eric said: "David, this is to be a merger of equals producing a club called Edinburgh City who will challenge the Old Firm and we should absolutely get right behind it." I didn't agree, not at all, and was pretty sure that privately Eric was envisaging Hibs being wiped off the map and that he wouldn't have been exactly devastated about it.'

Both men were in the ruling Labour group on Lothian

Regional Council, Milligan the convener. Begg was chairman of the finance committee and in that role was alerted to a plan to help out Hearts, cash-strapped at the time, by having surplus school pianos stored under one of the Tynecastle stands with the club receiving £90,000 in annual rent from the council.

In *The Music Box*, Laurel and Hardy were attempting a troublesome delivery to the mythical address 1127 Walnut Avenue. Just imagine Milligan and Begg at either end of a piano but with the latter attempting to drag it the wrong way along Gorgie Road, stymying the consignment.

Council officials feared the scheme would result in a red flag for auditors. Begg's view was that equivalent assistance would need to be given to Hibs. He said: 'The plan was quietly binned but for a while myself and the other Hibbies would wind up Eric and his chums by whistling Billy Joel's "Piano Man" around the chambers.'

Then in 1995 as part of countrywide reorganisation, Lothian Region was abolished with the pair moving across to the new City of Edinburgh Council for which branding would be required, and a colour scheme. This was likely to be contentious so the officials suggested neutral blue. Said Begg: 'Eric ruled that out right away because blue was Tory and also Rangers.' The next time the livery came up for discussion, the last item under any other business, there was cryptic mention in the papers of 'pantone 201'.

Begg and his fellow Hibby Angus MacKay were immediately suspicious. 'Mr Chairman, what colour is this? "It's pantone 201." Yes, but what does it look like? Finally we were shown it. Pure Jambo!'

This is precisely why we have elected representatives: to halt the march of Trojan horses in maroon caparisons. Okay, so if the coats were visible the horses wouldn't be Trojan ones and Trojan horses missed the jousting era by a couple of centuries and several thousand miles, but you get my drift.

Unfortunately, while the minutes of that meeting will show for evermore that Begg and his lieutenant voted against pantone 201, it was approved as Edinburgh's official colour. Later our man took over the transport brief. Begg was in charge of the council adopting bus lanes but while these are painted red in most cities he wanted the capital to go green. With a straight face revealing just the tiniest hint of mischief, he told me this was about Edinburgh showing its environmentally friendly colours, not any other kind. 'Although there was a wee moment when I did think that for the greenways along Gorgie Road I might have asked my neighbour to perform the opening ceremony. He's a guy you might know – Keith Wright.'

55

BECKENBAUER INVENTED THE ROLE AND LICENSED IT TO SLOOP

TIME-HONOURED rituals. Everything in its right place. The snug certainties of (football) life. It would have been strange for this boy, alarming even, if the journey to a game had been altered and for once didn't take the family saloon past the Fairbairns off-licence in Albert Street, or that there wasn't a gasping queue snaking round the block for the terracing refreshments of Tartan Special and Eldorado fortified wine.

And, even more alarming, enough to merit a late request for the match to be called off, if John Blackley hadn't run on to the park and, having reached the other side, played a one-two with Erich Schaedler then smashed the ball against the advertising hoardings. Ricocheting back to him, it was killed instantly. Of course it was. Other stoppers of the period would have aimed for the hoarding, missed horribly and struck a spectator full in the face, knocking his Bovril five steps back.

Blackley was a ball-playing defender, a radical new concept and there must have been some among the crowds, set in their ways, who found this bewildering and perhaps disturbing, and probably they didn't understand homosexuality either.

But the kids got it. They admired Blackley's ginger bangs, copied the dress sense – the aproned shirt – and mimicked the hen-toed walk, suggestive of their man having just dismounted from the trusty steed after a long time riding the range, or maybe a quest for the real Eldorado. Previously, impressionable youth would have all wanted to play centre-forward and fought over that jersey. But what – as Jimi Hendrix almost said – if nine was six?*

Blackley was the sweeper in Turnbull's Tornadoes. Franz Beckenbauer invented the role and for Scotland licensed it to Sloop – John B's nickname coming from the Beach Boys song – who took the position and added his own distinct cool. Defending didn't have to be perfunctory. You didn't have to hoof it anywhere and, in a tackle you favoured the scalpel over the sledgehammer. A swift, painless interception – e.g. Bobby Moore on Pelé, 1970 World Cup – could spring a rapid counter-attack and the instigator's shorts would stay nice and clean. Suddenly sixy was sexy.

Leith's libero was unhurried and unruffled. Well, most of the time. Blackley told me: 'The Tornadoes were a great team but we didn't manage to achieve all we wanted, couldn't quite manage to win at places like Ibrox every time. There was a game where Rangers scored a goal that was a mile offside. Pat Stanton (see ch. 64) and I rounded on the linesman. 'Tell us the name of your orange lodge,' Pat demanded, and then I took up our case with a barrage of non-stop swearing. I was sent off, naturally, and the SFA produced a charge sheet which listed every b-, c- and f-word. It went on for page after page.

'There were times when I was a proper radge – red hair, you see – although after Aberdeen scored against us at Pittodrie, a blatant foul in the build-up, I was aware the referee's day job was something in women's lingerie but in my rant bit my lip and didn't make any reference to it. Remarkable restraint!'

* Before 'six' signified a role, that being deep-lying midfielder, it was the number worn by the man who stood alongside the centre-half and, like in Blackley's case, no offence Jim Black, made him look good.

Blackley is proud to have made it all the way to the Scotland team and the 1974 World Cup from a tiny village in the high ground above Falkirk known as the Braes. 'My dad almost never saw me play because he got too nervous, but his last words before he died were: "John, you've made this family's name."'

Nevertheless, the No. 6 is somewhat embarrassed that there's now a street named after him, almost a unique honour* among Hibee immortals.

* In a new housing development close to the stadium there's Lawrie Reilly Place.

56

CHARGE DOWN THE SLOPE, TRAP THE OPPOSITION IN YONDER VALLEY

EYES HALF shut I can still see it. And because some years have passed, the drop seems that much greater. While in my mind I'm safely tucked behind the old main terracing wall, in my usual childhood spot on the halfway line, I feel like a cliff diver in Old Acapulco, peering over the edge, down and ever downwards.

The slope. It went south to north, a discrepancy of about six feet. Does that sound like a lot? Probably now, yes, with pitches pristine at all times of the year and, on TV in England at least, never looking less than glisteningly green. Back in the day and right across this land footballers were accustomed to mud and the odd hummock, but at Easter Road, if Hibs were so inclined, the decline could have them charging down the hill and trapping the opposition in yonder valley, much like the unfortunate Scots army in the Battle of Dupplin Moor in 1332.*

Hang on, though, surely both teams could enjoy the advantage of the slope over the course of a whole match. Technically true, but Hibs would invariably have it for the second half, when play became free form and the task set them was clear-cut. Then, Alex Edwards on the right could aim a trademark raking

* This was a key staging post along the way to English expansionism enabling Edward Balliol to seize the Scottish throne. At least England thought it was, for just three months later we gained revenge and Balliol's bum was oot the windae.

diagonal at the opposite flank – and even though he and all of us O-grade physics students knew the ball would pick up speed like a small boulder rolled down the side of a quarry – Arthur Duncan, nicknamed 'Nijinsky', never failed to collect it.

In my junior fanhood, Hibs didn't always turn around after 45 minutes to shoot down the slope, it only seems that way in misty water-coloured memory. Perhaps referees, in tossing a coin for choice of ends, had been handed fiendish double-sided florins. What is beyond dispute is that the momentous victories over Napoli, Sporting Lisbon and Liverpool came about like this, as did those of Barcelona and Real Madrid previously.

The slope used to be even more vertiginous. The six-foot discrepancy was an attempt, in 1924, at levelling up when the pitch was moved to allow for construction of a new grandstand. Before then, legend has it that for icy conditions, Hibs wingers had perfected a technique akin to speed skating on a luge run to whoosh past skittering defenders with the ball snugly between their feet.

But in 2000 came a ruling you'd have to call the Eiger Sanction. Euro officialdom was determined to move any mountain. Slopes had to be straightened out and non-conformity – that is, individuality, character, heritage, quirk and charm – removed. UEFA took their cue from the fun reduction officers at the European Commission earlier accused of attempting to unkink the bananas imported into the UK and reduce the virility of our vacuum cleaners. Chief accuser had been one Boris Johnson in his journalistic days as a Brussels corr. Some of his dispatches about threats to the British way of life were pure fiction but they stirred Euroscepticism and sowed the seeds for Brexit.

The threat to the Easter Road pitch and its wonky loveliness was all too real, so what a pity Johnson wasn't creatively scaremongering in its hour of need. That could have been his great Churchillian moment. Sloping parks – Oxford United,

Yeovil Town, Barnet – have all but vanished from the football-scape. Nowadays your town looks very much like my town. In your homogenous high street your skinny Starbucks latte tastes exactly the same as mine. But, eyes partially closed, I can still follow the path of Mickey's cross-fielder and Nijinsky in full flight is catching it on his toe without breaking stride.

57

SEEING THE LIGHT ABOUT THE EUROPEAN CUP, PART 1

FOOTBALL MANAGERS nowadays can sound thick. Admittedly they're invited to speak too much, for their own good and ours, so they end up spouting clichés on a loop. Alternatively, they come across as thin-skinned, condescending smartasses. But in 1955, Hugh Shaw found the right words, statesmanlike but allowing for some glee, when he said: 'The feeling is one of enormous pride that Hibernian are embracing a wonderfully exciting new European competition.'

And on 14 September, ten years after US infantry captured the city, cheered on by British squaddies based in Essen to deNazify the Ruhr, Royal Navy hero Eddie Turnbull scored his team's first goal in this grand enterprise of footballing endeavour with its side hustle of continental healing and reconciliation.

To be playing in Germany against Rot-Weiss Essen, with rationing having only just ended and national service set to continue into the next decade, the Second World War was not ancient history for Shaw's men. But Lawrie Reilly, too, was able to articulate the team's position going into the inaugural European Cup. 'We may not have been bearing old grudges,' he said, 'but we were harbouring poignant memories.'

Keep it tight, Shaw had told the team, but they were soon disobeying orders. Added Reilly: 'Eddie and Bobby [Combe] were supposed to lie deep. Ach, Bobby couldn't lie deep in two feet of water. I said to him: "This lot aren't that good. Let's have a go."' So

Hibs cranked it up against the West German champs, neutralised 'Der Boss', Helmut Rahn, the flying winger who'd netted the World Cup-winning goal the previous year, and won the tie 4–0.

A 'thrashing of the crack Rot-Weiss club,' raved Jack Harkness of the *Sunday Post*, something of an inaugurator himself, as henceforth all foreign opposition for British teams would be labelled 'cracks' (and, borrowing the language of the Cold War, all research to prepare for ties would take the form of 'spying missions', the findings compiled in 'dossiers').

Harkness reckoned this was the moment to dossier up Hibs' achievements: Peerless quality of football. Flying the flag in foreign fields. Challenging and beating the best here and abroad. Instituting a wage scale equalling the best in Britain. Installing Scotland's most expensive floodlighting. 'Since the end of the war, our most enterprising club,' he wrote.

Well said, Jack, but the *Daily Mirror*'s Jimmy Stevenson had a quibble because Hibs weren't reigning champions. 'I said they had no right representing Scotland in the European Cup. They went across to Essen and humbled Rot-Weiss 4–0. Am I red-faced? Not likely.'

What Rot-(Weiss). But Stevenson continued: 'I still insist that Aberdeen as champs are the team for the job.' Ah the Dons, who didn't want to participate in the European Cup and weren't viewed as a good fit anyway? But, despite the handsome lead, there was still a second leg to be played. Well, wasn't there? . . .

The tournament had always been planned for night-times, in the months requiring artificial illumination. The SFA well understood this when they sanctioned Hibs as Scotland's entrants. But bizarrely two months later, the beaks would ban competitive football under floodlights. Something had to give. The 'tremendously delicate' conundrum reached Belfast and the sports paper *Ireland's Saturday Night*. 'It would be tragic,' their editorial stated, 'if Hibs had to say, with their second-round place almost assured: "Sorry, we have to scratch."'

58

THE GROUNDSMAN MUMBLING FROM A HUT . . . THEN CAME RADIO HIBS

HERE'S ANOTHER story which seems very Hibs. They'd just lost at Hampden, again, and the pre-arranged party back in Edinburgh at the Dragonara Hotel was inevitably a glum affair. Then word reached the team from the far end of the lounge that an elderly guest had suffered a heart attack. They knew just who to summon in the poor fellow's hour of need.

'The guy was flat out on the floor,' remembered Bill Barclay. 'To try and improve blood circulation I was going to lift up his legs. Then his wife said: "Don't waste all your effort – one of them's artificial." I did my best not to laugh, same with the players, but it was a black comedy moment for sure.'

In the 1970s Barclay travelled with the Hibees as a sort of unofficial court jester. He was the folkie-cum-comic who had a novelty hit with the drinking song 'The Twelve Days of Christmas' and for Radio Forth interviewed manager Eddie Turnbull every Friday for a preview of the upcoming game. 'Before it could air, though, I had to edit out his swearing. I made up a tape of every f- and c-word and played it to him, saying: "This is all the work I have to do to make you a star."'*

* The polar opposite of Turnbull in the Hibs dugout was Derek Adams, No. 2 to Colin Calderwood, who insisted: 'I never swear.' That takes some doing in management, not least at exasperating Easter Road.

Barclay's association with the club began in boyhood. Lacking the admission money for the Famous Five, he'd wait with pals for the Easter Road gates to be opened, ten minutes into the second half. Then, if Hibs were awarded a penalty, they'd all rush behind the goal hoping to see a Turnbull cannonball rip the net from its moorings.

Full match access came with a job selling crisps inside the ground ('just plain, flavours hadn't been invented'), then graduating to chocolate bars ('again limited choice, but at least shrinkflation hadn't been invented either'). No one was demanding a 'full match-day experience', which was just as well, but later, after he'd sneaked into the Hit Parade ('No. 30 nationwide, top of the charts in Scotland'), after supporting Rod Stewart on the last-ever Faces tour when unfortunately he developed gout and had to perform in bedroom slippers, Barclay would do his bit to improve things.

'The public address at Easter Road was terrible – one of the groundsmen mumbling from a hut somewhere – so when I was at Forth I had the idea for Radio Hibs. There would be ads, jingles and most importantly proper DJs. Our booth was directly above the tunnel so we could be authoritative. There was no excuse for getting stuff wrong. So when I miscalled Jackie McNamara being substituted he was perfectly within his rights to shout "Fuckin' idiot!" at me.'

Barclay was billed as Edinburgh's answer to Billy Connolly. There was a rivalry between them and a few run-ins. The Big Yin was so big that divorce from his first wife placed him under permanent tabloid scrutiny, and anyone who'd spent even part of a night in the same pub as him could end up being doorstepped by the papers while in their pyjamas. This happened to Barclay.

Our man had an acting career. He went all the way from *Taggart* to *Gangs of New York*, the second Hibby to be cast in a small role in Martin Scorsese's epic (see ch. 67). This didn't daunt him. Nothing was more heart-in-mouth for this showbiz trouper of the old school than having to tell the Easter Road massive that George Best was – euphemism alert – indisposed and wouldn't be playing.

59

THE FORGOTTEN FIVE WHO PLAYED JUST ONCE

LET'S HEAR it for Willie Adams, Willie Allan, Alex Bruce, Jim Gunning and Dennis McGurk. You might call them the Forgotten Five. There were players before them who managed just the one game, and others who came after the same, but maybe these guys had the hardest job: deputising for the Famous Five when limbs were hanging by a thread and the superstars couldn't continue. In Hibs' golden years it had to be bad for a player to come off. Toecaps were lethal, referees were relaxed about GBH but players were far more resilient than they are now. And when the call did go out for a replacement, oh the pressure!

McGurk fared worst, having deputised for the injured Eddie Turnbull in the game reckoned to have cost the Hibees the 1949–50 title. The 1–0 loss at home to relegation-haunted Third Lanark was the only defeat in the final 14 fixtures, Rangers ultimately claiming the flag by a single point.

Stunned by the setback, *The Scotsman*'s correspondent described the team as 'inept', a 'sorry mess' and a 'mere gallimaufry of football talent'* in which McGurk's debut had been 'inauspicious'. Frustrating Hibs was their former goalie Lewis Goram, father of Andy, who left Easter Road without playing

* How many gallimaufries have I witnessed at Easter Road without having this superb word at my disposal?

a senior game and only managed nine at Thirds of which this was the best.

At least Allan's solitary outing away to Raith Rovers a year later was a 3–1 victory and he could say he played a minuscule part in that season's championship triumph. He even crossed twice for Gordon Smith's headed goals, although the *Sunday Post* wouldn't rate his performance any higher than 'unspectacular'.

The Five were gods and modest men from Lumphinnans like Allan would have to concede: 'We're not worthy.' At least he might have been offered a dollop of Smith's Deep Heat that Baltic January afternoon or better still a sip of his – purely medicinal – whisky. Roy Erskine – Andy Murray's grandfather – told me how he could only dream of such treats.

This centre-half-cum-left-back arrived at Easter Road from a works team representing Valleyfield Colliery in Fife on the juniors scene. 'They sent a motorbike for me every Saturday. I travelled pillion and never got to know the rider. The journey could be terrifying in the rain but I loved those games in Comrie, Lochore, Blairhall. Then one day this fellow Archie Gourlay whom we used to see on the touchline – an ex-Partick Thistle goalie, I think – asked me: "Is there any team you'd like to play for?" Well, it had to be Hibs. They were the best in the land.'

A part-timer, Erskine started out in the third XI, graduating to the reserves, but that was his limit. 'I didn't even get the chance to train with Gordon & Co. They were 9–11 guys and then off to the billiard halls. I was Tuesday and Thursday nights, trying to be an optician the rest of the time.'

He wasn't disappointed to leave Easter Road – 'Hibs were a great, great team' – and would turn out for Cowdenbeath and Stirling Albion. With the latter there was the ignominy of a doomed season when just six points were won, although he did score a Scottish Cup goal at Tynecastle. 'A truly spectacular OG!' Still, Andy's a Hibby – was an Easter Road ball boy – because of him.

Only one of the Forgotten Five might be a pub quiz question. Which Scottish footballer played his solitary match in the inaugural European Cup? This was Adams, the emergency goalie for the home leg against West German champions Rot-Weiss Essen. Regular No. 1 Tommy Younger – and Smith – had been abroad on international duty, Northern Ireland four days before and, just 24 hours prior to the Euro tie, Denmark. Despite manager Hugh Shaw's best efforts, with a fast car awaiting them at Prestwick Airport, the flight from Copenhagen was delayed by fog. Imagine how Adams must have felt when he saw his name on the team sheet. Could he hear the crowd when it was announced over the Tannoy that Younger would be missing – were they groaning?

Hibs were four-nil up from the first leg. One report read that 'Adams was seldom worried until the 18th minute when the much-boosted shot of Franz Islacker, the Puskás of Germany, had its first airing.' The return finished 1–1, Hibs were through, and Adams could slip back into the shadows, and like the others never play again.

60

'THERE WAS SUCH A CRUSH MY CHOCOLATE BARS MELTED'

WHAT'S THE ideal number of goals, and the perfect scoreline, for a comic strip-worthy dream game, a stone-cold classic? Seven, you say, producing a 4–3 outcome? No, too many, too whizz-bang; you're just being greedy and obviously Gen-Z, part of the instant gratification clips-straight-to-phone culture, expecting and demanding (and only really wanting) the money shot of the ball hitting the back of the net.

No, it's five goals with your team scoring right away, electric start, only for the opposition (wearing blue) to muscle their way back into the contest. They lead deep into the second half but your guys aren't giving this up. They level and right at the end, a glorious, soar-ious header.

What a game that was, 1972, vs Falkirk at Brockville (other 3–2 matches with headed winners are available). I keep coming back to it and yet no footage exists. No evocative images of Johnny Hamilton straight from kick off streaking through the middle, lank hair bobbing, for the ten-second opener, or right at the end Joe Baker diving full length and so low down to the slimy turf that his nose must have run a shallow channel. But to all you Insta kids for whom film validates every experience, I don't need it.

How could anyone forget Brockville? Stand-ites stomping on the wooden flooring like a censorious kirk assembly and across the pitch the claustrophobic, corrugated enclosure, similar to a long air-raid shelter or a giant sardine tin or a holding pen for desperate refugees. And this was 1972 BS – before segregation.

'I had chocolate bars in my pocket and there was such a crush that they melted,' is a favourite reminisce, not mine and not from that Bairns-Hibees game, but the teams' cup tie earlier in the season, nearly 20,000 squashed into the tiny, rickety ground. There were slightly fewer for the rematch although the stewarding still resembled a charity challenge of how many undergraduates could fit into a Mini Cooper.

Hamilton was a joker. When Eddie Turnbull sent a tray of watches tumbling – gifts for the team from Sporting Lisbon – he quipped: 'Time flies, eh, boss?' His goal was the quickest I'd ever seen, and the game just kept exploding.

Alex Ferguson was in charge of lighting the blue touchpaper, confirmed Hamilton's team-mates, recalling the contest with ease when I met them many years later. 'Fergie did me,' said Alex Cropley. 'Ned [Turnbull] thought it was an outrageous tackle and wouldn't talk to him for years after. But the referee kept telling me to get up! On the stretcher the home fans spat at me. That night I was in absolute agony – even the weight of the blanket on my bed was unbearable. My dad had to give me a fireman's lift down the stairs to run me to hospital. The ankle was broken, needed pins and I thought it was career over.'

Fergie was later sent off. Didn't he head-butt Pat Stanton? 'There was so much going on in the game that I honestly can't remember,' said the Hibs captain diplomatically. 'He elbowed me in the face,' laughed the more forthright John Blackley. 'The funny thing was before the game he'd given me a photo of our team for all the guys to sign. "Ya bugger," I said, "after me getting you those autographs." He just smiled. "There's nae friends in football, John."'

Fergie would go on to become the best friend to Scottish football there's ever been. Brockville became a Morrisons, which upsets Kevin McAllister so much that the Bairns legend, who also played for Hibs, makes the much longer journey to the supermarket chain's Stirling branch rather than shop there.

Meanwhile, the game is imperishable. Extra-special because it was the only one I saw with my mum.

61

UTTERLY FEATURELESS, PAINFULLY WEAK

GAMES CAN be better in the memory. You rev up footage of an old one and try not to wince at the slowness and the clumsiness. So a recent match – Argentina vs France in 2022 – sits among my recorded TV programmes gathering metaphorical dust, just in case rewatching would remove some of the glitz from what I want to remember as the greatest-ever World Cup final.

What then do we make of the Scottish Cup final of 1902? Well, nothing really because none of us saw it and no film exists anywhere. The most famous moving pictures in 1902 comprised *Le Voyage dans la Lune*, the French sci-fi flick where – money shot – the space capsule lands in the moon's eye. Alas there were no cameras recording the money shot of the final – Andy McGeachan's back heel bouncing into the Celtic net. Of course I don't even know if the ball bounced. I'm just guessing and attempting to add some colour.

Shame? Well, not according to the match reports. 'Ragged combinations . . . hollow passing . . . painfully weak shooting,' reads one litany. 'Utterly featureless . . . one of the poorest national finals.' There's more: 'Both divisions played rank bad football' and the Hibees, slightly less abysmal than their opponents, only claimed the prize with a 'lucky goal' from a 'doubtful corner'. Make no mistake, though, this was 'as dull and lifeless a struggle as has been seen between any two leading teams for a very long time'.

All of this comes from a single account in the *Daily Record*. We will just have to take the disgruntled hack's word for it being an absolute shocker. But in the entire history of Scottish football has there ever been a game referenced more often, subjected to greater scrutiny, quoted so randomly, and reduced to a buzz phrase so ruthlessly, to the extent that the mere mention of '1902' brings instant recognition both here and far beyond? Or at least it did.

After 2016, the hollow passing and the rest of the bad, bad football of 114 years previous stopped mattering. If 1902 had been a classic, would that have made the yearning for another triumph more desperate? Probably not. It was the distance back to the start of the previous century which lent the disenchantment.

Because the distance was so yawningly great there was next to no chance of 1902 standing up to any sort of critical rigour. There was too much pressure concentrated on it, too many gags surrounding it. No game could cope with such heat.

Cynics might claim that having Hibsed it for more than a century, how typical that even in that far-off success they were a joke club, blundering around to somehow end up with the trophy and that this was in its way yet another instance of Hibsing it. But that's rubbish. Countless times since 1902 there have been rotten finals, dismal affairs.

Fans who get to chase the Scottish Cup home don't care about the aesthetics and I'm sure that was true of the Hibs supporters in 1902. Flickering film exists of the FA Cup final from that year between Sheffield United and Bury. There's a lovely camera pan along the faces in the crowd which unsurprisingly prompts the voiceover to summon up J.B. Priestley's evocative description of a football crowd, how it 'turned you into a member of a new community, all brothers together for an hour and a half'.

The quote continues: 'Not only had you escaped from the clanking machinery of this lesser life, from work, wages, rent, doles, sick pay, insurance cards, nagging wives, ailing children, bad bosses, idle workmen, but you had escaped with most of your neighbours, with half the town, and there you were cheering together, thumping one another on the shoulders, swopping judgements like lords of the earth, having pushed your way through a turnstile into another and altogether more splendid kind of life.'

I bet Priestley's lyricism could apply to Hibs' triumph as well. And maybe, just maybe, an attic or a charity shop might yet give up the secret of a snatch of film. I'd love to see that, bet it's anything but dull and lifeless and would definitely watch more than once.

62

'I CARRIED INTO FOOTBALL WHAT I'D LEARNED IN BALLET'

IT WAS big news. 'Every paper in Scotland and some in England,' remembered Brian Marjoribanks with a chuckle. 'And then BBC Radio's *Today* programme wanted to speak to me. They were all astonished by what I'd done.'

Why would a footballer, just 21, who'd scored on his Hibs debut in an Edinburgh derby, give up the game for repertory theatre? 'I told *Today*'s presenter, Jack de Manio, that I thought I'd gone as far as I could in football and that theatre had always been my big passion, even though I was starting as the lowest form of life – assistant stage manager. Then Jack asked me to recite some Shakespeare. I chose the prologue from Act 3 of *Henry V*: "Thus with imagined wing our swift scene flies, in motion of no less celerity than that of thought."'

What a pity Marjoribanks flew the football scene so swiftly. Considering how football people love to copy each other, he could have begun a trend for Bardisms in punditry and post-match sound bites. If they're all going to say the same or similar things, then it might as well be Shakespeare things. Though much of the chatter around the game is anodyne, there's potential in the plays for world-class put-downs, such as these from *King Lear*: 'A brazen-faced varlet . . . a worsted-stocking knave . . . a finical rogue . . . an eater of broken meats . . . the son and heir of a mongrel bitch . . . a whoreson cullionly barber-monger.' And maybe worse, or worsted, of all: 'A base footballer.'

Marjoribanks was not a base footballer. As a striker, whose goal against Hearts in 1961 had him briefly wondering if he might be the man to replace Joe Baker, he definitely possessed celerity (it means 'swiftness'; I looked it up). He did not regard running on the pitch and treading the boards as mutually exclusive, telling me: 'What I loved about acting was the self-expression. It expanded my vocabulary and taught me how to communicate. Believe it or not, what I tried to carry into my football was what I learned in ballet, which was part of my theatre training and after all just another way of revealing yourself through movement. And I can tell you that an hour at the barre was no less gruelling than running up and down the terracing at Easter Road – often much worse.'

Hibs, the culture club, allowed Marjoribanks to play part-time while he studied at the Royal Scottish Academy of Music and Drama. And when the Glasgow commute caused him to miss training, they suggested he move to an Edinburgh college where they would pay his fees. Team-mates were interested in, and supportive of, his other life. 'Jim Scott was always asking what play was on the go and John Fraser came to see me in *The Happiest Days of Your Life*.'

Presumably Marjoribanks, at any given moment, remembered where he was and which craft he was learning for he was jumping from free-kick stratagems to Tennessee Williams's *Orpheus Descending* – 'The title role, I charmed women with my guitar.' Another Williams play was *Suddenly Last Summer*, attempting to save a girl with mental problems from the lobotomy ordered by her embarrassed parents. Heavy stuff.

Everyone else might have been amazed at Marjoribanks swapping Deep Heat for greasepaint, but not Pat Stanton who recalled him trying to coax the ball to recite Shakespeare. And although the appearance on *Today* hadn't been any kind of audition, he took a phone call that afternoon – how did he fancy starring in *Dr Finlay's Casebook*, the top TV drama of the period watched by 12 million? He played a footballer in that, and another in the soap opera *United!* Later, he brought the country flickering telly highlights of the Scottish League, including his old pals at Hibs, as anchor on *Sportsreel.* Here's the boy Shakespeare : 'All the world's a stage . . . and one man in his time plays many parts.'

63

JAMBO HEADS SWIVEL THROUGH 360 DEGREES IN SHOCK

THERE SURELY can't be many clubs whose embracing of inclusivity extends to a little brown ugly-bugly with saucer eyes, extendable neck and hydrocephalic head. And yet who *still* end up being accused of racism. But we're talking Scottish football in all its girny glory so I can give you one: Hibs.

In 1999, E.T. was revealed to be a Hibby. A TV commercial showed the alien from the Steven Spielberg sci-fi smasheroo sitting round the gogglebox with a family, all watching the Edinburgh derby. Everyone was a Jambo apart from the extra-terrestrial who when Hibs scored went absolutely berserk, whizzing across the room and twirling his green and white shirt above his massive noggin.

The star of – at that moment – the sixth highest-grossing movie of all time was seemingly in thrall to the 73rd best Easter Road full-back partnership of Paul Lovering and Michael Renwick.

Spielberg had no part to play in the ad or the football team conferred upon his creation, but perhaps he'd be happy enough with Hibs. Bit of early persecution, bit of romance, the odd calamity, some comedy.

So, a cute commercial? Jambos didn't think so. Noses were put out of joint. In fact, in Slateford sculleries and Shandon kitchenettes heads swivelled dementedly in the manner of E.T. at an unforgettable juncture of the film. There were protests to

British Telecom, whose ad it was, and threats of a boycott of the company's products.

Incredibly the gripe was this: E.T. loves Hibs, ergo Hearts and their fans are condemned as a sub-species, a whole different and inferior life form (count the toes). Even more incredibly, the protest made it to the in tray of top discrimination watchdogs.

The way the, um, story was written up this was the Race Relations Board. How quaint. That body ceased to exist after 1976, replaced by the Commission for Racial Equality, then the Equality and Human Rights Commission, so presumably forwarding addresses enabled the Tynie whinge to be carefully studied, then filed in the bin.

Or was it all just nonsense? I'm not sure because Hearts, the support at least, have a well-cultivated, long-standing superiority complex, believing as they do that they are masters of the Edinburgh universe and Hibs are the little green men. In civic life there is no other uproar quite like the one which rips fissures in the pavements and turns the sky black down Gorgie way if Hibs somehow contrive to win two derbies on the spin.

Then there's the whole issue of celeb endorsement, the backing of stars of stage, screen etc. Hibbies can legitimately tease the westside frenemies: 'Pray tell, do you have a Fish? Or by any chance a John Leslie?' This is one area where Hearts do have to admit defeat. Hibs boast more names, more glamour, and not just of this world.

There's also Scarlett Johansson's visitor from outer space in the film *Under the Skin* who lured young single men with the promise of sex in the back of her van only to end up harvesting them. Among the wretched souls – although let's face it, there are worse ways of copping your whack – was a Hibs fan. This fellow had the shirt. He had the mournful, hooded eyes of the season-ticket, life-sentence Hibby.

And, bless him, right to the end he probably felt the same about his team as E.T.'s human protector Elliott did the little brown ugly-bugly: 'I'll believe in you all my life, every day . . . I love you.'

64

INTREPIDLY PRODDED FORWARD, RIGHT FOOT CURLED IN SLIGHTLY

SIXTEEN YEARS old, Pat Stanton turned up at Easter Road for the first time. He'd been a regular on the terraces, usually without paying. 'To watch Lawrie Reilly I used to sneak over the wall at the Dunbar End.' But this was him walking into the dressing room as a young prospect.

He was awestruck and awkward in a new raincoat bought by his mother. 'Tommy Preston noticed this little boy lost and said: "Son, why don't you take that peg over there?"' Preston did not know this would turn into a permanent arrangement and Stanton had no idea he would become as revered as Reilly.

Well turned out on his first day, immaculate thereafter. He ran like a guardsman might, with impeccable upright bearing. The hair could never be disturbed, not by rain, mud or scoring with crashing headers like the one against Rangers in 1975, as pummelling as any shot.

These were Stanton signatures. There were others like how, in possession, the ball would be intrepidly prodded forward with the outside of the right foot, curled in slightly. Actually, thinking of this, a lot of players probably do the same thing. But how many performed as elegantly, swellegantly as the Hibee godhead? And how many were as handsome? No one said this about him back in the day, and certainly no man for risk of finding themselves in a reprise of a Dick Emery sketch and addressed as 'Ducky' or 'Honky Tonks'. But the world has grown up and Hibs are 150. It can be said now.

Stanton may have diddled the Easter Road turnstiles out of a few pennies but he paid back the club gloriously. In all, 617 games and though I wasn't at every one and am unashamedly biased, I bet he never hid or hurriedly shuffled the ball to some poor sap as if it was a bomb about to blow like in the *Beano*.

To those who knew him well he was 'Niddrie', after his Edinburgh housing scheme which he reckoned never disadvantaged him. As a boy, en route to Portobello's open-air swimming pool with his pals, a handwritten sign in a gift shop window caught his eye. 'It said "Direct from the contitent". So we went inside and asked to see these contitental goods. We may have been Niddrie boys but we could spell right. The shopkeeper chased us right down the street.'

Stanton also captained Scotland. In 1970, despite Hibs winning nothing and Celtic reaching the European Cup final, he was the football scribes' choice for player of the year – one of only two Hibees to win the prize.* Seven years previous to that, he'd scored on his debut as a teenager and seven years after it he was a double-winning Celt. For the Hibees he starred on the contitent 36 times.

The total doesn't include the 1964's conquering of Real Madrid, which was a challenge match, but Stanton still had to mark Ferenc Puskás: 'They were the best team in the world and didn't like to lose, ever, and I'd had Puskás's photo on my bedroom wall. He went over the ball that night and cut my ankle. I didn't want the wound to heal. I wanted to walk up Niddrie Mains Road with it still bleeding through my sock. The wee white scar is there even now.'

Stanton's legend is permanent, too, although, hang on, the cynics who must find slight fault with everything might

* The other winner was Leigh Griffiths in 2013.

mention that regarding leadership he was unshowy. Here's best pal from school Jimmy O'Rourke: 'Folk ask: "What kind of captain was Pat?" I think they expect me to say quiet, which he was, as if that couldn't be inspirational, and he was definitely that. You know there used to be a ground called Broomfield which we nicknamed the Bullring, and it was hellish to have to play Airdrie in November if the wind was howling down the park. But Paddy took games like that by the scruff of the neck. That's what kind of captain he was.'

65

THE WHIMSICAL PHILOSOPHER

DURING SEASON 1962–63 when Hibs were being duffed up home and away by Airdrie, Falkirk and Clyde and in the end very nearly tumbling out of the top flight, there was a moment of black humour when the ball went flying into the crowd, where it was grabbed by a long-suffering supporter and rather than return it to the pitch he marched to the top of the terracing and booted it right out of the stadium.

The reaction of Harry Swan was typical. 'At least the fellow knew what to do with the ball,' he said, 'and could do it.' And the Easter Road supremo made sure Disgruntled of Leith Walk might consider not giving up on the team by presenting him with a complimentary ticket for next time.

Typical because Swan wasn't about to pretend Hibs were something they were not. What they were not, in his opinion, when he joined as a director in 1931 was a serious-minded club. The ball-booter had a point and he reckoned he had a point, promptly resigning over the board's lack of ambition as the club languished in the second tier. But in 1933 he returned – as chairman.

Typical because, formerly a baker in Edinburgh, he must have reckoned he had a feel for customer demand, even if football is somewhere the audience can appear to think having your cake and eating it is possible.

And typical because of the humour in his remark. When Swan died in 1965, *The Scotsman*'s John Rafferty in an obituary mourned the demise of Scottish football's 'whimsical philosopher'.

It was Swan's relentless, visionary drive which dragged the Hibees out of their Depression Era doldrums. 'Give me ten years and I'll make Hibs great' was his famous boast. While completion date was readjusted because of the Second World War, and while Willie McCartney would pass away at Albion Rovers in January 1948, the spellbinding team the manager assembled, including four of the Famous Five, would clinch the title three months later.

When Swan took charge, Easter Road could hold 17,000. At the height of the Five's powers he'd upped capacity to 60,000. Everyone wanted to see Leith's superstars and just about everyone wanted to buy them. In one week the chairman turned down bids totalling £120,000.

Three decades in charge at Hibs, Swan loved a prediction. Even in the dark days he was telling anyone who would listen that sometime soon there would be light – floodlit football. There were almost as many sceptics for that piece of radical thinking as there were for continental competition. Swan prophesied that and passionately advanced the concept. And after the Hibee-backed European Cup started to fly he was able to say: 'It took a couple of years for clubs and their boards to recognise the potential of the competition, but I like to think that at Hibernian we've always been outward-looking.'

At Easter Road they seemed to be playing with a crystal ball. All-seated stadia? Swan didn't stand around waiting for that innovation to emerge from somewhere else. Advertising on strips? Swan was first to put his shirt on that. He was big on smaller leagues, too.

He was dreaming up too many schemes, and fizzing with too many ideas and opinions, for the game's administrators to ignore and in 1954 was elected president of the SFA. In 1962 came what he said would be his final grand plan – for a super league. And, once again seeing into the future, he said that if thwarted 'the alternative is for certain clubs to get together and disrupt the divisions as they stand and start new ones'.

John Rafferty signed off his tribute: 'We will miss, apart from his football wisdom, the straight, manly language he used to shatter the poseurs, the friendly slang and mock insults. For those who like a bit of fun with their sport his death is a shattering loss . . .'

66

SEEING THE LIGHT ABOUT THE EUROPEAN CUP, PART 2

IS THERE a magazine for the floodlighting industry? A for-the-trade quarterly which could figure in the guest publication slot on *Have I Got News For You*? I hope there is, and I think I know who its favourite football team would be.

Whatever the mag might be called, *Floodlighting Today* or perhaps more likely *Floodlighting Tonight*, there could be regular retrospective features on the friendly between the Hibees and an Edinburgh XI at Powderhall, illuminated by 'three Siemens dynamo-electric machines', a first for the capital, way back in 1878.

By 1955 and the first European Cup, the journal might have been amused by the sheer number of times the lights are mentioned in the reports of Hibs' ties. There's the novelty of them, same with the idea of continental competition. There's intrigue, and wonder, but also apprehension and maybe some fear. Lights, Euro, lights, Euro. The world was changing, too fast for some.

For instance, Celtic. As Hibs were taking on Djurgårdens of Sweden, the Parkhead programme notes read: 'Already interest in these floodlit evening games is on the wane.' Typical Celts, late to the party. They'd come round eventually.

The crowd for the second round, first leg tie was a not-very-waney 21,962. Remarkable considering it was played at Partick Thistle's Firhill, Djurgårdens' choice as the homeland was in the midst of a winter shutdown.

The Hibees' great Euro expedition has its sneerers and scoffers. Jambos, mostly, who point to the seemingly less-than-stellar opposition. Rot-Weiss Essen? They're hardly Bayern Munich. What, you mean the Bayern Hibs thrashed 6–1 in 1950, the first of five wins in a row against the team who would go on to anoint themselves FC Hollywood?

Djurgårdens prompt a similarly underwhelming response, but they boasted six internationalists with Sweden having beaten Scotland two years before. 'They're a well-built, artistic lot who're likely to make Hibs go all out,' warned manager Hugh Shaw. Djurgårdens trained for the match on ice – many were skilled at ice hockey – but Hibs won 3–1 in the west end of Glasgow and 1–0 at Easter Road in front of 31,346, just short of their floodlit record. Clearly the good folk of Leith did not mistake the glowing towers in each corner of the stadium for four giant wicker men, aflame with human and goat sacrifice.

Among football Europhiles there was excited chatter about a dream final of Hibs vs Real Madrid but for that to happen the Scots would have to get past Reims, their dazzling winger Michel Hidalgo and imperious playmaker Raymond Kopa. At the Parc des Princes, *The Scotsman* reported that Gordon Smith 'delighted the crowd with some dazzling efforts', but a last-minute goal doubled the French champions' advantage for the second leg.

This would be a stirring European night, establishing a long Leith tradition of them, but despite a 'gallant effort' (*Daily Record*) it would end in 'glorious failure' (*The Scotsman*). Predictably Kopa was the difference, setting up the only score, although according to Edinburgh's *Evening News*, how the Reims goal survived the evening was 'one of the great mysteries'.

That paper went on to praise the home fans among the 44,941 – the new record – for their warm appreciation of Kopa, the 'Little General' . . . 'a brilliant ball player' . . . everything revolving around him in his 'Pooh-Bah role'. Lawrie Reilly hailed him as 'the best I ever faced' and Smith lamented the European Cup coming a couple of years too late for Hibs who, back at the start of the decade, 'could have beaten anyone'. Nevertheless, this was a giant leap for footballkind.

67

WAS THE FUTURE KING'S KINK (ALLEGED) INSPIRED BY TURNBULL'S TORNADOES?

IN A word association game, what might 'peg' produce? Maybe you're among the curious and the salacious who hit Google hard in 2022 in response to the wild rumour about Prince William's sexual kink. As a result, searches for 'pegging' shot up by 400 per cent.

Me, I must have led a far more sheltered life, because in the game I'm sure I would think first of 'Peg', the Steely Dan song, and second, De La Soul's 'Eye Know', which sampled 'Peg'.

If true, how did Wills develop his dildo fetish? Yes, it could have come from Eton, or maybe he happened to be watching TV in 1997 when Channel 4 screened *The Granton Star Cause*, a clarty little Irvine Welsh yarn featuring a blasphemous, bevvy-merchant God, a Kafkaesque transmutation from human to fly . . . and pegging.

Everyone who saw the black comedy remembers the scene by the fireplace: stone surround, brass canopy, pretendy glowing coals in the hearth, demure figurines up top – and the very undemure Doreen Coyle banging her husband Boaby with a strap-on.

It's hilarious to think that the King's son and heir might have been among the audience, for this is what Boaby said between grunts as he gripped the mantelpiece: 'Herriot, Brownlie, Schaedler, *mmmph*, Stanton, Black, *nnnnggg*, Blackley . . .'

Presumably for Boaby, reciting the Turnbull's Tornadoes team softened the pain and enhanced the pleasure. Or maybe it ramped up the pain because by 1997 the Tornadoes had long blown themselves out and the Hibees were clattering towards relegation. Or maybe the moment was all pleasure because the middle-aged couple, their loafing son finally off their hands, were able to rekindle their passion with help from a marital aid (possible nicknames for it: Wullie, Nebuchadnezzar II and of course William Burroughs' appellation for his steam-driven version, Steely Dan). Or maybe it was all pain – 'Keep pushin', hen, ah need mair . . .' – because that is the essence of Hibbydom (controversial, I know, but see ch. 74).

The Granton Star Cause was written by a Hibs fan and the actor who played Boaby would have been thrilled to flaunt his fat, pimply arse on film if it meant he could namecheck players he adored. Alex 'Happy' Howden had been a miner, a whaler, a scaffolder, a boxer and a bus driver before turning to stand-up comedy. He was still driving buses while finessing his routine, sometimes telling his passengers he was stopping for a toilet break only to nip into Newhaven's Peacock Inn to crack a few funnies. And, having made the break from his old life, he would tell audiences: 'I quit the buses because everyone was talking behind my back.' (Geddit?)

After Boaby, Howden was able to squeeze out a few more acting roles including, phantasmagorically, Martin Scorsese's *Gangs of New York* in which he played the hangman. It is just too tempting, too delicious, to imagine downtime on that epic when he might have been invited into Daniel Day-Lewis's trailer to recount how a quip from the latter's Bill the Butcher – 'What will it be, then, rib or chop, loin or shank?' – could have been Erich Schaedler's battle cry seconds before thundering into a tackle. And then maybe it would be Leonardo DiCaprio's turn for a request: 'Go on, Happy, tell us the story of the seven-nil game – we love that one.'

When Howden died in 2015, a newspaper described the activity round the fireplace as 'a memorable scene'. Never has an obituary been more mimsyish, more euphemistic.

68

FINED FOR BUNKING OFF FROM AYR UTD TO WATCH HIBS

JINKY. THE Girvan Lighthouse. Elvis. Champagne Charlie. Shirley. Big Sadie. The Tinman. Choccy. The Chocolate Soldier. Jukebox. Jaws. Just some of the nicknames for Scotland's footballers that we know and love.

Were most if not all of these coined by team-mates? And do the less familiar, limited circulation but clever, funny and cute ones come from the fans? Ian Redford, a son of the soil, was 'Fermer'. Let's hear it for 'Greenock' Morten Wieghorst. Rudi 'Holy' Vata. And – love this – Marcus 'Blawna' Gayle. Motherwell's Abel Thermeus answered to 'The Flask'. Of course he did. Meanwhile Graham Fyfe was 'Johan' only for his brief stint as a Hibee to end in 1977 after zero evidence of total fitba, 180 degree switchbacks and just the one goal.

But who had the coolest nickname? Maybe Eric Stevenson. Easter Road's left-wing dribble fiend right through the 1960s who started off as a Hearts prodigy, signed for them unwittingly and illegally, then found himself cast as 'The Rebel'.

To quote the Marlon Brando film *The Wild Ones*, what was he rebelling against? It's a murky tale involving the player, then 16, putting his name to a form which was then stashed in an imitation teak Tynecastle drawer. Stevenson thought he was simply acknowledging a weekly £3 payment. Hearts actually had him on full pro terms but had to keep this a secret until his next birthday.

The ruse was rumbled by the SFA and club and manager, Tommy Walker, were heavily fined. There was a lengthy spell when Stevenson wasn't allowed to kick a ball. Not for Manchester United or English champs Wolves or Rangers or any of the other clubs keen on his intricate skills. But the fact he ultimately spurned Hearts for his boyhood faves who repaid his retainer in full seriously narked the Gorgie faithful. It gave them reason to boo him every time he came back for a derby and it gave the player the kudos of Brando or James Dean. The nickname was conferred on him by the *Scottish Daily Express*; Hearts might have preferred something stronger. Reject the establishment club? How dare he!

Unfortunately Stevenson, while much loved by Hibbies, also rebelled against sound professional habits. He hated training and loved Bacardi and discotheques. This devil-may-care attitude made for excitement may have bled into his game but was ultimately limiting. There was good advice around, he told me, if only he'd listened. 'Neily Martin got picked for Scotland's [1965] World Cup qualifier against Italy so me and Willie Wilson went through to Hampden to cheer him on. We gave a lift to Jock Wallace, then manager of Berwick Rangers, who said to me: "Stevie, you need a kick up the fuckin' arse. You could be playing in this game tonight – the potential you have is incredible. But you've too much nonsense in your head and you're aye out socialising." I said: "I know, Jock, I'll have to get a grip of myself." But a minute later I was asking: "Shall we stop at Whitburn for a couple of pints?"'

Regarded as one of Scotland's finest uncapped players, he could have been a Tornado but an exasperated Eddie Turnbull moved him on to Ayr United where he continued to rebel, albeit in a sweet, endearing manner, absconding from his new club to be at the 1972 League Cup final. 'Although I wasn't going to be playing for Ayr that day [manager] Ally MacLeod would have wanted me there but I was desperate to see Hibs win something. I was fined two weeks' wages and it was totally worth it.'

Stevenson died in 2017. The previous year, stricken with cancer with a tumour requiring the removal of his stomach, he was too weak to be back at Hampden. He said: 'I was born a Hibby and will be one to my dying day. I'm just glad I lived long enough to see them lift the Scottish Cup, too. At the final whistle, me and the wife danced round the living room in floods of tears.'

69

HIBS AS ART, BY MURIEL SPARK'S PORTRAIT PAINTER

THE SAFARI suit, once worn by gentlemen in urban scenarios who were unlikely to ever encounter *Daktari*'s Clarence the Cross-Eyed Lion, far less the non-cuddly variety, has fallen out of fashion. So too football's match programme.

What an odd pairing, you say. Well, not in my house. In the living room they're happily entwined in a portrait of my father. So every day I can see the programme, Hibs obviously, popping out of a pocket, with the way it's folded revealing the code on the back for the half-time scoreboard. This is more than I'm able to do at Easter Road for publication ceased in 2019. What a shame.

The painting, by Sandy Moffat, used to hang in the Scottish National Portrait Gallery in Edinburgh and after Dad died it passed to me. Yet again, surely, the Hibees can claim a first: the programme as art. Exhibited in a gallery. Viewed by the *culturati* (squinted at, puzzled over). The equivalent, on other walls, of some portly nobleman's faithful hound or Mary Queen of Scots' crucifix.

Moffat is the 82-year-old former 1960s radical and art 'suffragent' who, together with fellow student John Bellany, chained his studies of Scotland's working class to railings outside the posh, pillared buildings housing establishment culture.

They were rebels with paintbrushes, punk rockers in smocks, who demanded exposure for their subjects – captured in factories, pubs and bingo halls – and also for themselves. Moffat took the work seriously, became 'snobbish' about it, to the exclusion of all that had gone before for him, including football and a revelatory trip as a boy with his father to see Hibs thrash East Fife, the Famous Five in excelsis.

But football drew him back. Is there art in it? Of course. Gordon Smith's wing play had been balletic. 'When he was taking a corner kick, the crowd would surge and sway, all these folk trying to touch him.' Moffat had always loved the Hibs green ('The colour of nature') and the view from the top of the old main terracing ('Arthur's Seat, Salisbury Crags – that incredible landscape'). And thanks to Turnbull's Tornadoes the Hibees were exciting again.

Around this time my father, surveying the arts scene for BBC Scotland, put Moffat's work on TV. They bonded over Hibs and from their friendship came the portrait.

'I wanted to make it special because of all your father had done for me. The suit he was wearing was purple, which Hibs had just introduced to Scottish football as their second strip. But it's a helluva colour to paint. It's like orange: just one dab and it can entirely take over. Nevertheless, the painting was finished quickly in one morning, my most colourful up until that moment.'

Moffat has chronicled Scottish culture through his portraiture, most famously cramming seven great wordsmiths into 'Poets' Pub'. He was Head of Painting at Glasgow School of Art, bringing on the students who became the New Glasgow Boys, and when he retired, the school's janitors gifted him a Hibs shirt with his name on the back.

'I never want my sitters to be silent,' he explained. 'The aim is not to capture a waxwork dummy. What did your father and I talk about? Oh, Eddie Turnbull, Pat Stanton, how Alex Edwards never failed to find Arthur Duncan, one flank right across to the other. There was just one thing: the great swathe of purple needed to be broken up.'

Moffat can't remember how the genius idea of the programme came about; perhaps the most recent instalment had been lying around his studio. A 'wee aside' and he's used similar ones often. 'They shouldn't be rogue elements but things important to the sitters. For Sorley MacLean it was his 1930s beret. Not on his head – too obvious – just by his chair. For Hugh MacDiarmid it was a whisky glass. He was really quite ill with cancer and whisky was his most effective painkiller. But when I asked Muriel Spark if she wanted anything else in her painting she said: 'No, no, no. I only want *me*!'

This news just in: Dad's empurpled garb used to embarrass the teenage me, but the safari suit, or at least the jacket, is making a comeback as a 'shacket'. Hibs, it's time to revive the programme.

70

THERE WAS US LOT AND THEN THIS OTHER GUY, A GOD

IN THE Edinburgh of the immediate post-war years and for much of the 1950s, when there was rationing and national service, when TV was still in its infancy, rock 'n' roll hadn't been invented and movies were packed with unrelatable, unattainable glamour, and when the nickname Auld Reekie existed for a reason and large numbers of the populace perched on outside loos and all they could see was grey, it was understandable that the capital might want to big up its footballers.

Understandable and fairly straightforward. The city has never had it so good, either before or since. Hibs and Hearts have never been so winningly exciting. Though as Gordon Marshall, a goalkeeper for both clubs, told me: 'There was us lot and then this other guy. A god, really.'

Marshall went from Tynecastle to Easter Road with no fuss. The supreme being travelling in the opposite direction must have seemed like a miracle, truly divine intervention. 'I don't know how the hell it happened but suddenly the great Gordon Smith, Prince of Wingers, was a Hearts player,' said Marshall. 'He made his debut in a reserve game and 10,000 needed to see it. After training we were always given juice. I remember Gordon looking at it in mild disgust: 'But this is fizzy.' He didn't touch alcohol either. His body was a temple. He just wasn't like us ordinary footballers.

'Gordon had his roadhouse, his cottage in North Berwick,

his holidays on the French Riviera and his Porsche. I went everywhere by tram, the No. 27 for Tynecastle. And he mixed with Alfredo Di Stéfano, was good friends with the champion golfer Bobby Locke and famous jazzmen and for goodness sakes dined with Brigitte Bardot.'

If you know nothing about Smith, if you're naturally sceptical/cynical in the modern tradition, you might think he sounds a bit flash, a bit like fellow No. 7 Cristiano Ronaldo, albeit that the latter's only friend seems to be Piers Morgan. And you might wonder: 'Was he really that good?'

He was. These were extraordinary superstar trappings for a footballer of the era, for one from little old Edinburgh, so he could not have come by them if he hadn't played like a dream, firstly and majorly for Hibs. And the fact he was a handsome devil can't have been a hindrance.

Inspiring communal singing of 'A Gordon fir me', his magical skills were first noticed in Montrose. He was 16 when he made his Hibees debut against Hearts, scoring the first of 17 hat-tricks, and the final haul for the club would be 364 goals in 700 games. With the rest of the Famous Five he won three league titles. He led Hibs as they trailblazed into Europe and captained his country. Then, when Easter Road thought he was finished, that clumpy boot lunges by despairing full-backs had taken too much of a toll, he joined Hearts and claimed another title, and when they reckoned he was done, he moved again to inspire Dundee to the flag at the age of 38.

Was he superhuman? In 1950 he gave a pretty good impression of being Superman – at that moment 12 years into comic form – by bursting into the dressing room and throwing open his overcoat to reveal his green and white shirt when all had seemed lost.

Injury had sidelined him for the first leg of the League Cup quarter-final against Aberdeen, and 4–1 down with his shoulder still hurting, Hibs were surely done for. But with no time to lose on the afternoon of the rematch, he raced first to a hospital and then the scene of a road accident to track down the club's doctor who finally relented and allowed him to play. There was wild cheering from his team-mates when he reached the ground, and mild hysteria among his worshippers when the Easter Road announcer declared: 'Gordon Smith is back!' Hibs matched the Dons' score in the first game and after two Ibrox replays won the tie.

A god, really.

71

RAMPING UP THE BRIDGE OF DOOM'S MYTHOLOGY

THERE'S A fair bit of mythology surrounding bridges. One in Persian legend, supplying access to Heaven, is guarded by four-eyed dogs. Another had been built underwater to rescue a Hindu deity's wife. The construction crew? A bunch of monkeys, apparently. Yet another bridge pointing to the Promised Land, post-potted heidness in the afterlife, is as 'thin as a hair', according to Islam. So you're bound to tumble into the hellfires if you've been a sinner. Then there's the one in Prague, solid stone and real, commemorating the priest who died when he wouldn't reveal the – probably adulterous – confessions of the king's wife and was summarily thrown off it.

So what about the so-called Bridge of Doom? This is the little overpass linking Bothwell Street with Albion Terrace and a shortcut to and from the stadium. My abiding memory of it is being caught in a crush after the Inter-Cities Fairs Cup tie with Leeds United in 1968. Fans were squashed so tight they'd come to a complete standstill. It was a moment for a small boy to panic and contemplate prayers but I was with my father who was quick to act, clearing enough space to ring me with his arms and, clasping his hands out front, to push on through like a human snow plough or the Hulk.

What, you think I'm mythologising that moment? I'm not the one calling the structure the Bridge of Doom. The first time I heard the nickname was on TV. Danny Dyer was still unaware he was related to William the Conqueror and that this discovery would mean he could stop being a hooligan groupie and hang out with Harold Pinter. He was filming an edition of *The Real Football Factories* in Edinburgh when a reformed Hibs casual bragged about how rival fans never successfully made it across the bridge.

I didn't really understand the casuals cult. Why would you spend a small fortune on Italian designer leisurewear only to go fighting in it? When I dressed up as a boot boy in the 1970s to pretend being droog-hard and suedehead-tough, there was no way I was going to risk my Doc Martens losing their Cherry Red sheen or the collar buttons of my Ben Sherman shirt being torn off in some random terracing divergence of opinion. Of course there was no way I was ever going to find myself within a hundred miles of such a knicker-wetting situation.

So whenever I hear the bridge being discussed in hushed tones, being glorified, I think of Monty Python. For Bridge of Doom read Bridge of Death and the scene in the *Holy Grail* movie where John Cleese successfully answers three simple questions to be permitted to traverse a forbidding gorge but Graham Chapman gets: 'What is the airspeed velocity of an unladen swallow?' Stumped, he's fired into the air before plummeting down the abyss.

Unsurprisingly, those rival supporters continue to rubbish the Bridge of Doom's mythology. 'Never any trouble all the times I crossed it,' remarks a Jambo on social media, while another adds: 'I was always able to sit down with a meal deal and enjoy the ambience.' (Jambos and ambience together? Jambience?)

But Radio Scotland's Tam Cowan, *Off the Ball* presenter and Motherwell fan, insists that desperate cunning was required to defuse the peril of the bridge, which was real enough: 'We were absolutely convinced a doin' was coming our way. But there was an old boy alongside me so I grabbed his arm to make it look like I was his carer. He was mildly outraged at being dragged across the Bridge of Doom but thankfully the scam worked.'

72

'HE BESTRODE HAMPDEN AS HEROICALLY AS ANY MAN'

ON THE morning of 9 December 1972, the Hibs team bus trundled away from Easter Road to begin the journey to Hampden. It was early and the players weren't anticipating well-wishers on street corners and at first-floor windows, old-timers with gummy grins and babes being held up to the charabanc as if to be blessed. But nor were they expecting a flying half-brick.

A Jambo? 'Or maybe a disgruntled Hibs fan, fed up of us always losing through there,' laughed Pat Stanton. 'It was a freezing cold day. A draught blew through the great bloody hole in the window. But, you know, we arrived nice and awake and ready.'

The League Cup final was the seventh visit to the national stadium that year, including an early-round game against Queen's Park, generous hosts who enthused in the match programme of the Hibees' 'beautifully polished' football. Neutrals countrywide seemed to be urging the team to go out and win the thing for the general good. Stanton was desperate to atone for the heavy defeat by Celtic in the final of the Scottish Cup, the worst day of his career up to that point, although all the dashed hopes going back further than his era had got too much for his father.

'Dad was at every one of my games but decided to stay home that day after so many disappointments, thinking he was a jinx, so my mum wasn't there either. It was special when she came to see me play, although there was a match against Hearts where afterwards she asked: "Son, how's the lad who got hit with the ball?" This had been me, full on the face, knocked out, carted off. And I'm pretty sure I had the indentations "Hand-stitched in Pakistan" back to front down one cheek!'

Stanton would leave an indelible mark on a classic final, played at 100 miles an hour in lashing rain, two sides committed to cavalier attack, and this time Hibs staying with Celtic. It was 0–0 at the interval which seemed like a breakthrough, and the fans cheered them off.

At home games all season when the team were shooting down the slope in the second half, the old North Stand would sniff possibility through the pipe smoke and start a chant of 'Hibees, Hibees', usually bang on the hour mark. These were the implorings of grown men, not squeaky teenage boys, and the voices were stentorian, suggestive of professional lives, perhaps law and academia. The boys always joined in the chanting and invariably the team would ramp up the flair.

At Hampden, at the appointed hour, the chants came and Hibs wrested control of the final, skipper Stanton showing the way. From minute 60 for the next 20, Celtic couldn't live with their opponents, words rarely said about a Jock Stein side.

Stanton scored a stunning first, created a brilliant second and before, after and in between surged often and thrillingly. Ian Archer in the *Glasgow Herald* wrote that he 'bestrode the pitch as heroically and as imaginatively as any man who has ever played on this great stage before him'.

Two images from Hampden won't ever fade: the sheer blackness of the Centre Stand, as if Stanton for the cup presentation was venturing into a gloomy, dank cave to locate the trophy, and the players celebrating in the communal bath, the most unabashed display of male semi-nudity that I'd witnessed since finding a copy of *Health & Efficiency* naturist magazine stuffed in graveyard shrubbery.

Back in the capital that night the winter winds were again blowing through Hibs' mode of transport, though this time it was an open-top bus as the trophy was paraded joyfully along Princes Street.

Archer's report continued: 'The whole balance of power inside the Scottish game may just possibly be swinging across country from the coarse face of Glasgow to the finer aspect of Edinburgh.'

Time would tell. Meanwhile the commercial department, such as it existed in 1972, attempted to exploit the triumph with 'Pat Stanton busts – 50p'. Comb cases cost 10p and wallet covers just 5p so there would be change from a pound for a bag of chips, with brown sauce as one of those finer aspects, the capital's sophisticated preference. Oh happy Hibby days.

73

REVEALED: THE GREATEST-EVER HIBS HAIRCUT

MORE THAN just Haircut 100, what's the best Hibee barnet there's ever been? Borrowing the name of a long-established Leith Walk salon, who deserves the title of Tip-Top Tresses 150?

Possibly not Archie Gray, redoubtable right-back in the Scottish Cup-winning side of 1902, capped for Scotland, went on to play for Arsenal – he rejoiced in the nickname 'Baldy'. And not Joe Murphy either. For turning out in a wig in the 1890s he was dubbed 'The Judge'.

Gordon Smith sported a lustrous brushed-back, raven black mane, ideal for the movie star company he kept. Peter Marinello sported bangs which bounced when he ran, ideal for the pop star company he would keep when he moved to London, Swingin' Sixties epicentre. This was pretty much the same hair-style as Alex Cropley who followed Marinello there, douce little Edinburgh eventually proving too small for the Easter Road pin-ups.

Pat Stanton is a contender. His cut wasn't flash, far from it, but serene and immovable, just like him as a Hibee, the sort you'd see on the handsome male models on the front of knitting patterns, pointing keenly over yonder hill, or in Pat's case, down yonder slope.

Stanton, incidentally, told me a funny story about hair or rather lack of it from 1968, the Inter-Cities Fairs Cup and the away leg against SV Hamburg which ended in narrow defeat.

On the flight home the team were puzzled not to have been forewarned about the Germans' left-winger who'd shone in the match in keeping with his glisteningly bald pate. Pat said: 'We had a dossier on Hamburg, of course, but in his photo this fellow sported a full head of hair. No one knew he wore a wig which he took off to play.' This was almost certainly Gert 'Charly' Dörfel who after hanging up his boots joined a circus. It is not known if his trick was sticking his chromedome in a lion's mouth. Later, slaphead was a fad. Mixu Paatelainen had one, also Mathias Jack, and their Hibs ran out to "Song 2" by Blur ("Woo-hoo, got my head checked, by a jumbo jet").

Erich Schaedler's hair was Stantonesque but then he succumbed to the dreaded late 1970s fad for bubble perms. Bobby Smith was assumed to have artificial curls but his were natural. Willie Irvine possessed the straightest hair, worn in a daft mullet, which seemed certain to stay plumb-line true until he went kinky too. And we'll never know how fast Willie Murray, the wee stick insect on the right flank, could have run if he hadn't been weighed down by that heavy thatch resembling a snugly hibernating – Hibernianating? – woodland creature.

The natty dreads of Jimmy Boco merit mention before assessment of the claims of the young Leith team of Tony Mowbray when Easter Road was transformed into an aviary featuring the sulphur-crested cockatoo, the Eurasian hoopoe, the Victoria crowned pigeon and other exotic plumages.

'Fridays were Toni&Guy day,' confirmed Garry O'Connor. Every eve of a match, the players would gather at the uptown capital crimpers. 'I'd be sat next to Deek [Derek Riordan] and Scotty [Scott Brown] might pop in later with Thommo [Kevin Thomson] and Deano [Dean Shiels].' Imagine them in their capes, perched in a row under the big space-helmet dryers and drinking tea, flicking through *Woman's Own*, gossiping and bemoaning 'the change' (Mowbray's latest tactical tinkering). 'All of us went there. We had to look our best, our maddest.'

Ian Murray was part of that gallus team. He was the player with the sensible haircut until one day, one special anniversary at Tynecastle, he wandered over to the touchline for the first throw-in of the derby when the numbers cut into his hair at the back of his head and coloured green caused the home support to explode. Commemorating the events of three decades before, Murray could have displayed the scoreline but – subtler, classier – went for the year and so wins the coiffure crown.

Maybe a junior Jambo would have asked: 'Dad, what was so special about 1973?' And through severely gritted teeth the answer coming back: 'Well, son, Britain joined the EEC and VAT was introduced. Picasso died and Nixon, a big perspirer, was starting to sweat over Watergate. The Stock Exchange began admitting women, Princess Anne got married, *The Godfather* won the Oscar for Best Picture and that was also the year of the first-ever call on a cellular, cordless phone.

'Was that all, Dad – nothing else?'

'No, now watch the game . . .'

74

IS IT A HIBS THING TO SOMETIMES WANT YOUR TEAM TO LOSE?

THIS IS controversial. Some will think it insane. A few will insist: 'Attention seeker!' And others will conclude that it must be a Hibs thing. But is it? Is it really just us who every now and again want our team to lose? I'd be surprised if it was, though am happy to claim it as yet another USP. Further proof that supporting Hibs marks you out as a special case, and yes, I know that can be interpreted in different ways.

I will accept it's an age thing. Though we think of teenagers as being dramatic, overly so, I don't remember having these masochistic feelings, willing the team to muck up, when I was 14 or 15. But admittedly when I was 14 and 15, and 16 and 17 and a bit beyond, Hibs were great.

It didn't take long to appreciate that they weren't always great. I mean, that's Scottish football for most teams, right? Not always great. Most fans accept this as their lot; the crossbar they have to bear. For Hibbies, though, the Venn diagram of expectation and fulfilment rarely merges. The winger effortlessly escapes his marker.

Sometimes this gets too much. The long-running – 114 years! – Scottish Cup soap opera was like that. Actually, it wasn't a story at all until 2001 and the 99th attempt, Hibs actually reaching the final that year only to be casually undone by Celtic's Henrik Larsson.

After that, as a second century of failure began, it was *the* story. Every year, more questions (whenohwhenohwhen?), more pressure. Every year 129 teams don't win the cup but only Hibs were cast in the role of the soap's dependable, eternally unlucky in love, the tragic heroine, who has a plane fall on her as she's leaving the hospital where a terminal condition has just been diagnosed, thus denying her the chance to collect her lottery millions and meet the sister she never knew she had.

And this for the faithful, rather than intolerable, became strangely addictive. A support mocked in the wake of *Trainspotting* for injecting half-time pies with heroin had found a new drug. They couldn't fight the annual disappointment so they embraced it. And started to revel in it.

How many of the other flops were getting this kind of attention? The saga brought Hibs worldwide recognition. That they hadn't won the Scottish Cup for so long marked them as sad oddballs, 11 cat ladies. So every time they were bundled out of the competition, immediate disappointment was quickly followed by the consolation of the soap's narrative becoming ever funnier and even more sorrowful.

So what happened after 2016? Where did these perverse feelings go? Well, the Hibees finally winning the cup did not hasten a golden era and from the start of the 2020s the club began to beat itself up. From soap as a vehicle Hibs switched to those terrific old ultra-violent cartoons where the chump pursuer of the nifty hero – Wile E. Coyote, Officer Dibble, the cats Tom and Sylvester, take your pick – is reduced to self-harm: mallet in one hand and a large frying pan in the other while back-heeling themselves up the arse. Every blow represented a managerial sacking, a PR howler or a humiliating defeat – sometimes all of them combined in one utterly gruesome moment. And the fans, or some of them at least, wallowed in the misery, craving even more of it.

75

LAWRIE REILLY: 'I WAS BORN IN A GREEN JERSEY'

I'VE NEVER needed much excuse to wangle an invite to the trim sitting room of one of our former-and-forever association football greats, but when I met Lawrie Reilly it was virtually for therapy.

This was a couple of years before he passed away and the papers were full of hooker-addicted footballers, £200,000-a-week footballers, international-coinciding-with-groin strain footballers – and when Scotland's best hope of a goal against the unmighty Liechtenstein had been dubbed 'fat, lazy and selfish'. I wanted the Famous Five's centre-forward to whoosh me right back to, as the excitable journals have it, happier times.

'Player power?' Reilly said, settling into his favourite armchair and rubbing his bothersome right knee. 'Ach, we didn't really have that in our day. In 1949 I went with Scotland to New York for a friendly against the USA. We sailed on the *Queen Mary*, the journey took a week and there were three classes: first, for the SFA, cabin and tourist which was us.

'I'm an old man now, son, so you'll have to help me here. How come it's the players who decide if and when they'll turn up for their country? In our day it was the thing you dreamed about most as a wee laddie. And when you got to pull on that dark blue shirt for the first time? Boy oh boy . . .' His pale blue eyes sparkled at the memory. 'That lion on your breast was the greatest feeling.'

Reilly scored 22 goals in 38 appearances for Scotland and no one shook Wembley's Twin Towers quite like him. There were five goals in five games on England's cabbage patch, most memorably as 'Last-minute Reilly' in 1953 with an at-the-death equaliser for the ten-man Scots. Back at Wembley in '57, pre-kick-off, the Tommys Younger and Docherty were larking about and in the water fight Reilly trod on glass and sliced open his foot. 'The Partick Thistle doctor just stitched me up and a few hours later I was on the park.'

He returned to '53: 'After that one we got taxis to a restaurant and when I opened the cab door it blocked the way for some Scottish supporters so they banged it shut again. The funny thing was, without knowing they'd just passed me, they then started singing my name.'

Reilly told a few stories like this, seeking out the ordinary in the extraordinary. It was the era when a man at a bus stop could relay the news you'd been picked for your international debut. This happened to him and of course omnibus was Reilly's mode of transport, boots in hand. It was when, even though Wembley was jam-packed, he could hear 'the family whistle', look up and spot his dad waving in the crowd.

So go on then Lawrie, I said, try and illustrate the mundane in the Famous Five. 'Before games at Easter Road we played shuttlecocks.' With your feet, yes? 'No, table tennis bats. We'd rush down to the ground early to see each other. We couldn't wait. It was a great camaraderie.

'I was born in a green jersey. Hibs were the only club I ever wanted to play for. Mind you, I was brought into the world by a doctor called Fraser Lee who later became the Hearts medic. After a win at Tynecastle – I think I got a hat-trick – he told me: "I threw away the wrong part when you came out of the womb!"' I confirmed that, all told, he bagged 18 Hibee hat-tricks. 'Did I really, son?'

His fan credentials were just as impressive. By the age of

ten he'd seen Hibs play at every First Division ground, courtesy of free train travel. 'My dad was a guard so I went in his van although the real thrill was to go up front with the driver and the fireman – what a heat.' Wartime restrictions brought about the Southern League Cup and in 1944 Reilly saw his favourites win it against Rangers, 6–5 on corners. 'I remember our outside-left Johnny Aitkenhead being jockeyed at the byline, then playing the ball against a Rangers fellow for the winner. The rest of the team ran to shake his hand as if he'd scored with a fantastic shot.'

With his signing-on fee, Reilly decided to treat his mum. 'Electric carpet cleaners were all the rage so I got her one.' Reilly entertained the working man after himself completing a Saturday morning shift as a painter. Gordon Smith came straight from his shipyard, £12-a-week immortals one and all.

Out of respect, and fear, the Five's opponents would soak the ball. 'One time I headed the big mealie puddin' and could remember nothing else about the game.' He was proud of their achievements, but in his own modest way. When I pressed him for their magic formula it was several seconds before he answered, and then only to say: 'We were all different, that was the thing.' And don't forget the defence, he stressed. Only with that solid platform could they have performed.

Manchester United were great admirers of the Five, regularly having them down for friendlies. 'One time we beat them 7–3 in front of 70,000. Matt Busby – who'd guested with Hibs during the war – used to put an arm around me and say: "Would you like to play for Man United, son?" I was flattered, and I suppose I could have earned more there, but money didn't come into it. I was a Hibs man. Always will be.'

76

'WITHOUT TOM HART, HIBS WOULD HAVE BEEN INCONSEQUENTIAL'

THE QUOTE which is generally regarded as best identifying high-end watercraft as the ultimate statement of glamour and success comes from Carly Simon: 'You walked into the party like you were walking on to a yacht.' It's good but I think I prefer this from a visionary football chairman of the 1970s: 'I don't own a racehorse, I don't gamble and I've never bought a yacht. Hibs are my only concern.'

Tom Hart was a provocative and dynamic club supremo at a time when owners were neither seen nor heard. Nowadays these big boss guys are always being picked out by the TV cameras, best cushioned seats in the house, but it wasn't like that in Hart's era. Keepy-uppy on the pitch, landing helicopters on it, plotting to liquidate rivals – these flash moves came from others later (although our man did magic George Best out of a hat).

'Hart takes over Hibs' was the *Evening News* headline in September 1970, back when nobody had heard of Wallace Mercer either. Over the next 12 years until his death before a game at Pittodrie he was what *The Scotsman*'s Mike Aitken called 'the most colourful legislator in post-war Scottish football'.

Among his immediate contemporaries there was Celtic's Desmond White who was prominent because of the status of his club and the same for Willie Waddell at Rangers who'd also been a player and manager. But Hart was the miner's son from Tranent with boyhood dreams of playing for Hibs who became a self-made millionaire through the building firm bearing his name and then in the words of shaver king Victor Kiam when the opportunity arose at his Saturday afternoon favourites: 'I liked them so much I bought the company.'

His son Alan took up the story: 'I remember Dad coming home to Ravelston Dykes and telling me. "But you can't just *buy* Hibs," I said, as sure of myself as teenagers are. "Aren't there members who decide what happens to the club?"

'Dad had been a corporal in the Royal Scots, in charge of a Bren gun unit running alongside tanks on the France–Belgium border, when he was hit on the leg with a dumdum. That was the end of the dream, so he set up in business with his £100 war gratuity. He was a season ticket holder in the old North Stand when the Famous Five won their three titles. As a small boy I'd listen to him argue with his pals over who was the best. When he took over there was only one man he wanted as manager – Eddie Turnbull.'

Bobby Kinloch, the Barcelona vanquisher, reckoned that without Hart, Hibs in the 1970s would have been inconsequential. Certainly, as Turnbull fashioned them into a force on the pitch, he was a force in the boardrooms and the SFA's corridors of power, refusing to defer to the Old Firm and the old ways of doing things.

He once dubbed Celtic and Rangers 'cowards', later apologising. He said what most fans of other clubs thought, that Ibrox striker John MacDonald had an irritating habit of going down like he'd been shot, and was fined £500. But with his charisma and bold ideas he could carry his fiercest rivals with him, Waddell joining his campaign for structural revolution and the ten-team top flight which came into being in 1975.

He took on TV, blacking out coverage of the 1977 game which would win Celtic the title. Said Alan: 'His view was the cameras hadn't been at Easter Road all season. Also that TV paid peanuts. Celtic Films rocked up to finish their documentary and he banned them, too.' He took on the Department of Employment over their refusal to grant work permits to Hibs' Icelandic double act Svein Mathisen and Isak 'Vic the Viking' Refvik, forcing a rule change. He took on England's FA over their Wembley blockade of the Tartan Army. And he even took on Hibs fans after just 12,510 watched a week after the 1972 League Cup triumph, calling the turnout a 'disgrace' and questioning whether they truly wanted a top team.

Hibs, as he stated, were his only concern. If he got wind of the bonus offered to Hearts players to win the derby he'd double it. His wife Sheila's concern had been music. The lead violinist with Edinburgh Reel and Strathspey Society, she would duet with Yehudi Menuhin at the opening of the 1986 Commonwealth Games in the capital. But Hibs in the 1970s enraptured her, too, and she penned the Turnbull's Tornadoes song 'Hibernian (Give Us a Goal)'.

77

A WHIFF OF GORGEOUS GEORGE'S GENIUS

IT'S NOT difficult to choose the highlight of my early years in journalism. Cub reporters on weekly newspapers in my day were ambulance chasers and hopefully still are. They cribbed, from village noticeboards, breathless intimations of bring-and-buy sales and the names of the soon-to-be-wed. If your shorthand was up to it you might be trusted with the district court's litany of scuffles and kerfuffles which had 'disturbed the lieges'. So, yes: most memorable day? The opening of that tyre and exhaust depot in Restalrig, Edinburgh – no question.

Why? Because George Best was doing the honours. The fifth-placed player in FIFA's spectacular poll of the all-time diamond star halo world's toppermost. 'Georgie, Georgie – they call him the Belfast boy,' went the jaunty song from his TV show. Not a slip of a lad any more and no longer the fifth Beatle, heavier round the hips, appearing to play all his football from a standing position like one of those kids' toys operated via a wobbly button underneath a plinth, but still Gorgeous George and incredibly, cutting the ribbon at a garage.

Previously, he'd cut the ribbon at the grooviest of boutiques and the fabbest of discotheques. Where did it all go wrong, George? No matter. This was boffo news for the *Leith Gazette* and I was more than happy to work an (unpaid) Saturday morning shift in January 1980 for the chance to meet the legend, having just and no more managed to persuade my mother, who fancied him rotten, to allow me to go alone.

I'd witnessed his Hibs debut a few weeks before when he banged a goal into the bottom corner of St Mirren's net at Love Street. I'd been at his first game at Easter Road when he'd tripled the gate. I never did get a pair of Stylo Matchmakers, the white-streaked boots he advertised in his wing-wizard pomp for Manchester United, but this was better: George in green and white, playing for my team, not anyone else's. Bestie the Hibby. I have the programmes from all his 22 games. 'George Best needs no introduction,' insisted Meadowbank Thistle sniffily. Kilmarnock decided merely listing him as 'Best' on the line-ups page would be sufficient and Aberdeen were similarly grudgeful. Rangers grumped: 'Hibs' efforts to stir the Scottish scene by importing Best have been well recorded.' The wee Rangers of Berwick nearly rivalled the titanic parochialism of 'North-east man drowns at sea' with: 'He is of course a former team-mate of our boss Dave Smith at the LA Aztecs.' Ach, they were all probably jealous.

That afternoon, less than three hours after the official opening, Best was due to be playing against Celtic but, on being introduced to him in the tailpipe tycoon's office, I just couldn't see that happening. He still seemed hammered from the night before. His beautiful eyes were glazed and the reek of the booze wafting from his pores was overpowering. The pong nullified the Castrol GTX and the Blue Stratos* of the full sales force in

* Best that day required a dab of his own preferred scent and it's never left Gordon Rae's nostrils, as he reminisced for me: 'George lived in Edinburgh's North British Hotel, his club car was a crimson Saab 900 convertible and every Friday he'd have an ounce of this special cologne delivered to him from Paris. Each teensy bottle of the stuff was supposed to have cost a hundred quid, which was what I was earning a week. After games he'd splash it and then he'd let the young boys like me, Craig Paterson and 'Benny' Brazil share

attendance (district manager and, yes, regional manager, too). But it was George's genius which left me dumbstruck. What would Hugh McIlvanney ask him? Michael Parkinson? Jeremy Paxman? Eventually – and the memory makes me cringe – inspiration came from our surroundings: when was the last time he'd suffered a puncture?

Now I don't think even the garage boss would have produced such a fatuous line of enquiry. Not even the editor of *Tread Magazine*. George, bless him, laughed. The idea of him inconveniencing a beauty queen in this manner while she rode in his E-type Jag was plainly ludicrous. To help me out, he took over the interview. Was I going to the game? 'Great,' he said, 'see you there.' Then, after leaving his spotty inquisitor with twisted blood, he did the same to Celtic's Roy Aitken for a tremendous strike.

Bestie the Hibby. Statto dullards will point out that in those 22 games he scored just three times and didn't prevent relegation. They will question the wisdom of chairman Tom Hart paying him £2,000 a week from his own pocket. They will mention all the times he turned up too hung-over or not at all. But they aren't factoring in fantasy. They're disregarding imagination. Doesn't romantic possibility feature in their lives? And can't they acknowledge that if any Scottish club were ever going to attempt the wild and thrilling stunt of one last hurrah for George Best it would inevitably be Hibs?

---

the last few drops. George would be heading uptown for another night of untold pleasure while I was going back to Bonnyrigg and my local for the darts league, saying to myself: 'That can't just have happened. *Again*. He's the guy – the genius – from the *Shoot!* posters in my old bedroom!'

78

NOT A GOALIE CENTRE OF EXCELLENCE, NOT A BOOT HILL EITHER

AS A treat for my son's 18th birthday we pitched up in Birmingham to see his favourite ex-Hibee John McGinn's Aston Villa attempt a famous Champions League comeback against Paris Saint-Germain. Before kick-off, the stadium announcer repeatedly trumpeted Villa's goalkeeper Emiliano Martinez as 'the world No 1'. But the quarter-final second leg is just 11 minutes old when the Argentine dropped a clanger and his team fell further behind.

Who'd be a goalie? The cocksure Martinez, obviously, and I use that description advisedly if you remember where he stuck his World Cup prize for being the 2022 tournament's best keeper. Goalies nowadays are far more demonstrative (viz. England's Jordan Pickford). They're like modern referees in demanding to be noticed more.

Previous generations were a shy and retiring breed, near fatalistic about the nature of the job and accepting of the loneliness involved. George Farm helped see Hibs home to the league title in 1947–48. When he hung up his gloves he became a lighthouseman.

So what of McGinn's old club and goalkeepers? Do they get on well? Perhaps you wouldn't call Easter Road a goalie centre of excellence or even a goalie factory. A goalie boot hill? Maybe the best we can hope for is somewhere in the middle (and hopefully standing in the middle of the goal, not leaning on a post, cracking jokes for the ball boys).

Willie Harper was a celebrated Hibee custodian (see ch. 50) who could not be beaten en route to the 1923 Scottish Cup final. What happened next? He sailed serenely through the air to collect a cross and missed it, handing the trophy to Celtic.

Less celebrated was George Blyth, the goalkeeper in 1930–31 when Hibs were relegated for the first time. Midway through the season he lost his place to John Dudgeon. Blyth could hardly have been in high dudgeon about that, after letting in seven at Aberdeen, but he was reinstated when the other man conceded six at Motherwell, holding on to the fisherman's roll-neck jumper right through to the bitter end. Now, all these years later his handsome face adorns a fridge magnet, purchasable from a football memorabilia site for £17.95. It's the least he deserves, as thanks for his service.

There are no magnets of Zbigniew Malkowski, Andy McNeil, Simon Brown and Yves Ma-Kalambay. Guys, it's too soon. And you all blundered in noughties derbies so as members of a haunted grouping such recognition may only come ironically. Of course their mistakes were scrutinised to blazes by the TV pundits. (It beats me why we don't show the same concern over these ex-pros' dully repetitive behaviour as we do animals stuck in zoos and have the practice stopped. Such tragic creatures, every week delivering the same outcisive outsight.)

McNeil may be the most likely to win a reprieve from goalie hell, having been between the sticks for the 2007 League Cup triumph. But fans for whom these spillages are still too raw might be surprised to learn in an obituary for Lawrie Leslie, from the lost Scottish Cup final of 1958, that since the Second World War, Hibs have had ten Scotland goalies backstop the team. Admittedly they included the square-jawed Leslie, the fastidious Farm and Ronnie 'Faither' Simpson whose caps came post-Easter Road, and Jim Herriot and Willie Miller whose international days were over before they arrived. But both Alan Rough and Jim Leighton had Scotland careers revived by standing up to fierce shelling in Hibee colours in the 1980s and 1990s.

Regarding keepers, Hibs boast a number of unusual societies, all of them with select memberships. Andy Goram and Mark Oxley both boomed goals from kick-outs. Farm and Jimmy Kerr, No. 1 for most of 1947–48, both had games as emergency outfielders, Farm even scoring for Blackpool. And something else about him: with fingernails always immaculately trimmed, he liked to catch crosses with one hand atop the ball and the other underneath, not dissimilar to how a game-show glamour puss would show off a soda syphon, imitation Ming vase or some other low-grade consolation prize.

Kerr shared the Famous Five glory years with Tommy Younger who flew back from army service in Germany and in photographs is rarely without a big daft grin. But there's something the keepers from further back in the previous century had in common: with next to no job protection all the testimonies make mention of their bravery, and none more so than Leslie. Struck by a lorry as a boy and told he might never walk again, there were so many broken legs and arms in collisions with centre-forwards that by the time he was guarding the goal behind Bobby Moore for West Ham United, his wife used to joke about a bed at the Royal London Hospital having his name permanently stuck to the headboard.

So maybe Easter Road is not such a goalie graveyard after all. And we haven't even mentioned Conrad Logan.

Or Budgie . . .

79

TONY HIGGINS, HIS THIGHS AND FOOTBALL'S HAYS CODE

IT WAS as if Hibs had nipped up to Speaker's Corner next to the Royal Scottish Academy on Princes Street, overpowered the weediest God-bothering doom-monger to nick his sandwich board, and then on the way back down Leith Walk ordered a kwik-print shop to transfer its message on to the team's shirts: 'The end of the world is nigh.'

As far as purists and traditionalists were concerned, the Hibees had adopted the same shock tactics. The end of football, certainly as they knew it and wanted it to remain. Words on the front of strips were sacrilege. The words, or word, ultimately written across chests both strapping (Tony Higgins) and slight (Pat Carroll, Alex McGhee) was 'Bukta'. In 1977 the club teamed up with the sportswear firm for Britain's first major league sponsorship deal turning the players into walking – though hopefully mostly running or as it would turn out in big Hig's case lumbering – advertisement boards.

Bukta were founded in 1879 in Stockport. Before Hibs, their customers included the Girl Guide movement. In the football kit realm they were taking on an established order of big boys. Bearing in mind the year of the Easter Road tie-up, maybe the company adopted a punk ethos. And perhaps the production lines were encouraged to sing along to a Clash anthem rewritten for the struggle: 'No Umbro, Adidas or Ad-mi-ral . . . in 1977.'

It's hard to believe the stuffed-shirt SFA went along with corporate slogans. Harder to understand that STV, the commercial channel which screened ads every 15 minutes, with many of them sexist and showing that a woman's work was never done – were opposed to messages on strips and joined with the BBC in refusing to allow Hibs to promote their partners' products.

None of Hibs' other firsts were this problematic. The club were keen to avoid a telly blackout and as they wrangled with the broadcasters we wondered if there would have to be an equivalent of the Hays Code. This was the means by which Hollywood of the 1930s controlled what could and could not be shown to preserve moral decency. So if the leading lady in a movie's romantic scene where there was clearly a bed in view was required to keep one foot on the floor at all times, perhaps Big Tony would only be allowed lettering of a certain size if he covered up his muckle great hurdies, with the on-trend tight shorts in his case being likely to cause women, and maybe men, to faint.

In the end Hibs came up with an entirely different look for TV – in purple. The shirts were unveiled in a league game at Celtic although the first time the team had played in the colour was five years earlier in the European Cup Winners' Cup away to Sporting Lisbon. Although that match was lost, the performance persuaded them they might be on to something. The purplest of patches quickly followed.

Eventually TV relented and allowed the Bukta strips. And in no time at all footballers elsewhere would be blatantly plugging brothels, lap dancing bars and money lenders, rejoicing under the sponsor names Dong, Pooh, Wang, Bimbo and Mister Lady – and at Clydebank promoting warbling popsters Wet Wet Wet.

80

THE TICKET INSISTED: 'THIS PORTION MUST BE RETAINED.' I STILL HAVE IT

DID WE have tickets? It was Christmas-time, but this was all that concerned me. O-Grades were just around the corner, teenage romance was just around the corner, and soon pop music would take over almost my entire life, but in the countdown to 1 January 1973 and the derby, this was what really mattered.

Could my father just phone Uncle Don and ask? The game was at Tynecastle, so it was his turn. He usually lets us know he's got them and . . . what, he hasn't? They're all sold out? Disaster!

Don't worry, the message came back, being high up in the Lothian and Borders Polis – later rising to the rank of deputy chief constable – he would call in a few favours. And doubtless, Dad joked, squeeze a few handshakes that special, secret way.

They were best pals despite everything. Dad was Labour and Uncle Don was Tory. Dad in his youth had tried to burn down his school while Uncle Don, unsurprisingly, had always upheld the law. Dad was Hibs and Uncle Don . . . well, I think he pretended to be Hearts for the ritual banter. What he really liked was our two families getting together on New Year's Day, continuing a friendship which for the parents went all the way back to the 1950s, amateur dramatics and a summer holiday on Soay, off the coast of Skye – the latter so raucously reminisced as the whisky flowed that we kids, once aware of the concepts, would speculate amid our giggles on the stairs about the trip having involved naturism and possibly swinging.

And Uncle Don did get the tickets. And the stub is right by my side, as per the instruction of Hearts secretary W.A.J. Devine: 'This portion to be retained by the holder.' I've kept it all this time, along with the match programme. Checking eBay, the going rate for the prog – cover price 5p – is £150. Would I get slightly less for the stub, or even more? After all, only the centre stand required tickets, cost £1, so there must be fewer of them and, despite the direction of Mr Devine, they'd be less likely to have been preserved as mementos.

What, you think I'm more than a bit obsessed by this game? That claiming it as a rite of passage, working in mention of wife-swapping, is embellishment, sexing up and ultimately over-hyping its significance? And your point, caller, is what exactly?

Here's some more context: half a century ago, New Year celebrations were rather different. Edinburgh was not the self-styled Hogmanay capital of the world. Revellers did not descend from the four corners for a gigantic street party. Instagram did not creak with the sheer number of money-shot uploads of snogging in woolly hats against a backdrop of a lit-up castle.

Before all that, the welcome on 31 December had been: 'You'll have had your black bun.' At the chime of midnight, an exclusively local huddle formed outside a church in the Old Town, there to dodge the half bottles of Whyte & Mackay hurled skywards.

The next day, no one swam in the Forth in a self-congratulatory manner. No one had 'brunch' in a 'bistro', neither of these things having been invented, and nowhere was open, save for this day Tynecastle, so along Gorgie Road we came, drawn by the four floodlight pylons peering through Auld Reekie's grime and gloom.

Auld Reekin', more like. Apart from me, my little brother and Uncle Don's son, was everyone else still drunk? We giggled at the valiant attempts at forward motion: one foot anchored to the pavement, the other prodding gingerly like a blind man with a stick, the most stocious completing full circles, getting nowhere.

But eventually 35,989 of us reached the stadium (cont.) . . .

81

PICKED UP THE BALL, RAN ACROSS THE COPACABANA WITH IT

THERE'S ONE thing about Hibs that makes Hearts fans laugh. Actually there's probably more than one but let's concentrate here on Brazil. Jambos reckon we're obsessed with the idea that we taught the Brazilians how to play football. Not the corporate version the national team employ now but the game's most exuberant expression at the 1970 World Cup when even the centre-half from a deep position salsa-ed with the ball.

More than that, Jambos think we're convinced it was us, not Portuguese explorer Pedro Álvares Cabral, who founded the country. That we believe Rio de Janeiro's Sugar Loaf Mountain to be man-made and a homage to the old Easter Road slope. That we go around telling everyone how Lola, the showgirl in Barry Manilow's 'Copacabana', started out as an erotic dancer down at Leith Docks and that she sported a 'Persevere' tattoo with pride on her left arse cheek.

Okay, maybe we have got carried away. Picked up the ball and ran across the beach and into the warm Southern Atlantic with it. You know, all Hibbies are not actually married to the kind of smokeshows in itsy-bitsy buttercup yellow bikini tops that TV directors always pick out of the crowds. We wish.

But the football stuff, the flair influence, that's verifiable, right? Every time successive Hibs sides string three passes together the move can be traced all the way back to 1953 when the Famous Five guested at a prestigious Rio tournament.

According to Leith legend their scintillating displays were analysed and eulogised in a coaching manual and from its pages emerged the heaven-sent forward line of Jairzinho, Gerson, Tostão, Pelé and Derek Townsley . . . sorry, I mean Rivellino.

Well, the tourney was real and Hibs were invited as Scottish champs, admirable exponents of the Old World passing game: 'very nice, very intelligent, almost intellectual', according to one pundit keenly awaiting their arrival. But the rest? 'It's a good story, a great story – a Hibby story,' laughed Lawrie Reilly when we met, 'but I don't know what we could have taught the likes of Vava and Didi that they weren't doing already, and pretty well, too.'

The Torneio Octogonal Rivadavia Correa Meyer, named after Brazil's top blazer, was a sort of Club World Cup but much of the rest of Europe cooled on the concept so fair play to the Hibees for making the long trip. 'What an adventure,' continued Reilly. 'Edinburgh to London in a reconditioned World War Two bomber then on to Lisbon, Dakar, Recife and finally Rio. There was a lot of press to meet us and we were asked how it felt being in Brazil. Willie Ormond, typical of him, said: "Ah wish tae hell ah wis hame." I fell ill right away. We were capering about in the sea not knowing Rio had open sewers. But two hours after leaving hospital I was lining up against Vasco da Gama in the big old Maracanã. I scored one of my last-minute goals for a 3–3 draw. There was a moat round the pitch, wee laddies stretching out their hands, so at the end we kicked balls to them. I've often wondered if one of them grew up to be Pelé.'

And that manual? Like Shakespeare's *Cardenio* and Jane Austen's *Sanditon* it must go down as one of the great lost books. Eddie Turnbull, who also scored against Vasco da Gama, remembered Brazilian newspapers the following day containing diagrams of a strike which clearly astonished them. It had been a bit of a fluke. 'I shouted to Ormond: "Gie the ball tae me, Wullie, and I'll clock it." But I skited the shot and it swerved into the net.'

Maybe from a few illustrations the fanciful notion of an entire encyclopedia developed. By the way, Turnbull's recollection was relayed to me by a Scottish high court judge and Hibs fanatic who'd treated Ned to lunch at much-missed Easter Road trattoria Tinelli, so I'm not about to question it. And, having already speculated on what Dino Zoff might have said in the lead-up to Brazil's fourth goal in that classic 1970 final (see ch. 29), perhaps at the exact same moment Carlos Alberto issued this instruction: 'Gie the ball tae me, Edson Arantes do Nascimento, and I'll clock it.'

82

SCORED FIVE, BOOED BY HIS OWN FANS

WHAT'S JOE Harper doing in this story? It's not as if he was part of a glorious era. In fact he's best remembered for interrupting a glorious era. A wee, round, dumpy, shifty guy with a carryout who turned up at a swell house party and caused consternation. Eddie said it would be OK to come – Eddie Turnbull, the manager. Except it really wasn't.

But the episode – Harper was at Easter Road for just over two years – is instructive and revealing about the psyche of the Hibs fan and how the machinery of the brain grinds and groans.

It tells us about the high value this supporter places on loyalty (for all football, a flimsy concept at the time, completely antiquated now). It tells us he's sentimental – overly so. And just how demanding is he, how entitled – and how vulnerable to a visit from the loonies' yellow van? For what sort of mentalist boos a player at the end of a game where he's scored all his team's goals – and that's five of them?

Turnbull's Tornadoes, the original line-up, had not quite managed to win the honours their flamboyant football promised. Harper's sleekit goal-hanger ways would, it was hoped, make the difference. He joined in February 1974 and almost immediately embarked on a strike-every-other-game routine maintained to the end.

Hibs finished second that season. Could they go one better? The next campaign began promisingly with Harper raining down all those goals on friendly fodder Nijmegen. And that's when the abuse rained down on him.

Actually booing wasn't called abuse back then. This was pre-mental health. But why? What had Harper done wrong? Replaced favourite son Jimmy O'Rourke (see ch. 51), that's what. And the equally adored Alan Gordon (see ch. 31) would soon be sold as well. Still, the reaction from the stands seemed like cutting off lugs to spite mugs, football fans at their most S&M perverse.

Harper would net Ibrox winners, Edinburgh derby rockets, the goal to beat Liverpool and cup final hat-tricks – and yet at the end of his first full season, Hibs finishing runners-up once again, the surly fellow up front with the road-compressor physique, deadly when the ball was bagatelling around the box, scored a third against Airdrie and a clump of fans close to me on the old main terracing were still jeering as he returned to the centre circle. He offered the right-up-yooz gesture and they jeered even louder.

Harper couldn't win. Even if all his goals had been things of balletic beauty, even if he'd given his entire wage to deserving local causes, even if he'd unlocked life's inner meaning and even if Hibs had become champions, there's a sense that some among the cussed cognoscenti would still have had issues with him.

As mentioned, he was no wimp. He'd once played – under manager's orders – with 42 stitches in his face and three cracked ribs, this being the day after he'd flown through a car windscreen. When he and Turnbull were at Aberdeen together, a row with the boss left him with a black eye. A row with Alex Ferguson over him gutsing on a giant plateful of haggis and neeps ended with him slugging Fergie. Grounds around the land echoed to the chant: 'Harper's a barrel, Harper's a barrel of shite shite shite.' So his critics at Hibs weren't going to upset him and those well-stuffed cheeks simply formed into a wry smile. He even sympathised with the fans, was sorry for their loss of two idols having genuinely hoped he could have played alongside them. The next time he scored a hat-trick he was back at Aberdeen, his true home. The opposition? Hibs.

83

WINTER'S DIABOLIC UNLESS YOU HAVE A BLANKET ON THE GROUND

IN THE *Tomorrow's World* office, researchers were submitting ideas for the next edition but the producer was unimpressed and growing more and more impatient.

'Come on, what else?'

'Well, Hibs have something new . . .'

'Of course they do. What are they up to now?' The producer was very familiar with the club's claims to exciting newfangledness and 'firsts' but clearly a hard man to please. 'Don't tell me: half-time pies in pill form. Intravenous Bovril? A heat-seeking ball? Brain chips to blank out the bad stuff from fans' memories, i.e. Scottish Cup failure and Jambo domination? A reduced-gravity training pod in readiness for games on the Moon?'

He harrumphed some more. 'Shouldn't they be concentrating on trying to win a few matches?'

'Actually it's an undersoil blanket.'

'Oh . . .'

Now I don't think Hibs featured on the show in 1980. Michael Rodd may not have battled through a blizzard to report from a perfectly playable Easter Road, a verdant oasis in snow-bound Leith. And then to the strains of Billie Jo Spears' 'Blanket on the Ground' embarked on a dribble in his presenter's suit, sidestepping the old groundsman only to – ach – miss an open goal. The question is, though: why the hell not?

The club have always been about the green and white heat

of technology and the following year, on Boxing Day, they were the only game in town, in any town, thanks to their frostquake-beating initiative.

Football had been wiped out by a whiteout. In the words of the Scottish wit Bud Neill, noses had froze, noses were skintit. So were grounds all over Britain. (Winter's diabolic, intit?) A traditionally turkey-stuffed day in the season could not offer the great escape for fans desperate to get out of the house and see a match. Only *The Great Escape* on the box for the umpteenth time.

Undersoil heating was the whizzo idea of Easter Road supremo Tom Hart, carrying on the good visionary work of predecessor Harry Swan. The club had tried industrial-sized braziers by the touchlines and hot-air blowers under a polythene quilt – neither method worked. But installing a giant radiator one foot under the surface did.

Now, anyone fancy a game? That Boxing Day, Manchester United were up for one. Hart laid on a private jet to bring them north, a glamour team hoping new British record signing Bryan Robson would power them to title glory. It was all last minute and obviously pre-internet so word of mouth encouraged fans along to Easter Road, to chitter in sub-zero temperatures on the slippery terraces.

Man U were managed by a hot-air blower in Ron Atkinson though Hibs had a man in charge who could compete with his swagger and bluster – Bertie Auld. The friendly was competitive but fans were just as intrigued by the fashion face-off between the bosses.

Auld, the Lisbon Lion, had a thing about hats, having sported a trilby for Celtic's European Cup celebrations and a fedora for the Glasgow club's 'Battle of Britain' victory over Leeds United before modelling a selection of giant comedy bunnets in management. He told me: 'My favourite was made of cashmere and I needed it that day because it was absolutely perishing. Also because Big Ron was Mr Bojangles – herringbone coat draped to the ground with a big fluffy fur collar. We were two dandies keeping out the cold and I think I matched him with my camel-hair number, velvet collar – and when young Willie Jamieson put us ahead I flung the bunnet in the air and it hovered there like Sputnik.'

Man U came back through Frank Stapleton and this British battle finished in a draw. Really, Hibs should have won the Queen's Award for Enterprise with undersoil heating subsequently catching on everywhere.

84

GRAB YOUR ANKLES AND KISS YOUR ASS GOODBYE

IF YOU didn't know it you might wonder if Rotary clubs, by their very name, were helicopter enthusiasts. Semi-secret societies of guys who meet once a month to discuss choppers. Well, somewhat bizarrely, or maybe because Rotarians quite liked the allusion, they've come right out and published a list of their top ten copter movies. No. 1? *Blue Thunder*. That's the flick where Roy Scheider – who pounced on the role to avoid being in *Jaws 3*, apparently – polices Los Angeles from the skies in a swooping high-tech whirlybird until he stumbles across a chilling government conspiracy. The mid-air action is terrific, and usually trailed by Scheider saying something like: 'Grab your ankles and kiss your ass goodbye.'

The pilot of the helicopter whisking Jim Duffy to Easter Road in 1996 never uttered these words of caution. Or the warning issued in that later rotary-wing thriller *Black Hawk Down*: 'You shouldn't have come here . . . it's our war, not yours.' And that wasn't surprising. Duffy, in spite of a pugnacious mein, wasn't fighting anyone; he was going to manage a football club.

Still, it was some entrance. Rock star-esque, or like a world leader pitching up for vital detente. Or like Duffy was a gift from on high, a sexy alchemist come to transform the team after years of dourness.

There was a sexy victory over Celtic in the sunshine of a season opener, nomadic holy terror Chic Charnley seizing on a loose ball with the gait of near-namesake Charlie Chaplin for a scorching winner. Next game the bold Chico scored from halfway, a trick quickly matched by Pat McGinlay. This was fantasy football under Duffy, and in Edinburgh in Festival-time with comedians up every close, *Fantasy Football League*'s David Baddiel wanted in on it. Via my newspaper I arranged for the funster to train with Hibs, although the players refused to be star-struck by the TV personality, battering balls at his weedy frame and knocking his specs off. Then, lined up for a team photo in the traditional way, Baddiel squatting down the front, Charnley standing behind doused him from a bottle, only when he looked up nutter captain John 'Yogi' Hughes was dangling his cock above the comic's head, lending the impression it hadn't been water. Footballers, eh?

Also: Hibs, eh? The fun and fantasy quickly evaporated for Duffy who realised that flattering to deceive is something inherent at Easter Road, and sacked before the club would be relegated, he had to kiss his ass goodbye.

The story of that helicopter ride was another of the Hibees' cautionary tales, though 1996 was obviously a year of flash football gesturing, with Liverpool turning up at Wembley in ridiculous white suits only to end up losing the FA Cup final.

Such a big-shot unveiling wasn't Duffy's idea. Earlier in the day he'd wanted to say his farewells to previous club Dundee and the copter, laid on by Hibs owner Tom Farmer, was the only way he could have got to Easter Road in time for his unveiling. But I believe him when he tells me he didn't go all Lieutenant Colonel Kilgore on the flight down the east coast, mimicking Robert Duvall's character in *Apocalypse Now* – No. 3 in that movie roll call – and cranking up 'Ride of the Valkyries' as Leith hove into view.

In any case Duffy is more of a fan of the music I love, Steely Dan and Hall & Oates and what these days gets called yacht rock. Talking of which, it's as well he didn't swing into the Forth in a sleek schooner. That would have been even worse.

85

HIBS WERE EMERALD, HEARTS RUBY, TOGETHER: DIAMOND?

WHERE WERE you when you heard the news? Maybe, as chance would have it, when the report came on the car or van radio your workaday life had taken you to the wrong side of town, although as it wasn't a match day Tynecastle was quiet. The stadium could be glimpsed down the gloomy side streets and you might have wondered to yourself: 'How could they do this?'

Or maybe you were in the vicinity of Easter Road within sight of the floodlights. This ground – such a big part of your life, such a constant – was quiet too, eerily so, and something you hadn't thought about in a long while, if at all, the graveyard just a goal kick away suddenly acquired an ominous aspect.

How could they do this? As in: how could Hearts be contemplating a takeover of Hibs? We knew they liked to lord it around the Edinburgh football scene, but were they mental, actually certifiably insane? They wanted to end the derby, obliterate the rivalry, burn all the (history) books?

But also: how were they even going to be allowed to do it? Weren't there rules to prevent this kind of thing happening?

When Wallace Mercer, the Hearts chairman, launched his hostile bid, I was 1,200 miles away on a holiday from work at Italia 90. I saw Roger Milla dance elastically in Naples. I saw Frank Rijkaard launch globules of phlegm at Rudi Völler in Turin. I saw Murdo MacLeod and Jim Leighton come croppers – the former a free kick to the face which knocked him cold, the latter a tragic late spill which knocked Scotland out of the World Cup.

No one knew these two would star for Hibs later. Back in Edinburgh, no Hibs fan thought there would even be a later. Meanwhile in Italy news was frustratingly bitty and slow, though the bedsheet banners hung from the tenement-style towers of Genoa's Luigi Ferraris Stadium by supporters who'd just arrived and therefore knew slightly more spoke to the gravity of the situation: 'Hands off Hibs.'

The truth is football people – me and most likely you – are ignorant about business which is why the shock was off the scale. But a greater truth, and the one which saved the day, is that business people are ignorant about football.

Mercer, the businessman who ran Hearts, didn't reckon on bricks flying through his office windows (regrettable) or Joe Baker, Hibs' greatest centre-forward who'd gone on to play for Torino, Arsenal and England but emotionally hadn't left at all, kneeling down and kissing the Easter Road turf (glorious).

The kiss came at a rally. There were stirring speeches from club legends and famous fans and battle-cry songs from the Proclaimers. Hibbies packed the ground but there was room for fans from other clubs and some were Jambos, just as dumbfounded by their supremo's actions and just as agin them.

The emergency committee met nightly to discuss the following day's tactics. There were more protests, threats by fans on the branch doorsteps of the bank backing Hearts that personal accounts would be closed, speeches at miners' galas, questions in the House, petitions delivered to Tynecastle and also to Mrs Thatcher at No. 10. The prime minister notoriously didn't 'get' football or indeed community ('there's no such thing . . .'), but the situation was grave and dead horses needed to be flogged. So she was told, everyone was told: 'Hands off Hibs.'

During the diabolical plotting from the Gorgie boardroom there were code names. Hibs were 'Emerald' and Hearts were

'Ruby' while 'Diamond' represented Mercer's so-called united Edinburgh team, although everyone knew this was a sop. At best it would be 'Hearts, incorporating Hibs' like when two comics merged and your favourite, slightly less popular but way cooler, quickly lost all individuality and identity. Of course this wasn't *Hotspur* swallowing up *Hornet* only much, much worse.

But: it never happened. Mercer's Diamond was Ratner-ed. By the time I got back from Italy, Hearts were still Hearts, trying to pretend there had been nothing untoward, but with the rest of the football community thinking slightly less of them. And Hibs were still Hibs. Just and no more . . .

86

GREETIN' FACED, COULDNAE RUN, BUT OH THE VISION!

IT'S FAIRLY busy in the Clan MacLeod Society at Easter Road. There have been more of them than McDonalds, Mackays or McIntoshes, while the McKirdys have probably, er, peaked at one and it's highly unlikely we'll see any more Ma-Kalambays. All of the MacLeods have been notable. Murdo captained the 1991 League Cup heroes. Johnny netted five of the goals in a pair of megaboggling away victories within weeks of each other in 1959 – 11–1 at Airdrie, 10–2 at Partick Thistle – and also bagged two in the Nou Camp to help bring down Barcelona.

Hibs' first Ally of that name replaced Johnny on the left wing before a colourful career in management with Ayr United and Aberdeen. He then masterminded some of Scotland's most famous victories and, slumped in an Argentine dugout with a *villa miseria* stray his only friend, presided over one of the most notorious defeats.

That Ally, when things went well, exuded Pomange-standard effervescence, which isn't a phrase you'd use about his namesake, at least not in demeanour, but so what? When your skills are that mysterious, that magical, you can look as miserable as you like.

It wasn't that Alexander Hector McMillan MacLeod didn't enjoy his football. When he moved on to Dundee United where injury prevented him playing any part in their Premier

League-winning season and retirement quickly followed, the depression he suffered took five years to lift.

We met in 2016 on the eve of Hibs' Scottish Cup triumph and the man who'd previously come closest to smashing the curse when he hammered the post in extra-time in the third instalment of the *War and Peace* final (see ch. 136) listened patiently to the number of times he'd been euphemistically described as 'enigmatic'. And, yes, he smiled. Laughed, even. 'I'd no idea what I looked like when I played and wasn't trying to cultivate a mean and moody image,' he said. 'But so many folk have said that was what I was so I suppose it must be true.'

They said slightly more, evidence that the world was becoming more lookist: not just 'greetin'-faced' but with 'tiny wee legs' and a 'pot belly' so he 'couldnae run'. And these remarks were from fans who, like me, idolised MacLeod, for then they'd add: 'But oh, the vision!'

A university prospect in his younger days, an Ibrox-quaking four-goal sensation in his St Mirren days, MacLeod arrived in 1974 and by talent would have qualified for inclusion in the Tornadoes team if it had been any earlier. For eight years he was a cult favourite of discerning members of the cognoscenti, didn't scarper in the wake of relegation, scored 99 goals from a skulking, sulking midfield berth and seemed to exist in 'bullet time'.

This was the special effect in the *Matrix* movies where the world appeared to slow right down, causing shots from a gun to float and be dodged. For MacLeod it was tackles, his opponents seemingly paralysed by the drop of a slouched shoulder. He understood the exact moment to shuffle the ball from one foot to the other. Couldnae run? In this regard at least, working in milliseconds, living his life by them, he actually had something in common with Olympic sprinters.

Classic MacLeod was a 1982 game against Dundee when he banged a free kick over the wall and into the left-hand corner of the net only for the referee to spot encroachment and order a retake. What did he do? Nonchalantly popped the ball into the right-hand corner, of course. Surely that was the moment to smile, expand the celebration beyond the traditional single raised arm? 'Oh no. I never saw the need for any of that. Scoring goals was simply my job.'

87

POPJOYS, BLOOMERS, BIANCOS . . . THE HIBEE PUB CRAWL FROM HELL

PLANNING A stag weekend or a lads' jaunt? There are so many options now, the market demands ever more quirky themes, and window shopping in Amsterdam no longer cuts it. Check out Prague and there's 'Lesbian Strip Boat' and 'AK-47 Kalashnikov Shooting'. But Hibs fans: I reckon I've found you the perfect combo of history, hostelry and horror . . .

A pub crawl – or more accurately, wine bar wander – round some of the licensed premises in the West Country of England which were once owned by our club and might easily have ended us. Popjoys, Bloomers and Bianco's comprised a front three to strike fear and loathing into Hibbies during the late 1980s when the club became the first in Scotland to be stock market-listed. There were others, as many as a dozen more, and I should warn those contemplating a trip that they'll be lucky if they find any continuing to operate. Still, visit the former locations and console yourself with the fact that while the bars may have gone, Hibs are still around. And for a laugh, a macabre chuckle, maybe dress up like loadsamoney types – double-breasted suits with padded shoulders, Buggles specs, Filofaxes, little David Duff moustaches – to evoke the dangerous madness of the period.

The bars became Hibs' responsibility after Duff, the Hibs chairman, got into bed with David Rowland, variously described as a 'wheeler-dealer extraordinaire', a 'secretive property magnate' and – from the floor of the House of Commons by Leith

MP Ron Brown protesting about his involvement in the club – a 'shady financier'. The move into hospitality was hailed by Duff as 'the most important and exciting event' since he'd arrived at Easter Road, but it was the (cocktail) straw which nearly broke the Hibees, very nearly selling them down the River Avon some 400 miles away.

The bars were supposed to siphon money into the club but, on closer inspection of the books, they were found to be losing £80,000 a week. Rowland – who'd loaned Duff £800,000 so he could buy Hibs, providing the bankroller with a 30 per cent stake – hussled to protect his shareholding. Suddenly incoming: a mysterious figure, a predator. Duff's description of being taunted by Rowland's associates over this man's identity had him resembling a cuckolded husband sweating behind the bedroom door. 'Who's the worst person you can think of?' He never guessed it would be Wallace Mercer.

In the eyes of the support, Duff went from bad guy to almost good by refusing to sell his shares, prompting Hearts to back off, albeit he'd admitted to being naive, out of his depth and a mere 'puppet'. But what of the puppet master? I've stayed intrigued by Rowland, always stopping to read when business reporters have blown some of his cover, almost to the point of wanting to tell him: 'Spotty, you should have stuck with Hibs, learned to love them like we do.'

Spotty is his nickname. It refers to both the acne of his teens and the fact he was just 24 when he made his first million. The son of a London scrap metal merchant, who'd been convicted by a juvenile court nine years previously for stealing goods worth £2, had turned his life around.

He's a father of eight. You wonder how he can keep track of all the money when it's been shunted between the Bahamas, Panama, the British Virgin Islands, the Falklands, Idaho, Holland and Luxembourg – and sometimes he hasn't. At one point, just a single photograph of him existed, but there's a bronze statue in the grounds of his Guernsey mansion, unveiled by Prince Andrew, the 'door opener' for some of Rowland's deals. In 2010 the door of the Conservative Party was opened and, after donating millions, he was announced as chief fund-raiser, but the heat from newspaper revelations meant he never took up the post, leaving him with a portrait of David Cameron from an auction reportedly costing £20,000.

That's almost the equivalent of two Alan Gordons, but I suppose Spotty Rowland in backing the Tories and the Duke of York rather than sticking with Hibs made the correct decision, at least for him. An oft-heard jibe is that he displays 'all the emotions of an ashtray'. You simply can't do that spending any time at Easter Road.

88

'I NICKED SOME PIPING TO STICK IT IN THE CAR EXHAUST'

IT'S EASY to be ho-hum about pop stars and other showbizzers required to check in to The Priory. Not another one and, what, you want to tell us all about it? Your *journey*? But the footballers who have been patients comprise a smaller and more exclusive club, and those ending up at the drying-out clinic despite the longest of careers and the most cheerful of dispositions surely number just one.

'You've heard about the tears of a clown, haven't you?' asked John Burridge, the great goalkeeping eccentric, when we met. 'Well, that was me when I finished playing. I couldn't deal with it. I started at 15 so I didn't have to go down the mines like my dad. At 43 I was the oldest player in the English Premiership. At 46 I sat on the bench at Newcastle United in tears, knowing it was all over. So I thought my life might as well be over, too.

'I was going to get pissed, take some pills, hang myself, I didn't know what. I nicked some piping from a building site and was going to stick it in the car exhaust. I barricaded myself in the bedroom for four days. My wife Janet would come by: "Do you want a cup of tea, John? Do you fancy fish and chips?" Without football, without that three o'clock buzz, I had nothing to live for.'

Janet is the only person who calls him John. Oh and there was also Uday Hussain, the 'charming' son of Saddam who flew him to Baghdad in an old Russian cargo plane packed with sanctions-busting salad cream, hoping to recruit a goalkeeping coach for the Iraqi national team only Burridge had heard stories about players being flogged and forced to bathe in raw sewage so he declined the offer.

Later, Uday was 'removed' by the Special Forces. Burridge, though, came through his blackest moment, to the relief of the 30 clubs on his CV including Hibs who all know him as Budgie. Who were his favourites? Crystal Palace when Terry Venables bossed the 'team of the eighties'. But the Hibees, with whom he won the League Cup, were a close second. 'I'm not trying to flatter you. They really were.'

Burridge arrived in 1991 – by moped – and for two years was the pre-match entertainment with the penalty box his big top for crossbar gymnastics and walking on his hands along the line markings. But the clown was also a pioneer so Hibs – FC Innovaziones – were perfect for him.

There was method in his madness. 'I did my warm-ups on the pitch because, not going out until five to three, the size and noise of the crowd would hit you, also the cold. The walking on my hands dated from Palace where the head groundsman wouldn't let me take a ball out before kick-off. But, yeah, okay, I was also showing off. What do they always say but often forget? Football's entertainment, lad.'

Maybe the goalie fraternity didn't rush to copy his capering but he was the first in Britain to use dry gloves. 'And after I brought them back from Athletic Bilbao, Peter Shilton and Pat Jennings were quickly round my house trying to blag a pair.'

During his travels, studying soccer in America confirmed the importance of theatre and fun. 'I was revolutionary. I Bosmanned before Jean-Marc Bosman. When the staple football meal was steak and chips I was bringing my own blender to the team hotel. I studied the diet of African tribesmen and learned how the guava could help me. Mind you, I couldn't always find guavas in Grimsby and Lincoln and some of the other places I played.'

He was an early adopter of psychiatry. 'At Palace, feeling a bit stressed, I got a shrink to hypnotise me. I paid him 1,500 quid to listen to my life story and make me a motivational cassette. My team-makes took the mickey something rotten. But I was able to visualise games before they happened. I knew I was going to play well.'

Burridge played well in the League Cup semi-final against Rangers, the key tie in the run to glory. '[Manager] Alex Miller was talking up the opposition, as he tended to do. I was like: "But do they know they're playing against John Burridge?"'

The Hibs players, he said, would have seen two sides to Budgie. 'At training, in the gym, winning all the cross-countries, not smoking, hardly drinking, I was Mr Dedication. The guys used to tell me stories about my predecessor Andy Goram needing coffee poured down his throat in the changing room to sober him up. And at all other times of course I was Mr Jackass.

'But in the tunnel against Rangers I was warning Mark Hateley to keep out of my box and rubbishing "Super" Ally McCoist for being a failure at Sunderland. Our guys, Gordon Hunter, Mickey Weir and the rest, were like: "Go on, Budgie!" They ran out that night with right proper fire in their bellies.'

89

THE SMALLEST, SKINNIEST, MOST TALENTED AND BRAVEST

YOU MIGHT not believe this. You might think I've made it up or have just awoken from a delirious dream fuelled by Crabbie's Green Ginger Wine. But in an Edinburgh derby I once saw Alex Cropley score direct from a referee's drop ball on the halfway line, Hibs thrashing the old foes 11–1.

This wasn't a full-scale match but the semi-finals of a five-a-side tournament in the early 1970s, most of the big Scottish clubs competing, at the capital's Haymarket Ice Rink, long since gone. The ice was of course boarded over for the day. It wasn't as if players were required, like the cannon-fodder extras in Rick Wakeman's prog-rock mega-folly *King Arthur*, to perform on frozen water. Though you wouldn't have put it past Cropley, the smallest, skinniest, most talented and bravest of the Tornadoes, to cope just fine.

Now, younger readers will have to suspend disbelief here, and their usual go-on-impress-us attitude to newfangledness and innovation in the game. Five-a-sides had, for Scotland, just happened. Until Meadowbank Stadium was handed over to the capital's ratepayers after the Commonwealth Games for which it was built, there hadn't been an indoor space capable of embracing the concept. A couple of other halls followed, including the one at Leith Kirkgate, and for we tykes normally wading through school-pitch glaur in the Inspectors Cup, and just as long as we could cobble together the pennies for a booking, this was luxury. No, this was decadence!

Haymarket was the elite validating the reduced version of football and I don't think the drop ball was for a foul. In early fives tourneys this was how the ref restarted after a goal, so Hibs had just increased their lead and, in a flashing second, increased it again. Already high on Creamola Foam, the crowd, or at least the youthful Hibee contingent, screamed like a *Crackerjack* crowd.

Among small boys there were plenty of copyists or Cropleyists. The slight build was an encouragement to us and we would mimic the way our idol ran, hands fluttering at his chest rather like Larry Grayson, although I'm pretty sure the 'Shut that door!' comedian never stood his ground against John Greig, leaving the Rangers man to hobble away with a broken toe. Cropley did that.

Instead of that wonder goal I could have chosen one from proper 11-a-sides, such as the last-minute equaliser for a 3–3 draw at Dunfermline Athletic, joke distance and angle, in the season-end sunshine or the first of the team's eight in the snow against Ayr United (time: 12 seconds) or the fourth in the 7–0 game. This was a study in superior technique for a sumptuous volley of a high-dropping ball, something beyond lesser men whose attempts might have scudded the windscreen of one of the light blue disabled cars parked in the corner underneath Tynecastle's half-time scoreboard.

Really, for a special memory of Sodjer – the nickname coming from his upbringing in barracks-town Aldershot – I don't have to pick a goal or the slinky way he moved around the pitch. I could choose the slinky way he entered Bruce's, the grooviest record shop in town, to thumb through the new releases from Jethro Tull and Mott the Hoople. Or later that afternoon, leaving a denim boutique, the slinky way he held open the Wild West saloon-style swing doors for me. You know, I may have been stalking him.

90

'ARTHUR DUNCAN VERY NEARLY STARTED A WAR'

A FEARED dictatorship, a land in total turmoil. Some might argue when has Haiti ever not been, given its history of slavery, debt, corruption, violence and torture, to say nothing of it being in the eye of the hurricane, the earthquake, the flood, etc.? In 1981 the Caribbean country was still getting over a swine flu epidemic and an Aids epidemic was just around the corner. Poverty ran deep and so the people were scandalised by the Paris shopping orgies of the new wife of the tyrant ruler, 'Baby Doc' Duvalier, following a US$2 million wedding the previous year. But speak out against the excesses and you'd be arrested and deported, maybe worse with the dreaded Tontons Macoutes thug militia at the president's beck and call.

So for another end-of-season wind-down, guess which football club decided this would be the ideal destination? And what happened when Hibs pitched up in Haiti looking for some sun-soaked R&R?

'Arthur Duncan very nearly started a war,' laughed Alan Hart. The former Easter Road director, son of chairman Tom, was on the trip, and like many in the official party led by manager Bertie Auld, was unnerved by the chaos and the poverty of the place. Though perhaps not as unnerved as the players, sketchy about geography, who thought they had been bound for Tahiti.

As we know football teams on tour can make for great unintentional comedy. 'When you've seen one wall you've seen 'em all, haven't you?' was the immortal quote from West Bromwich Albion's visit to China, and the Great Wall, two years before.

Doubtless the experience of Haiti has softened in the memory and in the recounting during reunions for the side that bounced back from relegation to win the old First Division title. It just wasn't very funny at the time.

The players flew into the capital Port-au-Prince from the United States and a friendly against San Jose Earthquakes, latest stop-off for their old pal George Best. Hart said: 'Haiti were aiming for the next World Cup and the national team were keen to test themselves against European opposition. They were very pleased we'd come.'

Full-back Alan Sneddon picked up the story: 'The transfer from the airport was by a rickety, open-backed truck, past all these tin huts with prostitutes on most corners. And our hotel was an absolute dump. Tom Hart wasn't happy so he told Alan: "Find us one that's Hibs class."'

Hart Jr learned of a swanky joint at the top of the hill. 'It had been popular with Americans but they'd stopped coming to Haiti the year before so it was empty.' His father was summoned and approved. Ordering a Martini by the pool he told Alan to fetch the team.

Two friendlies were organised but only one was completed. 'The pitch was basically gravel,' said Sneddon. 'The first match took place in sweltering heat but right before the second there was a monsoon and we were trying to play football in a lake.' Although that wasn't why it was abandoned.

'Bertie calls time in Haiti hate game,' screamed the *Daily Record* headline with Auld ordering his men back to the dressing room after an hour of football with extreme prejudice. The paper's report quoted assistant manager Pat Quinn: 'It was absolute mayhem – the worst running battle I've ever seen. A tackle on Arthur Duncan was nothing short of bodily assault. You'd get jailed for that at home.'

Team-mates were just as shocked by what happened immediately following the GBH. 'One of their guys whacked him in the midriff and took the ball down the park,' said Hart. 'Arthur must have run 40 yards to drop-kick him. Then there was a 22-man punch-up. Thankfully we had Gordon Rae and Billy McLaren in our team to ensure we gave as good as we got.'

Coach John Lambie recalled a tense atmosphere before the game and suspected disgruntlement at Hibs' rubbishing of the first hotel as the cause. The players feared reprisals afterwards, not least since there had been the whiff of voodoo all around. But they were told by their guide that Baby Doc would ensure a speedy exit home. Haiti, the troubled land, didn't really need any more bad publicity, though plenty would continue to come its way.

Duncan's team-mates weren't the only ones stunned by the player's reaction. His record of 626 appearances will never be beaten now, and fans who watched him either as a flying winger or old head at full-back cannot remember him losing his temper, squaring up to an opponent or even fouling accidentally. He seemed to only want to run with the ball, run and run. The sarcastic would joke that if the gates were left open at the bottom of the slope he'd have sprinted right out of Easter Road. At the end of his career he ran all the way to New Zealand. Team-mates haven't heard from him for years. Like the supporters, they'd love to catch up with him and hope he's doing well.

91

BACK FROM THE WILDERNESS, BACK FROM THE DEAD

THE ANGEL Island mouse didn't stand much of a chance when a domestic cat was introduced into its Mexico habitat. Result: total wipeout. Native to the saltmarshes of Florida, the Dusky seaside sparrow was down to just a handful of males, their distinctive buzzy song a lament for the last female sighting 15 years previously. The Corquin robber frog of Honduras lived on the edge – the edge of mountains – and would end up paying the ultimate price for such a precarious domain. The Scarlet harlequin toad was just as picky, preferring not to stray from a single stream in an isolated Venezuelan cloud forest, before being hit by deadly disease.

These creatures with their lovely names were declared extinct around the same time as a football club with a lovely name were threatening to join them. Fending off the deadly Wallace Mercer, just and no more, they then plunged into financial chaos. But on 27 October 1991, Hibernian sensationally revived, winning the eighth major honour of their life cycle.

'Glorious Hibs back from the wilderness' was *The Scotsman*'s headline in recognition of the League Cup triumph. It was more than that, reckoned *Scotland on Sunday* who went with 'Back from the brink'. No, tell it like it is, insisted Alex 'Chiefy' Cameron of the *Daily Record*: 'Back from the dead'.

Back from the crossbreeding for sure. In the animal world this can preserve endangered species, but in Mercer's fiendish laboratory it would have seen Hibs subsumed into the dominant Jambo strain. Tom Farmer buying the club from the receivers prevented extinction or, in some fans' eyes, worse. (The Hibees as Hearts' gimps? We'd be better off potted heid.) As the saviour was the tyre and exhaust king, Farmer was more interested in crossply than crossbreeding and definitely more committed to Leith, community and Hibs' continued role in it.

The final against Dunfermline Athletic was no classic. Not intellectual like 1972's League Cup triumph, nor goal-tastic like the one in 2007. But it didn't have to be a chess match or a youth club rave-up; it simply had to happen and have Hibs involved. The back-story, about how there very nearly wasn't any kind of sequel for the club, provided more than enough drama.

Just a few short months before, the names on manager Alex Miller's teamsheet would have been found in the receiver's ledgers. What would the boyhood Hibs fans Mickey Weir and Keith Wright have fetched in a fire sale? Much-travelled goalie John Burridge, about to turn 40? Brian Hamilton, dirty work dependable? Or Tommy McIntyre, subbed after half an hour at Hampden previously and banished to the reserves for 18 months? Thankfully we'll never know.

McIntyre struck the penalty which broke the deadlock in a dour-but-so-what? match, his coolness contrasting with the clodhoppingness of fellow scorer Wright who always looked like he was running through treacle in tackety boots. Two goals, remarked Chiefy, which were 'like nails yanked from the coffin which had been prepared for Hibs the previous season when they nearly went bust'.

92

'THE GREEN JERSEYS WILL PLAY AGAIN'

SOME FOOTBALL club owners like to be out there on the pitch, tripping over the ball in tasseled loafers. Some earnestly believe a two-club merger called Thames Valley Royals to be a splendid idea, that it doesn't sound remotely speedway and are shocked when no one agrees. Some own more than one superyacht. Some hang out with the rapper 50 Cent then start dressing like him in garish shell suits and bling. Some are highly conspicuous, around all the time and love being the big I am, confronting the team manager in front of a packed stadium.

And then there was Sir Tom Farmer who claimed before taking charge of Hibs to have only ever attended five football matches in his life. Who probably didn't know the offside rule or, once *in situ* at Easter Road, the name of the main striker or the score in the previous week's game. Yet he was regarded as somehow the odd one?

Football may not have been important in Farmer's life, or even a thing at all, but Leith was important to him and community too. If the local club were cherished by the people, and they would be devastated if the team were suddenly no longer around, then he wanted to save them, which is what the Kwik Fit tycoon did.

Why do they do it? Why do hard-nosed businessmen, driven by the bottom line, get involved in football? Of course, some might have been fans since boyhood so it's their dream, but ego must come into play. If your life until that moment has been spent in boardrooms or surrounded by David Brents, then this is the chance to cast off the suit, pull club colours over your well-lunched belly and listen to a stadium singing your name.

But return on investment isn't guaranteed. Glory isn't guaranteed. And suddenly the fans are grumpy and ungrateful and wondering why you're not pumping in yet more millions and almost blaming you in that ill-fitting shirt for the open-goal howlers and comedy defending.

Farmer had his naysayers among a demanding support. He was basically an absentee landlord, but he forewarned about this, joking that having prised the club from the hands of the receivers he would be spending Saturday afternoons counting the cars coming into his repair depots.

In his near three-decade involvement, Hibs lifted silverware three times and were relegated twice. Over a comparable period pre-Farmer that worked out at more failure and yet more success, which once again seems very Hibs. Crucially, though, the club didn't disappear. They persevered. And Farmer passed them on debt-free.

His saving of the Hibees bookended dramatic intervention from a century before when two men called Farmer – his grandfather John and great uncle Philip – helped restart the club who'd gone bust following the loss of their original ground and many of their star players, lured away by Celtic (see ch. 21).

A more publicity-hogging owner than Sir Tom would have exploited this neat symmetry. But the facts are that his ancestors were vital to the great revival of 1892. It was a struggle – 'twas ever thus with Hibs – but Philip would not countenance colleagues losing faith in the enterprise before standing up at a meeting in Leith Assembly Rooms and passionately vowing: 'The Green Jerseys will play again.'

93

WATCHING IN STRING VESTS, JAMBOS SAW HIBS SCORE FOUR

YOUR FIRST day at school is one never forgotten – a staging post on the journey of life – and for a Hibby neither is the first great goal witnessed at Tynecastle's School End. These days the esteemed local remedial academy is hidden behind what Hearts prefer to call the Roseburn Stand and can no longer be glimpsed from the rest of the stadium, but the original nickname sticks.

Surely any goal at the home of our internecine nearest and dearest is to be savoured? That is true, and those up the other end are effortlessly recalled: Gordon Hunter ending 22-game winless woes in 1994, Steve Archibald's nonchalant left-foot scudder in 1988, Peter Cormack's uncanny contortions for a league-topping header in 1969 – and that sensational, stupefying beginning to the derby of 1965.

Before ground redevelopment ruined football's finest tenemental vantage points anywhere, what must those first nine minutes have been like for Hearts fans living on Gorgie Road with Jimmy O'Rourke and Eric Stevenson sharing four goals? Able to watch for free, able to watch in their string vests, they will have hurled suet puddings at walls, which then cannoned off mass-produced prints of woodland goddess 'Tina', bringing down formation-flying plaster ducks.

Then of course there were the first five goals in the seven-nil game. If ever an opening half of football was going to devalue these properties, sub-prime them at least among flat-hunting Jambos, then that was it.

But there's something special about the School End and shooting north, back in the direction of Leith, and invariably in the second period when a goal might be beautiful and – cherry atop the Empire biscuit – crucial.

Alan Gordon's second on New Year's Day, 1973 wasn't crucial, being the seventh overall, but it was definitely beautiful. Erich Schaedler performed his runaway armoured truck impersonation, crashed into Jim Jefferies, emerged without a dent and sent Arthur Duncan haring down the left wing for a fierce cross which Gordon met with a standing leap, a flick of his blond head and perfect precision for the aesthetically pleasing dunt off one post and then the other.

Duncan himself was a School End scorer in 1971, a sizzling shot winning a Scottish Cup tie following a mazy dribble retro-engineered in the memory so it gets longer every year and currently begins at the top of Robertson Avenue. And in 1985 another winger, Joe McBride, with big boots to fill as his namesake father had been a prolific goal-grabber, began with a sumptuous free kick as part of a School End double.

Leigh Griffiths' free kick in 2013 was even better, even further out, even harder hit and even cheekier, the harum-scarum hitman holding up a thumb in response to Jambos' mocking nickname for him.

Sullen sorcerer Ally MacLeod, who loved a maroon-neutering goal, blurred a volley to win the derby in 1977. He arrived at Hibs just as Alex Cropley left for Arsenal, the pick of the latter's 49 strikes from midfield coming at the School End in 1971. Think George Best against Sheffield United, running one way and shooting the other, turning the goalie to stone, and you've got some idea (though Cropley's beat the Manchester United genius by two months).

Our best School End goal? Perhaps, but the most ecstatically greeted one came from the head of Pat Stanton in 1975. For every yard Duncan's dash gains in the reminiscing, a minute is added to the lateness of this equaliser.

In the crow's nests of Gorgie Road there must have been blowouts of toasters and Teasmades leading to spontaneous human combustion. In Diggers and the other hostelries, in response to wild Hibby roaring back at the ground, mouthfuls of heavy will surely have been sprayed across the floors. Jambos keen to celebrate the presumed victory had only been allowed into the pubs at 5 p.m. Back then, a game not having concluded by that hour was rare. How great it was, how great.

94

'IF YOU WANT ENTERTAINMENT, GO TO THE CINEMA'

WHENEVER I think of Bobby Williamson now, and his stint as Hibs manager, I see Steven Seagal. Specifically, Seagal in *Half Past Dead*, the lumbering action hero's low-brow bullet-fest from 2002. The year, if not quite the movie, is highly significant.

I know, I know. How can an action hero be lumbering and how can a bullet-fest be anything other than low-brow? Well, if nothing else, Seagal should be admired for his bullishness and bloody-mindedness in carrying on regardless in defiance of critical opinion. And that was Williamson too when he declared – with *Half Past Dead* an available option at the time – 'If you want entertainment, go to the cinema.'

Williamson would probably most like to be remembered for blooding young bucks like Scott Brown, Kevin Thomson and Steven Whittaker, but in Leith it is that grouchy, grumbly sound bite defending the team's style or non-style which chimes with his name.

He arrived in 2002 for a rescue mission. A Red Adair – or Red, White and Blue given his Rangers connection which he maintained was a big part of the problem for the Hibs support – to save the club from relegation. He was replacing a Hibees hero in Franck Sauzée which also counted against him but he duly secured enough points for a scramble to safety, a feat which the fans celebrated in song: 'He's fat, he's round, he stopped us going down, Williamson, Williamson . . .'

What then? Dreary football, mainly. Not what Easter Road wanted. Did Williamson really believe in the kids? He tried to trade the inconsistent dazzle of two of them – Whittaker and Derek Riordan – for some unspectacular solidity from Inverness. So did he have a point regarding movies, which can be packed with crowd-pleasing moments and have happy endings guaranteed in a way that football by its very nature cannot?

I've looked back at the films released during the Williamson era and the comments on online review aggregator Rotten Tomatoes. There was *Big Fat Liar* ('Only very young children will be able to dive into the story without banging their heads'), *Big Trouble* ('Almost completely unfunny') and *The Big Empty* ('Muddled and weak'). Although *My Big Fat Greek Wedding* was a hit, Big Boaby's assertion doesn't acknowledge that sometimes film and film-maker are simply the wrong combo. And just as football matches aren't played on paper, so the successful transition from script pages to screen is not a certainty.

What else was on at the flicks? *2 Fat 2 Furious*. Sorry, *2 Fast 2 . . . The New Guy* ('Joyless dreck'). *Bad Company* ('This film has literally no cause for existence'). *Grind* ('Pretty much a complete waste of time'). And, yes, the tale of Boaby's Hibee reign could almost be written in film titles.

For the fans, those 26 months might have felt like *16 Years of Alcohol*, though not in a good way. A lot of the time they were *Touching the Void*. But if it was *Intolerable Cruelty* for them, it was hardly fun for Williamson who reckoned he was *Against the Ropes* from day one.

So we come back to *Half Past Dead*. It's set in a prison – Alcatraz, no less – and we have to wonder how much of an incarceration Easter Road was for Boaby, especially near the end. For Seagal in his cape, see Williamson in his big quilted manager's duvet-coat. Seagal is undercover FBI, posing as a Russian car thief, and for a while he gets away with it, but Boaby knew he was never going to be able to conceal his true identity, in his quaint words, as a 'weegie hun'. And there's a line from a crit of the film which, aimed at its sneering, snobby detractors, might easily apply to the demanding Hibby support with their high aesthetic principles who weren't quite able to put their arms around Boaby: 'Pantywaist liberals! Look upon his fleshy neck, his dodgy hair and his strangely puffy immobile face . . . and tremble!'

Definitely been called worse. Pantywaist liberal? I rather like it.

95

IT WAS 'BEND IT LIKE HAMMY' FIRST

DISREGARDING THE Famous Five. There, I've said it. Still sounds like treachery, mind you, but . . . *disregarding the Famous Five*, is there a Hibee from before my time that I wish I could have seen play? One has always stood out from talking to old footballers. He was the subject of the most colourful anecdotes – hilarious and outrageous with a tragi-comic aspect. How did he ever get himself on to the park? If it was to turn in a quiet game at left-back vs East Stirling that would be one thing, but this was the guy who vanquished Real Madrid.

Pat Stanton, who played alongside Kenny Dalglish, rated him the best. Willie Wallace, who played alongside Jimmy Johnstone, rated him the best. Jock Stein, passing a Celtic dressing room chattering about the most talented any of them had encountered and hearing mention of the usual suspects, stuck his head through the door and said: 'Willie Hamilton.'

What must it have been like, managing Hammy? Stein had to do this at Hibs and Hogmanays could be tricky, such as the one in 1964. Peter Cormack told me: 'Big Jock took the team to the Scotia Hotel. He wanted to keep an eye on us before the Ne'er Day game and Willie in particular.' But Hammy got stocious at the Scotia, availing himself of most of the champagne brought along by chairman Bill Harrower, a well-intentioned but dangerous gesture. 'In the morning of the derby at Tynecastle as we were coming down for breakfast, our physio Tom McNiven was carting Willie up to bed. Tom was a miracle worker – he could sort out plenty of injuries with his magic hands – but that day we all thought Willie would be beyond his powers. Then a few hours later the guy was bossing the game like only he could and scoring the winner from an impossible angle.'

Hamilton had come to Hibs from Hearts where Donald Ford remembered his ghost-like movement and off the pitch he was no less elusive: 'We were staying at Largs before a cup tie. Willie burst the curfew and slumped into bed. He was rooming with Bobby Kemp who said: "Come on, Willie, we've got Rangers tomorrow; be a good lad and get the light." So he picked up a shoe and threw it, smashing the bulb.' Like all quixotic geniuses, as fond of swilling Bacardis as he was selling dummies, Hamilton hated training, as Roy Barry confirmed: 'When it was running in the Pentlands I used to tie a rope around his middle and haul him up the hills. But the things he could do with a football! It was bend it like Hammy before anyone else attempted to use swerve.'

For Hibee karaoke his speciality was 'Twenty Four Hours from Tulsa'. Stanton: '"Do you know," he said to me, "that Gene Pitney and I have this one thing in common." Willie was from Airdrie, which is almost 24 hours from Tulsa, so I couldn't think what it might be. "Neither of us has won a Scottish cap."' He eventually did, away to Finland, when Gordon Marshall is convinced he would have packed nothing more than a toothbrush.

He lived out of his little A30 van and would drive it, according to Wallace, with the *Daily Record* spread across the steering wheel. No fool he, though: on the team coach for away games he never failed to complete the *Scotsman* crossword. Boats and planes provided more mirthful incident, such as when Hammy ignored the Norwegian ferry skipper's implorings for passengers to duck below deck as the fjords loomed. 'Willie stayed and grabbed a deckchair,' recalled Wallace. 'We found him later, completely covered in salt and very nearly potted heid.'

But the World Cup of Willie Hamilton stories comes from Hibs' 1965 tour of North America. Learning there was to be a prize for the top scorer in a game in Ottawa, Hammy responded: 'Will seven goals do it?' The handsome silver salver was a hassle to have to lug around. At the airport, ignoring team-mates' wails, he casually folded the plate in half so it would slip into his holdall.

Some doubt has been cast on this yarn but Cormack insisted it was true, adding: 'Willie ended up an alcoholic but when he played I think everything about his character – including the drinking – made him the kind of magical footballer he was.'

Plates, balls, they could all be bent to his will. It was back in Canada where he died as a bricklayer, at the tragically young age of 38.

96

PALS TALKED INTO HIS RIGHT EAR, ASSUMING HE WAS HALF-DEAF FROM THE ABUSE

DOES IT strike you as odd that in the story of Hibs, a crummy old sitcom like *On the Buses* figures twice? Well, I told you this was going to be an alternative history. After Ally Brazil (see ch. 32) there was Joe Tortolano. They were together in the team for six months, Tortolano's debut coming in 1985 at Clydebank's Kilbowie when Brazil scored a rare goal. The latter had transmogrified from frog to handsome(-ish) prince. The newbie didn't know it but this would be his journey too.

It began with a message from his mum. '"There's been a phone call for you," she said. "A Mr Blakey." I was like: "Does she mean that gormless idiot from *On the Buses*? Am I going to be offered a job as a bus driver?" Even though I sort of knew it wasn't going to be that Mr Blakey because he was a fictional character, I had buses in my head. One of my uncles drove a bus, you see, so it seemed logical. I called the number back: "Hello, Mr Blakey, it's Joe Tortolano." The voice on the other end said: "It's Blackley, Joe, John Blackley, the manager of Hibs."'

Like many Italo-Scots, the clan's roots were in ice cream, his great-grandfather setting up operations after the war in the Raploch district of Stirling. Starting out on the wing, Tortolano came to Hibs after knock-backs elsewhere including Tynecastle and quickly decided he was in the right place. 'One of my first questions was: "Don't you use old tyres here?" At Hearts they were strapped to your back for running up the sand dunes at Gullane. Training at Hibs you got to see balls – luxury!'

There was a promising start and in a titanic Scottish Cup tie against Celtic he looped over the cross for Eddie May's best-of-seven winner. Then he struggled, becoming the goad-to guy for the hard to please.

Pals would talk into his right ear, assuming he was deaf in the other one from all the abuse on his torrid touchline beat. Some of it was deserved. 'There was a game against Falkirk – don't know if you were there, hope not – when one, two, three, four times in quick succession I let the ball bounce over my foot and out for a shy. They were still getting the subby ready when I put the heid down and walked – I knew it was me coming off.'

Andy Goram, his goalkeeper, would put a vicious spin on the ball when throwing it to him to ensure he was paying attention. He failed to convince stadium car park orderlies that he was a player. 'This guy wouldn't let me use one of the bays reserved for the team. He even shouted over to his mate: "Hey, Wullie, have you heard of Joe Tortolano?" For Christ's sake, I'd been at the club eight years by then. So I had to park out in the street.'

He fared even worse under Blackley's replacement Alex Miller. 'I began to dread Saturdays. If I didn't find a green jersey with my first pass I'd hear one grumble. Next mistake, five more. "For Christ's sake, Tortolano! . . . Fuck off back to Italy." Hibs had a few guys who got it in the neck: Benny [Brazil], Snoddy [Alan Sneddon], Hammy [Brian Hamilton]. This'll sound terrible but I'd want one of them to be first to muck up and take all the heat, and maybe I'd be able to get away with an average-to-crap performance.'

For two years Tortolano was by his own admission 'absolute shite'. Overweight from too many pizzas, he trained harder, switched to full-back and improved to middling-to-respectable. Then came a further upgrade: decent-to-no' bad. An endearing nickname: Tartan Lino. Finally a song, which might have been ironic but sounded like Verdi or Puccini when picked up by his good ear after all the moans and groans from before: 'Joe, Joe, Super Joe! . . .'

97

'HOW THE HELL DID WE MANAGE TO SIGN *HIM*?'

A FRIEND calls it all differently. The league in which we play, at least most of the time, is the 'Pree-miership'. The song we sing, celebrating the club as mighty conquistadors, goes, 'Oh we've played in Morocco . . .' when strictly speaking it's the southern part of that exotic land. And the little Trinidadian trickster, what was he called again? 'Russell La-*tapy*,' insists David, channelling Henry Fonda in *12 Angry Men*, the lone, courageous voice fighting for emphasis on the second syllable.

None of this is important; it just makes me and my other pals smile. And in Latapy's case that's the automatic response to the merest mention of his name, however it's pronounced.

Besides, for -tapy read tappy, an old playground game of one-touch football in which our man would have excelled. And then read tippy-tappy, delicate kisses and whispery caresses of the ball which were his speciality, defenders unable to get it off him and reduced to chasing in and out the dusty bluebells. Or up and down an M.C. Escher staircase.

Every so often a club like Hibs get lucky and, attempting to keep the spluttered pie crumbs to a minimum, the faithful will cry: 'What's a guy like this doing *here*? How the hell did we sign *him*?' One such moment came in October 1998 at Somerset Park, Latapy peering into the Ayrshire gloaming, sizing up the rough playing surface, the rough opposition and the rough imploring of his skipper, John 'Yogi' Hughes. All of that must surely have seemed a long, long way from the Caribbean, sparkling sands and the other clichés of paradise. And soon it would be Greenock and before long, Clydebank.

Except Latapy came out of Port of Spain's most violent housing project. His dad abandoned the family when he was just two. His football pitch was a rock-strewn clearing not much bigger than a six-yard box. Games were restricted to three-a-side, winners stayed on. That's how he learned to become such a brilliant ball-hugger.

Crowded defences never bothered him. Thickets of pale, hairy Scottish hurdies never bothered him. He'd bob and bounce, skip and swerve, like he was dancing – cliché alert – Caribbean calypso. The classic Latapy goal was the final one in the 6–2 vanquishing of Hearts – totally tropical.

If only he'd stuck to Lilt, though that was never going to happen for a playmaker-slash-playboy, and especially after he'd been sold Edinburgh by manager Alex McLeish's guided tour of the New Town. Latapy made careful note of every fleshpot and hotspot, then was equally diligent about visiting them all.

He was nominated for FIFA's World Player of the Year. He won 81 international caps. Like the cricketer and childhood pal Brian Lara, he's feted in his homeland where a high school has been named after him. You wonder what he could have achieved if, as legend has it, he didn't smoke 40 fags a day or this wasn't a typical night out: 'Gin and tonic, brandy and coke, vodka and anything. It can get to the stage where even if they gave me petrol I'd probably drink it.'

And Hibs fans wonder what Latapy could have achieved in the 2001 Scottish Cup final if, riding with another good buddy, Dwight Yorke, and a couple of blondes in the back seat their car hadn't been stopped by police bouncing in the wrong direction down a one-way Edinburgh street. Without him – he was effectively sacked – the team lost meekly.

He told me how earlier in his career in Portugal he stayed in the house for six whole months. 'I lived like the book says but didn't notice any difference in my game. Couldn't run faster, jump higher, keep the ball any closer to my feet. And not having a bit of fun I was miserable. That wasn't going to help my football.'

Back in Trinidad, Latapy played in the wonderfully named Sunshine Snacks League. For Hibbies he was their sunshine snack, an explosion of effervescence, quickly over. All too soon it would be back to the pies.

98

'WE WATCHED ENCHANTED HIBS SUPPORTERS CHEERING THEIR TEAM'

CRINGE. GAME changer. 100%. Just three from the 2025 Banished Words List, the annual charge sheet produced by Lake Superior State University of terms and phrases which have outlived their usefulness and become, well, cringe. Some things you should never say, such as: 'There's no such man – or, hey, whatever the self-identification – as Santa Claus.' Another, especially in Leith and ever since 5 August 1972, is: 'It was only the Drybrough Cup.'

Only? *Only*? This was not the Full Members' Cup, the naffly named English tournament which got progressively more embarrassing with sponsorship (Simod, Zenith Data Systems). Nor was it the – hud me back – Autoglass Trophy or the Milk Cup, the latter of which these days sounds a bit like an inclusivity initiative to soften football's inherent machismo.

Drybrough & Co., who'd been in business in Edinburgh since before 1750, were warned off Scottish football's existing competitions by the game's beaks. Undeterred, they adopted punk's establishment-flouting DIY approach and instituted one of their own.

It wasn't inclusive – nothing like. You might have called it the Elite Members Cup because only a select few clubs who'd scored the most goals the previous season could compete. Normally Rangers would have expected to be involved but not in the inaugural year. Airdrie, despite finishing a modest ninth, five places below them, banged in more goals thanks to the two Drews, Jarvie and Busby, and a last-day 7–1 thrashing of Falkirk, which would go down in history as then Bairn Alex Ferguson's worst-ever result in football.

Hibs – and Rangers – were invited the following season. Alan Gordon inspired the Hibees to victory in the stormy semi-final between the sides and then it was back to Hampden and Celtic again, their conquerors in the Scottish Cup final three months before.

Gordon – the best centre-forward in the country who'd be a Rest of the World pick for German World Cup star Willi Schulz's testimonial – netted another double and harassed Billy McNeill into an own goal. 'What the hell's going on?' wailed the Celtic fans. 'We normally win everything!' Some of them swarmed on to the park attempting to have the game stopped. Hibs being Hibs did toss away their handsome lead, and press box veterans must have been formulating intros for a complete collapse, but the team shook off their dwam to lift the cup in extra-time with a couple of crackers.

An eight-goal final. It had been revolutionary, with lines drawn across the 18-yard boxes to reduce offside calls. It was effectively summer football with the crowd in short sleeves, Simon shirts omnipresent. And for Hibs – the sunshine bathing the players in the greenest green – a major psychological barrier had been smashed. 'The greatest show on earth' was the headline on Allan Herron's match report in the *Sunday Mail* while *The Scotsman*'s John Rafferty opined: 'One wished all managers and referees had been there so they could see how attractive football can be.'

Only the Drybrough? 'There was much pleasure to be found at Hampden,' Rafferty continued, 'as we watched enchanted Hibs supporters cheering their team as they took away a cup at last.'

The club almost didn't know what to do with it. Next home game there was a victory parade, although this was the trophy plonked on to the groundsman's lawnmower with the sponsors' name on the side misspelled.

The following season, Gordon again the hero, the cup was retained. When Drybrough's Craigmillar brewery closed in 1987, last orders were watered down with tears.

99

'THE TEAM MEAL WAS CHICKEN BASICALLY RUNNIN' ABOOT'

IT SEEMS highly unlikely when Derek Riordan and Garry O'Connor were tearing up youth football together with Edinburgh's famed nurseries Hutchison Vale and Salvesen that they would have been fantasising about how far, geographically, their gallus talents could take them in the game.

Everyone assumed that here were a couple of proper homebodies, probably with ambitions confined to playing for Scotland – both of them did – and if lucky, running out at Hampden with Hibs, although losing the 2012 Scottish Cup final prompted O'Connor, on being handed his runners-up medal, to chuck it away in disgust.*

But Deek made it all the way to China and, equally gob-smackingly, Gaz to Russia which makes you wonder about the catch-up conversation between the skinnymalink and the sizeable unit possibly beginning something like this: 'Mate, we've both played under dictatorships. Superpowers feared the world over. Ginormous, overbearing, snooping, silencing, fuck off empires. How did that pan out for you?'

Their stories chime. Both mentioned corruption to me,

* There was a sad Hibee symmetry to O'Connor's actions. His Hibs lost the final 5–1 to Hearts. Forty years previously John Blackley's team were hammered 6–1 by Celtic and he would discard his medal in the same fashion.

and chaos off the pitch. O'Connor at Lokomotiv Moscow had to get used to four different managers while for Riordan at Shaanxi Chan-Ba it was 'a new guy every month'. As Riordan explained, they could have shared the same story. 'I turned down Lokomotiv when maybe I should have gone there. Gaz, my best mate in football, was desperate for me to buddy up with him. But he had the girlfriend and the bairn and I thought I'd end up playing gooseberry.'

The Muscovites' sales pitch to O'Connor went like this: 'In this apartment block, our great and glorious former president Yuri Andropov lived – choose your penthouse.' He went for one with chandeliers and a Jacuzzi. On top of the tax-free basic of £16,000 a week, there would be £100,000 bonuses for winning derby games (14 of them in a season) and £250,000 if he lifted the Russian Cup, which he did, scoring the vital goal. But being able to watch from the hot tub as Vladimir Putin's motorcade rumbled to the Kremlin quickly lost its glamour. The language was a problem, constant police checks highly irritating and when O'Connor's partner fell pregnant everyone began pining for home.

Riordan's Chinese adventure left him far from sated. More sour than sweet and the food was definitely an issue right from the welcome banquet when the chicken was 'basically runnin' aboot'. Then the menu at a team dinner was 'some strange animal's feet, what I was told was frog and other no' right stuff'.

Riordan was relieved Xi'an had consented to having a handy branch of Subway but the place was much less tolerant of footballers from the West being swearie-mouthed. A censure left him grumpy and the club were forced to admit: 'The man has disappeared.' There were lots of frustrations, uppermost being the modest quality of the team. 'I was playing with guys you could have pulled out of The Gunner* and that's no joke.'

* Riordan's Granton local, at the time we spoke run by his Aunt Maria and Uncle Frankie.

Veteran coach Donald Park had his hands full with two enormously talented kids who also had a flair for mischief. 'They both should have achieved much more. Garry's a decent guy, just daft. He got carried away with his success, made a load of money and frittered it away.* Deek's mistake was staying in Edinburgh; he had to leave his friends behind. But he was the most gifted young player I've ever seen.'

Riordan and O'Connor taught Park something important: 'The significance of a youngster's environment to his development. I remember [fellow coach] Ian Westwater saying: "Deek's just looked me in the eye and told a whopping big lie." I said: "He comes from Granton, that's what a boy has to do there. He's not Corstorphine or Currie like you."'

Riordan was ballsy enough to want to see what the world had to offer and so was O'Connor, continuing a fine Hibee tradition of being open to new opportunities and new lands. 'Aye, maybe we could have done more,' admitted Deek, 'but dinnae forget it was a dream to pull on a Hibs shirt. For me that was massive, as it is for loads of laddies where I'm from.'

* Among other things, on a Ferrari (crashed), a Bentley and a £2,000 tracksuit. 'That's exaggerated,' he's claimed. 'More like £1,000.'

100

THE DIRECTORS PEED IN A CHAMPAGNE BUCKET

'CENTENARY SPECIAL,' boasted the match programme, but in truth it wasn't any different from other editions with the usual, dependable ads: Butlin's, Kensitas ciggies, the Americana discotheque, holidays in Yugoslavia, the Fairbairn's offy, ex-Hibees goalie Ronnie Simpson's sports shop and 'cut-price LPs' including *Cat Stevens' Greatest Hits* at £2.19 from Sound Centre, 17 Easter Road.

But the game would be special as the editorial explained: 'Hibs could not have found more suitable opponents for this celebration than England's champions and we are indebted to Derby County for accepting the invitation without a moment's hesitation.'

What, you're thinking, Derby don't exactly sound glamorous? Maybe not these days but listen, kids: real, actual life did not begin with 'the Prem'. English football excited us in 1975 without all the hype and overkill of © 'the best league in the world'. It was strictly rationed on TV, pundits hadn't been invented and *Shoot!* magazine was all the comment and analysis we needed. Scots were prominent in every team and in cross-border skirmishes Scottish sides took plenty of scalps, in the grisly terminology of the era. So, yes, we were excited by English football though by no means in awe of it.

But exactly how had Derby become champs? That was still a puzzle, adding to the intrigue of the challenge match. The playing surface at the Baseball Ground was atrocious, the last clump of grass disappearing deep into the primordial mud by mid-October, meaning a permanent gluepot thereafter. And there wasn't one obvious superstar, though Francis Lee had scored an 'interesting . . . very interesting' goal against Manchester City, strangely denied the award for the season's best.

But they did have the clever . . . very clever duo of Kevin Hector and Alan Hinton. The Scottish . . . very Scottish Archie Gemmill and, less obviously so, Bruce Rioch, while the manager was another Scot, Dave Mackay, who would be strangely denied some of the title acclaim due him, as if the team had been on automatic pilot since the departure of Brian Clough, the precise course plotted and left on a chalkboard by Ol' Big Head.

There was, I reckon, none of this cynicism or suspicion wafting around Easter Road on the balmy evening of 4 August, two days before the 100th anniversary of Hibs' founding – no matter that Mackay had once been a Jam Tart with a derby record of W14, D1, L3.

He'd left Edinburgh for England apprehensively, recounting when we met his shock at being summoned by Tottenham Hotspur while at home with his parents – the phone hardly ever rang and never during *Sunday Night at the London Palladium*. Then, in Big Smoke dwellings previously occupied by ventriloquist Terry Hall, his panic at finding Lenny the Lion in a cupboard, not realising it was almost certainly one of many spares.

But Mackay quickly became a mighty force, winning a league and cup double, charging up and down terraces to rehabilitate his snapped limbs, grabbing an extremely irritating Billy Bremner round the throat – and at Derby knocking heads together after a players' sit-in protesting at Clough's exit with directors too frightened to face the mob, barricading themselves in the boardroom where they had to pee in a champagne bucket.

Perhaps unsurprisingly, the back-story was better than the tale of this match. Derby had paid Hibs the compliment for the centenary of not turning up slightly flabby and still in hols mode like Manchester City and Coventry City in 1979's Skol Festival Trophy. Unperturbed by finding lush grass under their feet, they won 1–0 thanks to a goal from Rioch.

101

LIKE SUBURBANITES WANTING TO BE FIRST WITH HOT TUBS

ON THE road out of Tranent, on the way to Ormiston past fields, it's easy to miss. The sign is small, sinisterly so, and surely the minimum possible lettering size without contravening road safety regulations. Countless episodes of *The Avengers* began like this. And then Steed and Emma Peel would infiltrate the semi-rural terror lab to thwart the evil boffins with a rolled-up brolly and sexy karate. 'HTC'. What can it possibly mean?

Hungarian Telephone & Cable Corp, maybe, or Hyperbolic Time Chamber? Help The Community? Honda Total Care? Housing Tax Credits? Hear The Cheers? Hipster Troll Carwash? Hebrew Theological College? Horribly Troubled Contraption? High Tech Crap? All of these and more turn up when you Google acronyms and abbreviations, but strangely not 'Hibernian Training Centre'. These guys really don't want to be found. What do they have to hide?

Oh, just the tactics for Saturday. If a football club are serious about competing these days they need their own physical jerks complex. And, regarding what's in these complexes, they're competing with each other. Like suburbanites wanting to be first, or if not that then better, with bi-fold doors or decking or corner bars or hot tubs.

Rangers opened Murray Park in 2007, Hearts moved training to Riccarton in 2004, Celtic started setting out the cones at Lennoxtown in 2007 and that was the year Hibs decided they needed to keep up with the Rob Joneses, East Mains becoming operational a few months after the big baldy Englishman had lifted the League Cup.

The thing about all of them, all such facilities everywhere, is that they're nowhere near stadia and far away from fans. To interview Kevin Thomson when he was at Middlesbrough I had to go to Darlington. Sunderland's centre is at the seaside. I had to add another hour to my journey to meet new Birmingham City manager Alex McLeish with the hefty taxi fare displeasing my editor – and Big Eck wasn't too happy that day either. He thought he was done with Hibby pestering re the 2001 Scottish Cup final ('If only you'd forgiven Russell Latapy – we could have won it!' See ch. 97).

In the old days footballers trained on their pitch. There's grainy footage of the Famous Five bending and stretching at Easter Road. Think of the stress that put on the grass. And think of the stress on the home dugout roof from Bertie Auld stomping on it, shirt slashed to the waist to show off his European Cup winners' medal, and supervising his Hibs men as they ran round the perimeter. 'We had to do four miles every day with him roaring at us from his podium,' Gordon Rae told me. 'Derek Rodier got it the worst, and because he'd been to university Bertie called him a poof. "He's cut that corner! Right, everyone start again!"'

Not being bothered, either by groupies or the grudgeful, should allow players to get on with sessions which nowadays are presumably far more sophisticated. That's the theory behind the complexes. But if players only visit the ground on matchdays there's a risk of a disconnect between team and supporters.

What's wrong, every now and again, with the under-performing centre-back being subjected to a bit of friendly(-ish) fire from a big, hairy-arsed fan who spots him in the street? Ivan Sproule from Tony Mowbray's team was smart enough to realise the importance of players not becoming too remote and chose to live near Easter Road and use the local buses, co-op and barber's shop for immediate insight into what the fans were feeling.

When we weren't feeling good about Hibs it became tedious to hear one new signing after another rave about East Mains. They were only being polite, and thinking they were saying the right things, but what the hell was everyone doing out there all week when the results were dire?

When David Wotherspoon was at Hibs there was a funny story that an auntie of his worked at a Tranent baker's shop and every Friday he'd be dispatched on a cake run. But the story was only really amusing if the team were playing well.

And when Ben Williams was the goalkeeper he admitted the side were too soft and identified part of the problem: 'We have a fantastic stadium and a fantastic training centre. We're spoiled.' As soft as Spoony's fondant fancies in the Terry Butcher era, they would end up being relegated.

Williams's admission didn't go down well with Pat Stanton. When he was captain Hibs had to scrabble around for somewhere to train. 'We got chased by the Easter Road groundsman, we got chased by park-keepers all across Edinburgh. Sometimes we'd end up on the beach at Portobello, just as long as the tide was out.'

This would be the Hibees' lot, even when they were eclipsing Real Madrid. 'The day after that game, what did the Madrid guys do? Retreat to some splendour, no doubt. Maybe we'd have been daundering down Craigentinny Road, wondering if the Seafield parkie would be in a charitable mood.'

Stanton is mindful of not sounding like one of the Monty Pythons in their sketch where each tried to outdo the other's impoverished beginnings ('Hole in the ground, you say? We got evicted from ours!'). State-of-the-art centres like East Mains are viewed as essential for the modern footballer, but just so long as HTC doesn't mean High Tech Crap. Otherwise the team won't Hear The Cheers.

102

JOE BAKER'S WHITE BOOTS

DESPITE IT being my dearest wish, there was never a Johnny Seven* under the Christmas tree. But I did get Adidas Santiagos. My first football boots. Well, the first ones not from Woolies. Which weren't called Winfields. Which didn't have moulded soles. Which lacked the naff band the colour of on-the-turn liver. Which weren't plasticky and provoked peer-group abuse.

Now I could play with the big boys. Now I knew the capital of Chile. I loved my Santiagos and, while my bedroom remained a tip, loved cleaning them. The studs – screw-ins! – would be removed so I could tease specs of dirt from the threads with the awl of my Swiss army knife. A Zurich watchsmith couldn't have been this painstakingly precise, and for getting into the perforations on the famous three stripes, the knife's toothpick worked best. I've never cared for anything like I did those boots, the Dubbin-ing going on for hours until they were returned to their box-fresh state and an unmistakably black sheen.

And then what happened on 16 January 1971? Joe Baker walked out on to Easter Road in *white* boots. Down by the terracing wall, hundreds of little pairs of eyes – some in NHS specs, others behind balaclavas, many encased in parka snorkels – gawped in wonder.

* 'Seven guns in one! You're a one-man army!' The toy that was every warmongering whippersnapper's dream.

A few years before, these eyes gawped at TV going colour. My memory of the seismic transformation is of a London bus trundling into view in an old movie and not being grey. The thing is: we all knew that London buses were red, that grass was green and that tigers burned bright. We might have guessed that Big John Cannon's youngest son in *The High Chaparral* was nicknamed Blue on account of his eyes. And it seemed safe to assume that *Batman* and *The Monkees* had been hiding their light under the bushel of monochrome transmission (though we hadn't anticipated quite how pop-art fantastic they really were).

But boots? They were always black. Never deviating, as black as the Good Book. Baker's sacrilege, then, was sensational.

Well, it was to us. Older fans might have reacted with suspicion, even alarm, much like Terry in *Whatever Happened to the Likely Lads?* when camp hairdressers expressed not just an interest in football but comprehensive knowledge of Bulgarian over-physicalness.* We, on the other hand, craved those white boots.

But could Baker, back at Hibs for a second spell, play in them? In highly conspicuous white, sclaffings and miscontrols were going to be so much more obvious and unfortunate, not least after our fathers had filled our heads with great stories from the centre-forward's first spell – his four goals at Tynecastle aged 17 to blow Hearts out of the Scottish Cup, the nine in another tie against Peebles Rovers and the double in the Nou Camp in the victory over Barcelona.

The crowd for that game in '71 was huge. Aberdeen hadn't conceded a goal in aeons, or lost a match for even longer. It was a dank afternoon, in spite of our pioneering floodlights (see ch. 29), but the fabulous Baker boy dazzled in his choice of footwear. And, perhaps to ensure the boots stayed as clean as possible, he netted the winner with a flying header.

* The classic episode where Bob and Terry did their darndest to avoid the result of an England game so they could watch it on TV later.

Nowadays boots come in every colour under the sun so it may be difficult to appreciate the shock and awe caused by a player smashing convention like this. And safe to say my mum wasn't the only one pestered by pleas for a pair just like Joe's.

103

BREXIT MEANS BREXIT AND SCHAEDLER MEANS SCHAEDLER

WAS THAT it? Six and a bit months? Was I and thousands of others just too obsessed with Turnbull's Tornadoes? It must be rare in sport for a team to be so raved about, so revered and so remembered – to have been celebrated in songs, books, VHS, the hippest movie since *Easy Rider* and not forgetting the quirky subversion of gendered bedroom dynamics (see ch. 67) – and for that to be the sum total of their time together.

I'm being ruthless with the stats here. The last Tornado to arrive was Alan Gordon in January 1972 but because of a long suspension for Alex Edwards and then a long recovery from injury for Alex Cropley, they didn't take the field as an eleven until 9 September of that year at Tynecastle. Then on 21 March of the following year at Hajduk Split's Stari Plac, which translates as 'old ground', the old goalkeeper Jim Herriot played his final game and strictly speaking the Tornadoes were never the same again.

That said there were plenty of stirring performances from the others both before and after that six and a bit months, and some that were sensational. A big shout-out goes to their deputies including Johnny Hamilton, John Hazel, Des Bremner and Tony Higgins, the latter two going on to achieve permanence in the side. But for the record this was the team enshrined in the iconic* Harry Gilzean poster glimpsed in the bedroom of *Transpotting*'s Renton during the cold turkey scene where a baby only a mother could love crawls across the ceiling before swivelling its head through 180 degrees: Herriot, John Brownlie, Erich Schaedler, Pat Stanton, Jim Black, John Blackley, Edwards, Jimmy O'Rourke, Gordon, Cropley and Arthur Duncan.

In my O-grade year I knew this line-up better than just about anything. Certainly better than the 'E, et, est' song my French teacher attempted to hammer into us, and the 'Estonia, Latvia, Lithuania' chant when history lessons reached the Baltic War, its only rivals for rote learning, while the Stanton-Edwards-Brownlie triangle was far sexier than geometry ever was.

But a great team can't get by on sex alone. Someone, maybe a couple of guys, have to do the heavy lifting and make the tackles. I mean, all the Tornadoes could tackle. In those days no footballer was allowed to slip a note to their manager requesting they be excused. But Black and Schaedler could *really* tackle.

They were the most unsung, the least quoted, the most underrated, the least likely to score a goal. Schaedler from left-back managed five in 13 seasons, all because there was no one still standing in his immediate vicinity who needed to be tackled. Black was the centre-half, a hugely unglamorous role. These days as a No. 5, top level, you're probably assured of a celebrity travelogue and your own clothing range. Our man netted just the once.

Black hailed from the most ordinary-sounding village in Scotland – Plains in North Lanarkshire. 'Cilla was our centre-half and thank goodness,' said John Blackley. 'Pat and I were sometimes paired together at the back but that never worked as we both wanted to step off and read the play. Neither of us wanted to attack the ball but Cilla did.'

* Overused, pretty much flogged to death, please note that this is the term's only appearance in these pages.

The son of a German prisoner-of-war, Schaedler was the Tornado most like an actual tornado in the ferocious way he played. There are old right-wingers dotted around the country who feel sharp twinges in their legs when they bend down to pick up the cat litter tray or fasten the Velcro on their slip-on shoes which can be directly traced back to a thundering challenge from Shades.

Remember 'Brexit means Brexit'? That was Theresa May's slogan on becoming prime minister in the fallout from the 2016 Euro referendum. She was attempting to demonstrate firmness in her determination to follow through on the vote and take Britain out of the EU. Instead what transpired were three and a half years of prevarication and confusion. Back in the day, though, Schaedler meant Schaedler. Few things in Scottish football have ever been more definite and unambiguous.

Oh, and in answer to the question about whether we were too obsessed with his Hibs team, the answer, just as unambiguously, is no.

104

RELEGATION, GOOD FOR THE SOUL

PROTECTED SPECIES. That's what we think of goalkeepers now. They know that at a corner kick if there's so much as a narrowing of the eyes or a curl of the lip from the opposition then the referee will immediately blow for a foul. This is why goalies slick their hair with immaculate partings. Sculpt and curate their beards. They can groom and groom safe in the knowledge there will be no more stramashes. Guys, you're looking kinda hunky, even with your skinny, under-developed legs, which of course stay hidden, though never again with Hamish McAlpine's bobbly joggers.

So thank goodness, in 1933, for a centre-forward's right to steamroller the custodian into the net. Hibs were in the old Second Division, trying desperately to get out. Their first attempt hadn't gone well. A seventh-place finish behind Forfar Athletic, St Bernard's, Stenhousemuir, Raith Rovers, St Johnstone and East Stirlingshire, champions thanks to Jimmy Hart's 33 goals.

The following season the much-travelled Hart – Glasgow-born via Crewe Alexandra, the Welsh League, Bradford Park Avenue etc. – brought his prolific plundering to Easter Road and hit a hat-trick to down St Bernard's which seemed to be returning Hibs to the big time, only for Armadale and Bo'ness to be banished from the division meaning the wins against these sides were expunged from records. The Hibees had to claim the title all over again.

In their report of the key match against Dumbarton, *The Scotsman* described how visiting keeper William Simpson had fielded a cross then was 'promptly charged by Hart. He eventually managed to clear but the referee agreed with the Hibernians' view that the ball had been over the line.'

Just 3,000 witnessed this licensed thuggery and the team made good their escape. Hibs were waiting for Willie McCartney and they were waiting for Gordon Smith. A flamboyantly attired manager and a flamboyantly skilled winger. But until the outbreak of war they'd flirt with relegation again.

Now, what's coming next might seem patronising and perverse, but I am not devastated when Hibs tumble through the trapdoor. I probably don't want them to make a serious habit of it but every now and then is fine.

Top-flight clubs shouldn't be a protected species, and we've already avoided the drop once through league reorganisation. Our mighty Premiership – heavenly table of succulent skills and some sclaffing – can engender snobbery. Relegation – and Queen of the South, Montrose etc., you'll hate this bit – is good for the soul. It's humbling. It makes you appreciate the dedication, resourcefulness and quiet ingenuity that goes into a scene which might have to be categorised as sub-diddy.

It makes you appreciate proper football grounds, old-school and quirky, history wrought from corrugated iron, which you might not have visited before and for some supremacists, beyond the odd cup tie, never will.

I remember a game at Parkhead, Martin O'Neill's Celtic having handed out a casual 3–0 beating, and a Hoops supporter and friend of a friend was giving us a lift back to Queen Street Station. All around the country car radios were tuned to the afternoon's results, but not this one. None of the other scores would affect our driver; none of them really interested him. Hibs fans have to be interested; their future is not assured. As 1980, 1998 and 2014 confirmed.

The gaps between our relegations are about the same, so successive generations of supporter have forged paths through what must seem the unchartered interior to reach the likes of Alloa Athletic. In 2014, feeling like the American railroad pioneers of the mid-19th century, Hibbies successfully negotiated a change of train at Stirling, located Recreation Park, bonnie Ochil Hills at one end, KFC at the other – and witnessed their team being duffed up.

On the journey home the result exacerbated the general disorientation, which must have been the same for the travelling fans of 80 years before. These fields. This . . . Clackmannanshire. It was all too strange for one poor soul. 'I need *coast*,' he wailed. 'I need to see *coast*.'

But the club haven't sulked through their demotions; they've treated the lower league with respect and treated the wee toons to glimpses of some sumptuous talents: George Best in 1980 and Franck Sauzée and Russell Latapy in 1998. And from their position in steerage they've lifted the Scottish Cup, becoming the first second-tier winners since East Fife 78 years before.

105

'A GAME AFLAME WITH ANTAGONISMS'

BE CAREFUL what you wish for. Hearts lost a title on goal average and moaned about it, only to lose another later by the replacement method – goal difference. Switching round the systems would have meant two Gorgie Road parades. Instead the open-top bus stayed in the garage.

We may snigger but goal average did for us too, Rangers claiming the championship in 1953. Our goal difference was superior, also our goal tally – 13 more – although there is no record of Easter Road coming over all entitled and whingeing.

In 1961 the away goals rule would have seen the Hibees into a European final. Unfortunately UEFA had not yet come up with the wizard wheeze to reward teams for boldly going continentally. This was Hibs' second Euro semi in five seasons and yet while the earlier one (see ch. 66) is always referenced, the clashes with Roma are almost forgotten.

And they were clashes. 'A game aflame with antagonisms' wrote *The Scotsman*'s Hugh McIlvanney of the first leg in Leith. 'The Italians were given to charging and lashing out at anyone who got in their way, and one or two who did not.'

It had all begun so civilly the day before with the *Daily Record* admiring the fine Italian tailoring of the *Giallorossi* as they dined in their Edinburgh hotel on 'tomatoes and mushrooms with rice, steaks and trifles', washed down with 'rich red wine'.

The chief troublemaker in a match witnessed by 35,000 was Roma's Argentinian midfielder Francisco Lojacono who according to McIlvanney 'flew into a frenzy, hurling kicks', his targets including the referee. There was a serious threat of a riot to rival the Barcelona blow-up (see ch. 109) before the game finished 2–2.

For the return in Rome's Stadio Olimpico, the pre-match centered on Hibs' centre-forward Joe Baker, still only 20 but seemingly promised to Torino after the tournament although Roma, with the Eternal City's paparazzi following him around eternally, were threatening to gazump their Serie A rivals.

The photographers were much better at tracking Baker than the Roma defence who, in a game played in a freak thunderstorm with giant puddles holding up the ball, were left flummoxed by a simple switch of shirt numbers. Two goals in three minutes from the star striker had Hibs tantalisingly close to the final. 'Instead of a couple of men constantly on my tail I got some room to move,' he told the *Record*'s Tom Nicholson.

As lightning flashes zigzagged overhead, Hibs fought with 'tremendous gallantry', according to *The Scotsman*, but 'did not receive the best of the refereeing decisions'. Roma rallied for another draw, 3–3, although instead of quiet relief the home fans pelted Baker & Co with fruit. A play-off was required, but where?

The Italians insisted they 'could not possibly' travel back to Edinburgh and proposed Switzerland or France. Crazy as it seems now, Hibs opted to return to Rome, the board swayed by a 50–50 split of the gate money which would exceed anything from a neutral location.

Eddie Turnbull was the Hibs trainer. In his memoir, *Having a Ball,* he wrote: 'The Roma officials got hold of chairman Harry Swan and let's just say he was very easy to deal with. I don't know if money actually changed hands but some deal was done and there was also the promise from Roma of a week's holiday in a five-star hotel.'

Maybe embarrassment explains why this campaign is rarely mentioned. Baker for one lambasted the board for 'selling the team down the river'. And then there was the scoreline – a 6–0 hiding with *The Scotsman* reporting Roma fans 'whistling and laughing' at Hibs' attempts to retrieve a hopeless situation. In place of the earlier monsoon there was a heatwave and the stadium bowl sizzled like a giant skillet pan. Idle for an entire month, the Hibees were risotto-ed.

106

YOU TOO CAN HAVE A BODY LIKE MINE

THE BALL is round. The abs are ripped. The chest is carved. The arms are sculpted. The thighs – the thighs! – are marble-esque. What are we to make of the reign of John Collins who definitely uttered one of these things?

'The ball is round, it's meant to roll' is his. When he said this in 2006 there was a huge collective sigh of bliss round Easter Road. He gets us! He's one of our own! He's just flown in from glitzy Monaco and he's going to be great! But it's the other stuff that did for him as manager. So the story goes, anyway . . .

Collins the player looked after himself. At Hibs, he was a full-time midfield prodigy and a part-time model. Team-mate Joe Tortolano told me: 'I thought I had a no' bad physique but John's was something else. He'd pose in the mirror in just his jockeys. "Call me The Viking, Joe." "Aye, you would suit horns coming out of yer heid."'

In the narcissistic New Romantic era, the toothsome two-some were in demand to be the faces, and bodies, of boutiques and tanning salons. 'Electric Beach in Lothian Road promised us ten complimentary shots on their sunbeds,' added Tortolano. 'We're still waiting for our vouchers.'

When Collins got his ticket out of Easter Road and progressed his career most fulfillingly, 'upper body strength' entered the game's lexicon. Previously, no one had really used these words in the context of footballers who by and large were still knocking off from training at noon and calling that a day's work.

So when he returned to Leith he seemed like the perfect mentor for Scott Brown, Kevin Thomson and the rest, impressing upon young, cocksure talent the importance of good habits.

It didn't quite work out that way. There was a mutiny over his methods. Much of that talent would leave, which would probably have happened anyway. And after little more than a year, Collins himself quit. The official reason was frustration at not being permitted the funds for new players, but he must have been hurt by the rebellion.

The popular Leith myth is that he sauntered around training showing off his six-pack and urging his charges: 'You too can have a body like mine.' Thomson told me: 'He was certainly big into sit-ups, press-ups, pull-ups and dips. Because he was such a cultured, creative player I think the boys were surprised he put so much emphasis on the gym.'

Michael Stewart was another disappointed in Collins: 'When John arrived he would have commanded instant respect because of his achievements as a player. But he lost that almost instantly. The training wasn't tough. It was the same thing every day, not progressive, just crap.'

Befitting his captain's role, Rob Jones was more diplomatic. 'I think John wanted to influence the players in a positive way. He was teetotal, had an incredible career and was still very fit. I never saw him challenge the guys to beat his sit-ups record or anything like that. He tried to tell them: "If you live your life this way, you'll do well." But, you know, maybe that could have been explained better.'

Perhaps. But fundamentally wasn't Collins, scorer of a World Cup goal for Scotland against Brazil, correct about how the game should be played on the ground rather than in the air? The man qualified for a description which has fallen out of fashion in the game's phraseology – he was a 'carpet artist'.

One more time: *the ball is round*. It should be the Hibs motto, inscribed underneath the club crest. *The ball is round.*

PR firms would charge a fortune to dream up a slogan that simple, that brilliant. *The ball is round.* The thing is designed to rotate across a flat pitch, or indeed a flat stomach.

107

'THEY CALLED ME TROTSKY AND A WEE COMMIE BASTARD'

AT THE height of Covid, Jason Cummings had had enough. Exasperated like the rest of us by the prime minister's special adviser and his smugness as the self-appointed cleverest man in the world. Aiming an Instagram potshot at Dominic Cummings, Hibs' Scottish Cup hero opined that the No. 10 chief of staff was 'tarnishing my name' by dragging it through the mud with his lockdown-flouting actions – all the way to Barnard Castle and back again.

This was typical Jason, a footballer with a keen sense of humour, who went on to propose that he – 'Cumdog', his nickname and wrestling moniker – should take over the government gig. He was also displaying political awareness, something rare in football, although once upon a time the Hibees were led by 'Jackie the Red'.

Jackie McNamara was handed one of the toughest jobs in the Scottish game when he arrived at Easter Road in 1976 from Celtic. Unbeknown to him, this was a swap deal and Pat Stanton was travelling in the opposite direction so he would have to replace a legend. But when you're a card-carrying communist very little daunts you.

That was the year McNamara was outed. 'I remember the headline on the back page of the *Scottish Daily Express*,' he told me. '"Two sensations rock sporting world". One story was about the ice skater John Curry being gay, the other was about me being a commie. My dad said: "Think yourself lucky the paper didn't mix the pair of you up."'

I remember my dad alerting me to the revelation about our new signing. He seemed impressed whereas I was mystified by the 'card-carrying' bit. Did McNamara hide this card in the heel of his shoe? Was it made from rice paper – or doused in cyanide? At the time the only communists to have entered my world were the sworn enemies of two laconic Scots secret agents – Sean Connery as James Bond and David McCallum as Illya Kuryakin in *The Man from U.N.C.L.E.*

McNamara explained: 'The old man was an engineer at Harland & Wolff, one of the youngest shipyard shop stewards on the Clyde, and big mates with Jimmy Reid. He was a communist so as soon as I could I became one too. As a kid I delivered the *Soviet Weekly* and *Morning Star* round Easterhouse and got abuse for it.' When he took his politics into the dressing room the abuse continued, although mostly it was good-natured.

'At Celtic, Billy McNeill called me a "wee commie bastard" and to Kenny Dalglish I was "Trotsky". While the rest of the team were playing cards, I'd be reading *The Ragged Trousered Philanthropists*.' He was just 22 when he tried, and failed, to turn Parkhead into a collective, possibly an independent socialist state. 'It was the Drybrough Cup, we'd just beaten Rangers, and Jimmy Johnstone told me in the bath: "Grand a man, Jack." I thought: "Brilliant, I can pay off the house." But then it transpired that me as one of the young bucks would only be getting 250 quid. My view was that wages were wages but if you were out there on the park, bonuses should be the same for everyone. It had to be a fair day's pay for a fair day's work. Unfortunately Billy and Jock Stein didn't quite see my point of view!'

At Celtic he was injury-hampered. 'I was left on the scrapheap by them so Hibs saved my career.' Eddie Turnbull was a 'genius' with a superior football intellect to Stein. 'I loved Big Jock too but Jim McLean at Dundee United used to phone up my centre-half George Stewart after training: "What did Eddie have you doing today?"' Typical of Turnbull's vision was successfully switching the player he nicknamed Jackie the Red from midfield to the role of sweeper.

McNamara is still bolshie about fairness – and greed. 'Every breath you take is political.' Every breath he took as a Hibee was hugely appreciated in an uncompromising era. 'There was an Edinburgh derby when Derek O'Connor broke my leg. A complete accident but Bertie Auld, who was manager by then, told me to keep playing. "It's all in your heid, son. Just have a jag and a lump of sugar."'

108

THE DADDY DAYCARE BOSS OF THE SUGAR-HIGH HIBS

MAYBE TONY Mowbray's Hibs didn't achieve all they could and should have. They lost one Scottish Cup semi-final from a winning position and were humiliated in the other. But nothing bad will ever be said about the man, the daddy daycare manager whose permanent sugar-high charges jumped over scattered plastic toys to produce many highlights, both on top of their heads and on top of the pitch.

The most astonishing performance, the most brazen, came at Ibrox in August 2005, a few games into a season which had already featured another hammering by Hearts. It was astonishing for many reasons, not least for how Scott Brown ran and ran at the Rangers defence like he was in his native Hill of Beath, relieving the teenage boredom of a late summer's afternoon by challenging a rival scheme's speediest: race to the Slim Jim statue* and back again.

(Astonishing, too, that when he moved to Celtic their fans never saw Broony rampages like these ones. One of the great sights of noughties Scottish football simply disappeared, like the insistent, clamorous song of some rare woodland bird.)

Back to Ibrox: another astonishing thing was Garry O'Connor's opinion on the 63rd minute substitution. Passing

* Jim Baxter, another famous son of the Fife village.

the player replacing him, Gaz dead-eyed Mowbray: 'What the fuck's he gonnae do, eh?'

Astonishing of course for Ivan Sproule's gleeful hat-trick but also for the fact he was at Ibrox that day and not back in Northern Ireland, his brief Hibee career ended in disgrace.

A few days before the match on a wild club night out, Sproule head-butted Guillaume Beuzelin. 'Footballers do stupid things, especially footballers who've been bevvying,' Sproule told me. 'I wasn't proud of that and the next day, in floods of tears, my bags were packed and I was for home.

'Born in a village of just 300, I'd been Crocodile Dundee in Edinburgh, out of my depth and knowing nothing. I thought it would make life easier for the manager if I cleared off.

'Tony called me in to Easter Road, sat me up the top of the empty main stand and we had a heart-to-heart. I wasn't the easiest player to manage – Jesus how many times was I sent off? [Four, Ivan] And yellow-carded? [29].

'I was frustrated at always being subby. But Tony knew what kind of boy I was. Knew about my dad dying when I was young and about my big brother being killed in a car crash. Knew how desperate I was to do well at football in their memory.'

None of us was earwigging but it's easy to imagine Mowbray's soft, slow, kind, encouraging words to his jet-powered winger, one man who'd suffered personal loss to another.* More difficult to comprehend is how he kept the playgroup happy, head-butts to a minimum. Sometimes it must have been like herding cats.

Mowbray's Hibs would not have beaten Eddie Turnbull's Hibs but I reckon their fizz, flair, flamboyance and fearlessness might have been too much for Alan Stubbs's Hibs, even Alex McLeish's Hibs.

* Mowbray lost his first wife Bernadette to breast cancer in 1995.

Sproule again: 'We had an exciting, crazy, fun, mad, brilliant dressing room but, just as well, there was this mellow guy who was our manager and he was a genius. If Tony had told me to run up and down Arthur's Seat ten times I would have done it. Actually he once did tell me to do it – right after I'd crocked wee [Merouane] Zemmama at training. But after that lovely chat we had I gave him a big hug. For me and a few boys he was a wonderful father figure.'

109

THE GERMAN REF WAS BEATEN UP, DITTO THE LEITH POLICE

DAVID BECKHAM cruises round bustling Manchester in his car. Nice and slow with the window down. His hair, a national obsession but for once not demanding attention, is flat and scraped back off his face with an Alice band. It must not detract from what the superstar wants the world to see: the little, ickle scrape on his cheek after a difference of opinion with his manager when a flying kick from Sir Alex Ferguson sent a pile of jockstraps hurtling in his direction.

So was Hibs not repairing the dents in the door to the referee's room caused by incandescent Barcelona players kind of the same thing? Not really. Becks was engaged in a PR tyranny, as he's been his entire career, in this instance attempting to show that player power, or rather celeb power, beats the dinosaur roar of the last great disciplinarian manager on earth. The Hibees were, without any hoo-ha, leaving the damage as a little reminder of the most momentous of victories and, if anyone asked about it, perhaps a source of inspiration to the next generation.

At the end of 1960, and the first half of a season when Hibs had leaked four goals to Airdrie, Kilmarnock, Motherwell, Hearts and six to Celtic to sit unremarkably in mid-table, they travelled to a daunting encounter in the Inter-Cities Fairs Cup. Barca were the reigning champs. As well as defending their trophy they were going for the European Cup and had just seen off Real Madrid who'd dominated the latter tournament since inception. In the Nou Camp Hibs conceded four again, but also scored four of their own.

They led 2–0 then 4–2, Tommy Preston netting the third goal. 'It was a pretty good left-foot shot which went in off a post,' he told me. 'Their guy was catching up so I said to myself: "Come on, Tom, you'd better skelp it." I think we shocked Barcelona. The crowd were certainly upset. At the end they were all waving their white hankies.'

Joe Baker scored two of the four and, alarmingly close to kick-off in the return, was spotted by fans sprinting to Easter Road from his engineering works, still in dungarees. No one expected to see Barça's Luis Suárez in such a state of high anxiety – he'd just been crowned winner of the Ballon d'Or.

But during the match, Baker only stopped running when he was hacked down, which was often and by increasingly desperate means, and from one of the free kicks his header put Hibs ahead. The roar must have been heard in Fife. Back came Barça to level then lead in the tie for the first time. Preston scored again before, five minutes remaining, Hibs were finally awarded a penalty. Cue Catalan conflagration. The German referee was beaten up and when the Leith police rushed to his rescue they were attacked too. The game was halted for 12 minutes. How on earth did regular penalty-taker Sammy Baird ignore the almighty rammy and maintain equilibrium?

He didn't, telling team-mate Bobby Kinloch: 'I'm shite-ing myself.' Don't worry, said Kinloch, just pick a corner. 'No, Bobby, you don't understand, I'm *actually* shite-ing myself.' Who could blame him with a linesman next to be knocked to the ground?

Kinloch, who'd been calmly sitting on the ball in the centre circle, assumed responsibility and it was 7–6 to Hibs for the most notorious, most explosive, most thrilling win in their history, at least until 21/5/16. The ref officiated from the mouth of the tunnel for what time was left then dashed to his room.

Despite Barça's attempts to break down the door, he got out of the stadium alive.

The coolness displayed by Kinloch would have been evident pre-Hibs as an RAF airman and also afterwards when, to supplement his puny wage playing football stateside, he joined the cops and was involved in a shoot-out with Detroit gangsters.

Back at Easter Road the severely holed door went with the rest of the main stand when that came down some 40 years after the conquering of Barcelona. History in a skip – did we Hibs it again?

110

TYNECASTLE WAS AN ASHTRAY

IRVINE WELSH has lost it. That's what I was thinking when, on his way back from an extended American stay, he proposed a venue for our meet-up. What, Gleneagles? That posh golf hotel in the middle of the very unradgey Perthshire countryside? Then I remembered where he'd been holed up over the previous month and decided he'd utterly, completely lost it. Florida. Trump country. He'd been Mar-a-Lago-ing it in a two-speed, reverse functionality buggy with POTUS!

No, no, Gleneagles Townhouse, what used to be Vlad the Mad's* bank in Edinburgh's St Andrew Square. There's a members' club and they wanted Welsh for it. Well, there he was, slurping an Americano after a boxing workout and it was a cast-iron certainty that no one in this plush lounge or in any confab anywhere in the Golden Rectangle – before, or in the future – would be talking about the sacking in 1990 of Millwall's supposedly impregnable Cold Blow Lane by Hibs casuals.

'And the following day,' he said, 'some West Ham United hard nuts took out an ad in the *Evening Standard* saying well done to the Hibbies for an impressive job.' The Hammers are the *Trainspotting* author's English team, though he initially chose them because of old-school Upton Park and now London Stadium is 'just terrible, the hardcore next to the football tourists waving their camera phones and no one enjoying themselves'.

* Vladimir Romanov, bonkers boss of Hearts of Midlithuanian.

Still, there will always be Easter Road for Welsh. Except he was soon telling me how he could have been a Jambo. *What*? Stop all the clocks. Especially the Memorial Clock at Haymarket and the one above the bar in the Diggers.

'Folk think of Leith being a Hibs district and it is now, but pre-war it was very Jambo because of the docks where you had to be a mason to get a job. So my dad's old man, a docker, was Hearts, as were his three brothers.' Smiling, he added: 'The Famous Five converted folk to Hibs but my grandad and my uncles were kind of legacy Jambos. My dad was the only Hibby in the family, the first of a new breed for the Welshes. He was the youngest so he maybe went his own way to get attention or as a wind-up. Whatever, Hibs were the greatest gift he could ever have bequeathed to me!'

Welsh's first game, the one which hooked him aged nine, was the last of the 1967–68 season, a 3–3 draw with Kilmarnock. 'Colin Stein hat-trick, Gerry Queen, Eddie Morrison and Tommy McLean for Killie.' That's anoraky recall and he was quickly kitted out in strip and scarf (knotted round wrist), followed by the quintessential piece of memorabilia for his generation – Turnbull's Tornadoes in poster form, caricatured by Harry Gilzean, which was pride of place in his bedroom, above the bed . . . until one day it wasn't. 'I was back from London. Kitchen-portering, working the cross-Channel ferries, some building sites. Mum had had a big clear-out. She told me: "You're 27, not a laddie any more; it's time you grew up." David Bowie went as well.'

In the lead-up to that moment the laddie had followed Hibs everywhere. By train with the prospect of scraps ('British bulldogs, basically. You got mobbed up for self-preservation but you sensed your own power'). By bus ('You could get on with cans, wine, anything – even as a 14-year-old covered in plooks. I preferred the excursions to official supporters' club buses with their grumpy committee men: "Sit doon and shut up ya wee bastards!"').

While still at school young Irv bunked off for power-cut games* and excursions to Kilmarnock lasting three days (maybe as a consequence of missing the geography lesson about map reading). Hitch-hiking from the Big Smoke for the 1979 Scottish Cup final, he and a mate were tripping on acid as they stumbled up the A1 wondering why no cars would stop for them and were later arrested face down in their service station egg and chips. Banged up in a cell for the night at Grantham on the eve of the game, he still made it to Hampden.

It took him three years from the poster incident and his mum Jean's pep talk to find his path. 'It was never going to be nine to five. I really wanted to be a pop star but Pubic Lice never made it. We were sub every crap band that played the Vortex. I tried every instrument and couldn't sing a note. The rest of the group progressed but I never did.' So: books, fiction, stories from the schemes.

Welsh has featured Hibs almost every time, even if only to name a dog Cropley. Thrice married, the club have been more than anything else the big constants in his life, even when living far from Easter Road. 'In Chicago I recruited mates to the cause and they all had the shirt. Dublin was good for a Hibby in exile as it has a lively supporters' club. I'm back in London now so I watch the games at The Sheephaven Bay, my Camden local.'

He returns to Leith often to catch up with a dwindling coterie of football pals. 'Jimmy is just the same – a massive indestructible drinker, he had a key to Carrick Knowe golf club and our match-day sessions used to start there – but some are dead or dying.' The passing seasons have brought maturity and perspective. Well, almost. 'When you're a kid, before you discover girls and pubs, you're obsessed with football and your team losing is the end of the world. As you get older you become more

* During the 1970s miners' strikes when the floodlights had to be turned off, evening games took place on weekday afternoons.

mercenary. Win, great. Lose, ach it's all a lot of shite, back to the more important things. But recently Hibs have been stressing me out. Or maybe they always have. As a Hibby you can be this highfalutin renaissance man, but every now and then you'll revert back to being an idiot.

'I feel so lucky they're my team. They're of the community, invested in it. Leith has changed but Easter Road is a smart stadium in an area that nowadays boasts every kind of diversity.' Once again he thanked his father, Peter, for passing down Hibs. 'Dad was of the generation that watched Hibs one week, Hearts the next. I went to Tynecastle but the smell from the breweries made me sick. Tynie was confined, like you were trapped in an ashtray – a big, piss-stained ashtray. But at Easter Road looking over to Arthur's Seat there's always been that beautiful expanse of green. It's like what [*The Football Grounds of Great Britain* author] Simon Inglis said: "The green of Hibernia merges almost imperceptibly into the green of Caledonia." Easter Road symbolises freedom.'

Peter passed away when Welsh was young and Jean a few years ago. 'I wanted to do something to mark her death. From being a kid with my *Oxford Atlas of the World*, Alice Springs had always fascinated me so the next time I was in Australia I decided I was going to do a Jim Morrison, walk out into the middle of the desert and feel her spirit, maybe Dad's as well, to thank them for life and for Hibs. I was the only fella there and what I felt was . . . nothing.

'That was disappointing but then a few days later in Perth I snuck into a matinee of *Guardians of the Galaxy 3*, no one else there either, and pretty soon was crying my bloody eyes out. I was like: "Sorry for being such a bad son . . . Mummy come back! . . . Daddy I love you!" How bizarre is that?'

Very, but it also seems very Hibs.

111

HE COULD PLAY KEEPY-UPPY WITH A SOAP BUBBLE

AS AN example of the shifting complexion of football, consider Hibs' three League Cups. In 1972 the goal heroes were sons of Niddrie and Clermiston. In 1991 the clincher came via Craigmillar and the man of the match hailed from West Pilton. And in 2007 the players on the scoresheet were born in Stockton-on-Tees, Shrewsbury and Fez, Morocco, home to Tommy Cooper's headgear.

'Just like that', as Tommy would say, the game changed. Less local, more international. Five home-bred players still featured in the victory over Kilmarnock but in February 2024 at Aberdeen when Jojo Wollacott replaced David Marshall in goals for the last eight minutes, Hibs, for the first time, had no Scots on the field.

Does this matter? In principle, yes. It is not being insular, or worse, to have as an ideal a Scottish club majorly made up of Scots. You could ask what an academy is for if not to be a conveyor belt towards this end. You could ask – though this is not just a Hibs problem – why so few kids break into the first team. But it's worth remembering that any disconnect between club and fans might not be the fault of the players, wherever they've come from. A faceless hierarchy can cause it, nincompoop PR can exacerbate it.

However . . . principles, shminciples. They matter less if the team are winning. And winning a cup. And winning it with a full-back like Englishman David Murphy, perhaps the only real challenger to Erich Schaedler for a place in the all-star Hibee select of the last 50 years. And a Frenchman like Guillaume Beuzelin with a touch so delicate he could play keepy-uppy with a soap bubble. And Abdessalam Benjelloun, the fellow from Fez.

Maybe '07 had less drama and urgency about it than the other two. In '72 Hibs hadn't won a major trophy for 20 years. In '91 they'd come back from the near-dead. But the best side since '72 kept stumbling to semi-final defeat and needed something to show for their exciting football before breaking up completely.

Already Derek Riordan, Garry O'Connor and Kevin Thomson had gone (though all would return later). It's a parlour game to try and fit every bonnie talent from the noughties into an eleven. Can there be places for Michael Stewart, Chris Killen and Dean Shiels, all absent from the final, as well as Benjelloun's countryman Merouane Zemmama? Not unless defensive berths are jettisoned, and sometimes it seemed that had already happened, so committed were the Hibees to the top end of the pitch.

Imagine the side with a commanding goalie. And a commanding centre-back alongside Rob Jones, scorer of the first goal against Kilmarnock. And maybe John Brownlie at right-back behind the cavalier Steven Whittaker, although of course Onion was no less of a frustrated winger. And should there be an enforcer in the midfield or would that be treacherous to Tony Mowbray's total flair concept? What if . . .? What if . . .?'

As it was, and by '07 managed by John Collins, they didn't need to worry too much about defending in the final. Steven Fletcher, who described to me a perfect connection with his left foot was him having 'paintbrushed it', scored two of the goals in the 5–1 win and the other two came from Benjelloun.

Chucked into the side three years previously, Benji seemed absolutely clueless. The opinion quickly formed that here was another foreigner completely ill-suited to the rough and tumble of the Scottish game. When he scored his first goal he didn't know how to react and so sprinted back down the field alone as if fleeing a burning building.

By the final, however, he'd got the hang of things and his sand dancing bamboozled the Killie defence. At the final whistle he celebrated by donning - what else? - a fez. In Scotland. In a howling snowstorm. It was perfect.

112

'I VISITED THE PLAYERS IN THEIR BATH AND APOLOGISED'

IN 1962, Decca Records told the Beatles: 'Don't call us . . .' It was the most notorious kiss-off in showbiz history, prompting much speculation over the identity of the cloth-eared exec with Dick Rowe the prime suspect.

Two years later *The Scotsman* looked forward to Real Madrid's visit to Easter Road and declared: 'Hibs will get a thrashing, probably 7–2 against.' What in its broadsheet days was the esteemed journal doing, getting involved in the messy predictions game? Best leaving that to the small funnies. Maybe, though, the paper couldn't resist. After all, Real were the football celestials who'd won so many European Cups they were using one as a waste-paper bin, another for rice for the paella and a third for the Persil ('Washes whiter than white!') It was fun to speculate on how many goals they would score, and perfectly safe, though the author couldn't quite put his name to the piece which was bylined 'Our own correspondent'.

What happens? Sen-sation. Jock Stein's team do score twice but the mighty Real with Ferenc Puskás, Paco Gento and José Santamaría not at all. This is unprecedented. Europe's most glamorous, most successful rarely lose and never to a Scottish side, so: yet another Hibee first. There's an old song: 'Barcelona, Real Madrid, they will make a gallant bid . . .' It's sung all over the place but really, few clubs get the chance to play these Spanish giants, never mind topple them. Hibs, though, had achieved the double – *el doble*.

There might have been nothing at stake although at no stage did it feel like that. Pat Stanton told me how all day excitement in Edinburgh seemed to ratchet up every hour. Before TV drenched us in football and its biggest stars this was a genuine event. Stanton's father reported from the top of the main terracing that the turnstile queues snaked back all the way to Lochend Park.

The previous 24 hours had been thrilling enough for 400 youngsters squashed up against the stadium gates and trying to peer through the slits at a Real training session. Hibs chairman William Harrower ordered the gates to be opened and the kids swarmed on to the enclosure. This impressed the *Sunday Mail*'s Rex Kingsley: 'From gestures like these Hibs' old glory may one time spring again.'

Real were impressed by Hibs with Kingsley quoting club officials being 'shaken' by the skill and speed of a side they expected to be able to scrunch up and pop in the bin. In recognition of his fearsome pace, Gento might have earned the nickname 'the Gale of the Cantabrian Sea', but the Madrid defence could not tether the flying colt of Leith Walk, Peter Cormack, just turned 18, or the flicks and feints of Willie Hamilton, a player who'd been 'discarded by so many clubs' according to *The Scotsman* but on this night of nights showed he was 'worth six of Puskás'.

The paper that forecasted a clobbering couldn't have been more effusive about the 'spectacular' and 'glorious' 2–0 win: 'The terracings were alight . . . the roof was almost lifted off the stand . . . never before had the dour citizens of Edinburgh displayed such ecstasy over a football victory.'

Then the scribe, W.H. Kemp, revealed himself to be the man who'd written off Hibs so spectacularly: 'With Jock Stein I visited the players in their bath immediately after the game to compliment them and apologise for underrating their potential. I was grateful for the opportunity.'

113

IN THE INTERESTS OF BALANCE, THE TIME WE LOST 7–0

IT'S NOT all glory, glory, you know. There are times following Hibs when things will get gory, gory. You have to learn to take the Roughie with the smooth. Alan Rough was not the goalie, goalie on 30 December 1995 when the Hibees' most celebrated and sung-about scoreline was done unto them by Rangers. It was Jim Leighton, at the time the Scotland keeper, who picked the ball out of the net on seven occasions.

Meanwhile at the other end, just about the only effort to make the match reports was a sclaff from a distance of 35 yards, struck by Joe Tortolano 'in the manner of a Ronnie Corbett 6-iron' which bobbled past the post. To extend the metaphor, presumably Bruce Forsyth was guffawing so much he toppled backwards into a bunker, taking Jimmy Tarbuck with him, while Kenny Lynch, also in hysterics, drove his buggy straight through the pro's shop.

Ibrox guffawed that day. From the home fans there was what *Scotland on Sunday*'s Graham Spiers called 'derisory snorting . . . donkey noises . . . mooing and crowing'. All of it aimed at Hibs and 'absolutely dripping with hot sarcasm'.

For fair-minded observers of Scottish football, however, those always with a protective blanket at the ready, this was no laughing matter. Not just humiliating for the Hibees but the credibility of the league. 'Murderous' was a word used in more than one paper. For while this was nine-in-a-row Rangers, the team of Brian Laudrup and Paul Gascoigne, Hibs at that moment were third in the division so purportedly best of the rest.

The manager was Alex Miller. If the 1991 League Cup was his zenith then that might have been his nadir. 'The most embarrassing experience of my life,' he groaned, and while he saw out the rest of that season, a few months later he would be gone.

Miller time – and there was ten years of it – forms one of the strangest chapters in our story. A trophy winner who was never loved. A dull pragmatist who signed Steve Archibald, Keith Wright, Darren Jackson, Michael O'Neill and Kevin McAllister, often playing most of them at the same time, and when he didn't, chucking on Mickey Weir or Kevin Harper. A manager with the demeanour of someone who'd been bundled off to Siberia, this before he went there of his own free will. And when we met, not miserable but funny, not cautious but unafraid of voicing bold opinions, a rounded man who talked movies and very much his own man (when he wasn't being henpecked by his wife).

After five managers in succession who'd all played for Hibs, he was the first in a long while with no previous connection to the club. More than that, more Vladivostok-remote than that, his team had been Rangers, a red (white and blue) flag on the CV for many Hibbies.

Let the record show, though, that he didn't desert the club in their darkest hour as the finances imploded and Wallace Mercer spied what to the bon viveur Hearts supremo was a Béarnaise-sauce-coated business opportunity. Maybe the football under 'Squeaky' wasn't supersexy but some pretty frigid bosses would follow him. Unlike them he hoisted the League Cup. Unlike them he didn't get Hibs relegated.

Let the record also show that in the middle of that Ibrox collapse, when Gazza for a giggle picked up the yellow card dropped by the referee and pretended to book the official, and when Tortolano would have been forgiven for wallowing in his own misery, it was the luckless Hibee who tried to avert the censure of the Geordie japester which still stands as Scottish football at its most constipatedly crabbit.

114

'THIS IS SHEER FOOTBALL DELIGHT!'

AM I obsessed? Do I imagine myself right back there? If I close my eyes can I visualise the exact colour of the sky, the precise shade of gloomy grey, and would Farrow & Ball call it 'Civil Service Suit' or 'Hippo's Dismay' or perhaps 'Meat Paste Surprise'?

Can I recall the punctuation error on the match programme's front cover and how it would have been red-penned by my English teacher although that wouldn't happen now? ('Maroon's Journal').

Do I remember how alarmed I was by Hearts' fast start although Tommy Murray's shooting proved as skew-whiff as the programme editor's positioning of apostrophes?

What, then, about the greater alarm provoked by the much easier opportunity which fell to Donald Park and when I see him around now, which is quite often, do I still wonder, if he wonders, how he ever missed?

So can I say with some certainty that despite these fluffs the Hearts fans were sufficiently encouraged to chant 'Easy! Easy!'?

And is it just my memory playing tricks or was Tynie's Shed actually singing 'Donald Ford, give us a goal, a goal, a goal . . .' just as Jimmy O'Rourke banged in Hibs' first?

Was Alex Edwards' back-heel his moment of peak impudence or did that tie with the free kick he flicked up and over the Jam Tarts' wall which, contrary to their club song, was not 'as strong as the old Castle rock'?

After the third or maybe the fourth goal, what was BBC

Scotland commentator Alastair Alexander's considered verdict – perhaps 'This is sheer football delight!'?

Was I impressed when, after a rare save by Hearts goalkeeper Kenny Garland, Alexander free-formed: 'The best continental style . . . fittingly for the first of January as we are now in the European Economic Community.'? (It was the political contextualising which was impressive, not the save, which these days would be termed 'one for the cameras'.)

Could I name seven – unrandom number – of the companies/organisations/products advertised round the track? (Queen Anne whisky, Remington shavers, McEwan's Export, Esso, Royal Navy, Player's No 6 cigarettes and last but not least 'Hot Bovril'.)

Do I accept that Arthur Duncan's first goal was a mishit which Garland in Lev Yashin's all-black should have gathered and that his second was an attempted header which came off his shoulder?

Did I see Alex Cropley's volleyed fourth as travelling in the most painterly of arcs, mimicking the curve of a Botticelli nude in languid repose, although this thought only occurred a few years after discovering pretentiousness?

Do I recollect the dark mutterings the half-time score of 0–5 prompted from the Hearts supporter sitting nearby in the main stand, possibly a self-made Gorgie businessman in his Sunday best even though the game was on a Monday, the look completed by a fine camel-hair coat? ('Fuckin' IRA bastards', repeated several times.)

Do I still smile at what the other Hearts supporter within earshot said to his son, partly to dam up any likely tears from the lad but also, assuming irony was involved, to lighten the macabre mood? ('Have faith, Johnny. We'll get Ernie Winchester back on an emergency loan for the second half.')

Am I willing to acknowledge that O'Rourke's second – the one he shamelessly stole off Pat Stanton – would probably have been nixed by VAR but what a horrible tech tyranny we live under now?

Can I, from that glorious afternoon of Hibee exceptionalism, list the minutes of every goal, including the seventh and The Greatest Header Of All Time, courtesy of Alan Gordon, and yet occasionally struggle to remember the birthdays of a couple of my kids?

And what about the pay-off in the *Daily Record*'s match report by the normally hyperbolic Hugh Taylor who on this occasion was absolutely spot-on – did it go something like: '. . . All the flair of a top team – and by a top team I MEAN ONE OF THE TOP TEAMS IN THE WORLD'?

The answer is yes.

115

THE OTHER TIME WE LOST 7–0

WHEN SCHOOL atlases and globes still contained a fair number of pink bits, but in any case most geographical knowledge was coming from continental adventuring on the football field, there was a memorable 1970 victory for my brave boys. 'Wonder Hibs rout Swedes' proclaimed the *Daily Record,* with the 6–0 scoreline vs Malmö in the Inter-Cities Fairs Cup the most goals I'd seen them score in a single game up until that moment.

Unfortunately the most goals I saw them lose in a single game happened 43 years later, a gruesome Scandi-noir revenge psycho-chiller which screamed out for the headline 'Turnips 0, Swedes 7'.

Malmö were two-nil up from the first leg of the Europa League qualifier but an emotionally charged Easter Road was ready to roar the Hibees to a stirring comeback in tribute to Lawrie Reilly who'd passed away a few days before. The Famous Five's sainted No. 9 would surely be gazing down on his old patch of green, willing continued involvement in the European contests which he helped found. Unfortunately the task was in the hands of Pat Fenlon's Hibs.

Upon this manager's appointment, chairman Rod Petrie, who'd come to football, a business like no other, hotfoot from, er, accountancy, declared: 'I looked into his eyes and I saw a winner.' But before Malmö, the little Dubliner had already presided over the worst-ever result in the club's history – the

2012 Scottish Cup final – and this would turn out to be the second-worst.

Europe's finest began playing each other competitively in 1955 and around the same time came the Eurovision Song Contest. Fenlon's countrymen, and women, had proved themselves brilliant exponents of crap tunes but only grim notoriety was available to him for presiding over Scotland's heaviest aggregate defeat in any Euro tournament. See firsts and standing apart? Sometimes they're overrated.

It was a sultry July evening. The kind, a few years before, where there would be no football and no one was missing it. We would have been perfectly content watching *Seaside Special* with the prospect of verifiable TV fool's gold: Tony Blackburn locked in a cage singing 'Tie a Yellow Ribbon' to four ravenous lions. But an expanded continent had brought extra qualifying rounds for the likes of Hibs and Malmö.

High summer it may have been, though long before the end the haar descended. Had the east coast sea mist ever swallowed up a game whole, causing it to be abandoned? There was a first we desperately sought.

Now, it was easy to call this a freak result and Malmö, who surely couldn't have believed the ease with which they scored virtually every time they attacked, didn't have to be sensational. But maybe the night produced another unwanted first with the lowest player ratings anywhere. Footballers claim never to read papers but they all check their individual assessments. According to the *Daily Mail* every man in green and white was an irrefutable one out of ten.

Hopes of a goal or two so the outcome could have appeared slightly less horrendous had rested on the slim shoulders of Rowan Vine. With Reilly being remembered, the responsibility was too great, and the striker would exit Easter Road meekly – then miss his unveiling at next club Morton after filling up his car with the wrong fuel.

By the way, Vine's rival for the most barn door-avoiding frontman of the twenty-tens was James Collins who, refusing to be outdone by him in the embarrassing postscript stakes, would be caught peeing in a glass at the Cheltenham Festival.

116

COULDA BEEN A CONTENDER, SHOULDA BEEN A HIBEE

IS THERE a Jambo who could squeeze into this incredible story? A prominent, persistent foe swathed in maroon whom we fear but, dammit, grudgingly admire? I think, showing 'beauty and kindness' as it says in our anthem, room can be found – but squeezing will definitely be required and the man knows this. As his calling card for the Edinburgh derby used to proclaim: 'It ain't over until the fat striker scores.'

The terrifying gonk powers of John Robertson can't hurt us any more. Mercifully, he stopped after 27 goals. But he's the Easter Road legend who got away, and not the only one. If the all-star, coulda-been-a-contender, coulda-been-a-Hibee fantasy eleven had played together, then Gordon Strachan would have dinked craftily and even if Willie Pettigrew's snap volleys struck post or bar or arse, then Robbo, skulking like a street-corner knock-off goods imp, would have jabbed home the last-gasp winners.

Coulda been, and deep down really wanted to be? This was the word on the terracing. And I must admit that, just as in another journalistic life when I was forever attempting to convince Bryan Ferry that Roxy Music were best with Eno in the band and couldn't he just give him a call, every encounter with the Tynecastle idol was me trying to get him to address the love that dared not speak its name.

'Here's what it was,' he told me the first time we met. 'My dad, who died when I was 14, was a Hearts fan. Big brother

Chris, who played for them before me, was a Hearts fan. But my eldest brother George supported Hibs. He was, after all, the only one of us seven Robertsons born at Leith Hospital.

'George took me to see Hibs who as you know had a great team in the 1970s. And aged 12 to 15 I trained at Easter Road. Eddie Turnbull wanted to sign me – 50 quid a week. Chris at the time was at Rangers. With the old man no longer around, I needed to show him the contract. Wasn't [chairman] Tom Hart anti-Rangers? He said: "Sign today or you'll never play for this club." He was adamant. Forty-eight hours later I joined Hearts.'

Next time we talked I wanted to know more about George.

'He does everything different. Dad was Labour, he was SNP. And with Dad being Hearts he had to support you lot. He could have been a footballer. He played in the same juvenile team – Melbourne Thistle – as Gordon Strachan. He had trials with Sunderland. Dad told him: "Don't drink, don't smoke and keep away from women." Of course these became George's vices. He's been married four times. A published poet, and a good one. The intellectual of the family, that's George.'

Of course, a Hibs fan *and* a poet! George may have preferred that Easter Road contract to have been signed, but he's been proud of his kid brother, and protective, such as the occasion of Robbo's first derby goal in 1983.

'This Hibby shouted, "Robertson, ya bastard," so George decked him. "You can call that guy a wanker, you can even call him a cunt," he said, "but he's my wee brother who's not long lost his father so never ever call him a bastard."'

And while there were 26 more where that opening strike came from, we shouldn't forget that Robbo went from 'The hammer of Hibs', as the headline writers had it, to 'Hands off Hibs' and fronting up for the protest against Hearts' takeover bid in defiance of his chairman. Beauty and kindness, indeed.

117

THE SECRET CODE EXCLUSIVE TO ABSOLUTELY NO ONE

'MEN LIE, women lie, numbers don't.' So said rapper Lil B. Shakuntala Devi, India's 'human calculator', reasoned: 'Everything around you is numbers.' John Nash concurred, insisting that you didn't have to be a mathematician like him to have 'a feel for numbers'. And Beyoncé, not a mathematician, summed it up: 'We all have special numbers in our lives.'

Hibs fans have a feel for the number seven; it is the special number in their lives. Now, they all loved *Trainspotting 2*, how it continued the Easter Road references from the first film, and also for the bit where Ewan McGregor and Jonny Lee Miller cleaned out the bank accounts of that pub full of Rangers supporters. Because these two knew every pin number would be '1690', Hibbies could laugh at the utter predictability of the Ibrox saddos. But a split-second later they were like, bloody hell, if that was us? . . .

'0762'. The two biggest and most ecstatic victories over Hearts make up our secret sequence, exclusive to absolutely no one. This is the means by which we function in a hectic modern world requiring so many passwords and by which we aim to keep our data, and it follows, our loved ones, safe and secure. If an alternative to the four digits is required we are fairly relaxed about this, just so long as the 7 can be retained in some form. If a word is required for the code then, unfailingly, that will be 's-e-v-e-n'. Honestly, a three-year-old girl playing hide-and-seek who ducks behind the first available tree, big curls showing either side, has applied greater ingenuity and cunning than the Hibby in his attempts to outwit cybercrime.

For years the Ne'er Day derby of 1973 was a seven-studded cudgel with which to beat the maroon-ites. Every mention of the magic number induced a warm glow, occasionally an erotic charge e.g. the *NME* review of David Bowie in the Broadway production of *The Elephant Man.* Lacking the freaky prosthetics of David Lynch's movie version, Bowie conveyed Joseph Merrick's terrible deformity by contorting his body into a seven. What a star!

A new century began with that 6–2 scudding but then Hearts came up with some big scores of their own. From open windows in Tynie tenements, Helen Reddy could be heard on ancient Dansettes with Jambos singing along to the shrill Canuck's anthem of second-wave feminism: 'I am woman, hear me roar/In numbers too big to ignore!'

Four was their greatest margin of victory. 'Pleasing,' as the Gorgie phrasebook would have it. But these wins didn't stop the Hibby taunts about getting to seven. Until that is 19 May 2012, a day that will go down in infamy when 5–1 felt like ten and should have been, only Hearts seemed to take pity on their useless opponents and eased the boot from the windpipe. Jambo veteran Jim Jefferies, bearing the mental scars from having been on the pitch in 1973 and managed in 2000, was raging about that.

Now the Hearts hordes play the numbers game. They revved up smartphones for selfies of them flashing the 5–1 gesture atop global landmarks or while sneaking behind unsuspecting Hibs men, grinning gormlessly. Most prized were the shots where they'd pestered/tricked/sweet-talked/intimidated celebs into displaying all the fingers of one hand and a single digit of the other.

Hibbies just had to suck it up. After so many years of seventh heaven, finally Hearts had a decent comeback. Bizarrely, though, shortly after being snapped as honorary Jambos for a day, it seemed that every single one of the notables would experience a dramatic fall from grace.

Heavily rumoured to be among them were Bill Cosby, Oscar Pistorius and Rebekah Vardy. This motley crew: Prince Andrew, Rolf Harris, R. Kelly, P. Diddy, Boris Johnson. Wait, there was a whole bunch more: Kevin Spacey, Huw Edwards, Morrissey, Post Office chief executive Paula Vennells, Lance Armstrong, Kanye West, Harvey Weinstein, some bloke who looked like Fatty Arbuckle, cancelled a long time ago, Apu from *The Simpsons,* Phillip Schofield and – she really fiveone-d the country's economy – Liz Truss.

Bad luck, them's the breaks.

118

PENALTY KICKS, SUCH A CONTRIVED, CONFECTED CEREMONY

THE GOALKEEPER'S Fear of the Penalty is an art house movie which is partly about the existential crisis provoked by spot kicks, so often an ordeal to be endured because of a team-mate's crime. The other part involves an actual crime – murder. There's a sequel begging to be made right now though it would be more of a black comedy, or perhaps a hagiography in weird tribute to the penalty-takers.

When did penalties, the whole procedure, become such an enormous big deal? How did this start? I like to blame David Beckham for most modern ills and maybe it was when he took a penalty for England against Argentina in 2002. He wasn't just trying to score from twelve yards, stationary ball, no opponents allowed near, keeper required to stay on his line. No, after being sent off in an earlier match against Argentina, and being blamed for the defeat, he was seeking the nation's forgiveness so that he could, you know, *live again*. That was how the penalty was hyped at any rate, and Beckham would have cheerfully given his consent to such a schlocky, Hallmark-scripted scenario. And of course from that moment he was able to stabilise the Becks brand and build, build, build!

And that's a penalty, isn't it? No interference, no distraction, a straightforward, routine function. It's certainly how Joe Davis approached them. He scored the first penalty I witnessed in my very first Hibs game. He scored another in my second game, also in my third, and netted the winner from the spot in my first Edinburgh derby. But there I go using a word like 'witnessed', inferring a penalty was some kind of spectacle, capable of inducing awe. It was perfectly perfunctory. Even at the age of ten I got that. There was no fuss about spot kicks, not like now.

Now you watch them on TV and they involve such a contrived and confected ceremony. The elongated build-up, indulged by the commentators. Look at the chosen one, see how heavily he's breathing as he stands, readying himself. Does he seem confident? What are the shoulders saying, the eyes? Body language expert – help us please! What. A. Moment. This. Is. Classic reality-show pause-for-effect dramarama. It's as if this man, this hero, is about to push Captain Oates back in the tent so he can be the guy to utter the immortal words: 'I may be some time.' He's going to walk through the valley of the shadow of death, he really is. With a vital book, an instant pop-philosophical classic, ready for publication and optioned by Netflix when he emerges through the other side: *Zen and the Art of Penalty-Taking.*

Football's greatness is it's nearly always moving. Rugby has lots of stoppages, which might be why there's so much hullabaloo around its kicks now, all the nonsense with clasped hands as if in preparation for wrenching a sword from a stone or dragging an especially stubborn wheelie bin down the driveway. Footballers are not playing rugby, nor are they golfers agonising over four-foot putts, two sports where slow play is a major issue.

Now back to that penalty and . . . and . . . goal! He's scored! Look at him: he's levitating with the self-congratulation of the logic of his Oneness!* But I repeat: twelve measly yards with everything in his favour. He's celebrating like he's cured cancer, rescued a toddler from a terrible inferno and cracked – not the

* A pinched line from a very funny spoof of *Zen and the Art of Motorcycle Maintenance.*

atom, that's been done – but the unfathomable appeal of light entertainment jobby-wheecher *The One Show*.

Davis, needless to say, indulged in absolutely none of this. No player of his era – the 1960s – behaved with such oneness. Admittedly celebrations – of any goal – were not the freed hostage reunions or *Long Lost Family* money shots they are today, but players back then well understood that marking the successful execution of a penalty with any more than a no-nonsense handshake would have been the height of self-indulgence and the nadir of decadence – and no one knew this better than Davis, a humble left-back.

All told he slotted 39 penalties for Hibs and, though not present at every game he played, I can't remember him missing one. He sported a bank teller's short back and sides, always scrupulously neat and tidy, and there was never any danger of anyone ruffling up that hair as the team filed back smartly for the restart.

119

DON'T MENTION THE WAR

WAR HAS been weaponised and fascism, the word, has been desensitised. Once – in actual wartime – it described pure evil. Now, if you criticise someone for not visibly honouring, in the traditional manner, those who died in battle then you risk being accused of poppy fascism. What must old soldiers, the ones who came through war and were eyewitnesses to real fascism, think about that?

These heroes – and there's another word that's been cheapened by so much casual usage – are dwindling in number. We *should* remember them. But there's an argument that remembrance ought to be a private act and that a public display, an overt one, can look pretty much like a celebration of war. It's a minefield. Not literally, obviously, but probably best to avoid. Unless you're a football fan. Then you wade right into it in big army boots. Not literally, obviously.

Rangers love a man in uniform. Celtic don't love poppies. Hearts think they won the First World War by themselves. These are the kinds of things rival supporters say, not always in jest. Now it's highly unlikely any of these factions consulted the boy Beevor (Antony, author of a dozen war books) or the boy Hastings (Max, approaching 30) to back up their claims. Fandom, after all, is predicated on many things, some of them good (passion), some amusing (one-upmanship, wind-upmanship) and some which are less good (paranoia, jealousy, nastiness).

At an Edinburgh derby at Tynecastle a few years ago the half-time entertainment was a man with a guitar singing about McCrae's Battalion which included in its number 16 Hearts players, seven of whom did not return. The song was loudly booed by Hibs fans.

What a phoney war it is when we squabble over real war. Maybe some booed because war commemoration seems to cover all conflicts and the ones in Northern Ireland and Iraq have no shortage of dissenters. Some supporters of course will boo at anything.

But if the Hibs lot had been irked by a suspected Jambo hijacking of the Great War, turning it into a Hearts story, then as the stadium announcer was at pains to stress, Hibs also served and suffered losses.

And if Sandy Grosert, the Easter Road right-half in McCrae's Battalion, was still alive, he might list for their benefit all the clubs the unit represented including Raith Rovers, Dunfermline Athletic, Falkirk, East Fife and St Bernard's with many fans choosing to march alongside their favourites. Also all the sports – rugby, cricket, swimming, archery, bowls, billiards and just about every discipline in track and field including Scotland's fastest man over 100 yards, plus Scotland's strongest man.

This was Murdoch McLeod who would die on the first day of the Somme, the terrible battle which did for the Hearts quartet of James Boyd, Duncan Currie, Ernest Ellis and Henry Wattie.

Grosert, who enlisted after the 1914 Scottish Cup final, served as a second lieutenant and his bravery in France was recognised with the Military Cross. His citation read: 'For conspicuous gallantry in charge of a platoon during the operations near Roeux on August 27, 1918. When the troops on his left flank and the enemy made a determined bombing attack on his position, he continued to go over the open under fire from one post to another directing and encouraging the men. He held on until only four of the men were left and he was almost surrounded. He behaved splendidly.'

It's funny reading about him back playing for Hibs, such as in the report of a match at Raith when, hit by injury, he was 'compelled to shelter in the pavilion under medical supervision for the rest of the game'. He might have smiled at the depiction of 'suffering' after everything he and his squaddie mates had endured – and maybe too at the monumentally petty disputes between football fans there have been ever since, so often dubbed 'wars'.

120

MICKEY WEIR'S *ANGELS WITH DIRTY FACES* MOMENT

IT'S A gangster classic, and 1930s Warner Bros social conscience at its most urgent: two boys in New York's Hell's Kitchen attempt to rob a railroad car, one evades arrest by the skin of his teeth, becomes a priest and devotes his life to keeping the next generation out of trouble – a job that would be a helluva lot easier if his friend hadn't been caught, hadn't been seduced by money and guns, hadn't turned into the worst kind of role model.

'*Angels with Dirty Faces* – what a fantastic movie,' chirruped Mickey Weir when we met to talk about how his Hibs career owed something to him being much less Jimmy Cagney and a little more Pat O'Brien.

Growing up in the tough Edinburgh scheme of West Pilton, Weir got in with the wrong crowd. 'We were involved in "setting up" houses for break-ins – keeping shoatie for older boys who'd do the stealing,' he explained. 'That paid 20 quid a time – a fortune for wee toerags like us.

'Then one night something went wrong and we were rumbled. We were chased down the Granton Ramps but luckily I had my bike and was able to get away. If I'd been nicked, could I have ended up in a life of crime? One hundred per cent. I screwed the nut after that.'

Weir, who clearly knows his Hollywood history, obviously didn't follow O'Brien's character into the priesthood. Instead his good fortune became the good fortune of aficionados of classic Scottish wing play who thought that the deedle and dawdle, weeble and wobble of tiny touchline loiterers had all but disappeared because of improved diet and everyone getting bigger.

Weir only reached 5ft 4ins. Lionel Messi's growth hormone injections weren't around during his early development – in any case the family couldn't have afforded them – and despite his mother feeding him up with platefuls of tripe, he would suffer the time-honoured rejection, also classically Scottish: 'Sorry, son, but you'll never make it – you're just too small.'

Weir seemed even more dinky than Jinky – Celtic's Jimmy Johnstone, the prototype, pint-sized patter merchant, the imp imperial – and that was probably down to the baggy shorts, fashionable in the era but ludicrous on him. A ship chandler in Leith may have stitched them together from sails. All that superfluous, billowing fabric should have restricted his dribbling, rendering him little more than a novelty act for the final ten minutes of games, before being fitted with a spring and a suction pad to be plonked on the dashboard of the team bus, the driver's lucky charm.

Instead, full-backs found themselves cast as grouchy schoolteachers or skittering policemen or farmers missing apples from their orchards and Weir was the scamp driving them demented with his dribbling, just as fast as his little legs could carry him.

In West Pilton he also escaped the scourge of hard drugs. But his appeal was more than comic or nostalgic. He won a trophy, the 1991 League Cup. And he was very much from a club tradition. Kenny Davidson, Willie Murray, Jamie McCluskey – these guys way out wide weren't big and strapping either. And from further back and before the war let's have a big hand for Lil Arthur Milne (see ch. 49). Hibs have often been a safe house for skelfs, an equal opportunities employer for slips of laddies. The stunted but talented will find a refuge at Easter Road.

121

BETTER THAN MATTHEWS, BETTER THAN FINNEY

THEY KNEW each other's game, how in an instant it could be their game. How they could interchange, chameleonise and swap roles like kids would trade cards bearing their faces. This was the genius of the Famous Five, or at least part of it.

And when, at Ibrox in the Scottish Cup in 1951 in front of 102,342, Bobby Johnstone sneaked into the towering Rangers defensive wall at a Hibs' free kick, a wee guy from the Borders loitering under a row of Govan cranes, he wasn't surprised by Eddie Turnbull's improvisation. 'Ned would normally have blockbustered it but this time he popped the ball along the ground to me,' Johnstone said. 'So I just flicked it up and hit it over my shoulder and into the net.'

Johnstone, the last of the Five to arrive, the final piece of the wondrous jigsaw. Growing up in rugby country and becoming a painter's apprentice at 14, he never contemplated a career in the game, far less Twin Towers heroics and team-mates insisting he was better than football's great knights, but manager Willie McCartney charmed him into giving it a go with the Hibees.

Gordon Smith raved about his balance and his dribbling, two qualities on which the Prince of Wingers could be said to have been Scotland's foremost authority. For Turnbull, what set 'Nicker' apart was his football brain. The man himself reckoned: 'Maybe I was the slowest on the ground of the five of us but I might have been quickest in the heid.'

The quintet's first time together was on 15 October 1949. After leaking five goals in the Edinburgh derby and losing the League Cup semi-final to Dunfermline Athletic the week before, the *Daily Record* predicted 'sweeping changes' for Queen of the South in the league at Easter Road. The big story, according to the *Sunday Post* which began its report by quoting the Tannoy pre-kick-off, was Bobby Combe moving to half-back. But there was no mention of the player replacing him up front.

A Hibee hot streak followed, indeed there were just two more defeats. Clyde were hit for six on the penultimate Saturday, all the forwards scoring, only for Rangers' 'Iron Curtain' to squeeze out the point needed for the flag. But then came two titles for Easter Road and Johnstone's first honours, by which time he was a Scotland player, scoring on his 1951 debut against England.

He relived that 3–2 victory at Wembley when back in his native Selkirk, the local fleapit showing the Pathé newsreel with Bob Danvers-Walker hailing the 'Hibs wonder boy'. At Wembley again two years later he set up Lawrie Reilly's last-minute equaliser. Then in 1955 he was playing for Manchester City in the FA Cup final, losing that one but 12 months later scoring to lift the trophy.

City's Roy Warhurst rated Johnstone the finest player he'd ever seen up close, superior to Stanley Matthews and Tom Finney. He returned to Easter Road a little heavier round the middle but with that brain still sharp to load the bullets for Joe Baker and push his own goal tally past the 100-mark.

Total Famous Five haul: 1,083. Total Leith takeover of the Scotland front line? Didn't quite happen. Nicker moved on to Oldham Athletic where fan sites still hum with fond memories: 'Little barrel . . . ran games from the centre circle . . . transformed the team and the town.'

Club official Bernard Halford recalled: 'Bobby was the

cause of me regularly telling lies for the only time in my life. Matchdays the phone wouldn't stop ringing. "Is Johnstone playing?" He might have been sitting in my office with his ankle in plaster but I had to say he was fit otherwise no bugger would have turned up.'

122

THE GREATEST HIBBY WHO NEVER PLAYED

TAMSONS BAR on the corner of Easter Road and St Clair Street, a couple of hours before a 1997 derby.* A Hibs fan in a replica strip orders two pints of lager and stands with his back to us holding the drinks, waiting for his pal to join him. What's on his shirt? Not 'Miller' after Willie, the psycho right-back of the era who in a film would be played by Joe *Goodfellas* Pesci though without requiring a snub-nosed Smith & Wesson to bring down irritatingly tricky wingers. Not 'Gottskalksson' as in Oli, the calamity goalie whose manager once described his attempts at retrieving the ball as being 'like a drunk trying to catch a balloon'. No, it's not a name but one word: 'Remember.'

Remember who? Remember what? Remember, remember the fifth of November? Remember you're a Womble? 'Remember Me This Way', Gary Glitter's 1974 switch to self-pitying balladry after all those stack-booted stompers of glam rock?

By the time we'd exhausted all possibilities, the pal arrived, also wearing a team jersey. There was a clinking of glasses between them before the second Hibby was very deliberately moved by the first Hibby so he was standing on the right side of his friend. And what was on the back of the second Hibby's strip? 'Albert Kidd'. We burst out laughing, the whole pub did. 'Remember Albert Kidd'. How could we possibly forget?

* Minor consolation for Hearts, they won that derby.

On the last day of the 1985–86 season, every Hibs fan had trudged along to Easter Road with a little cartoon black cloud of unutterable gloom hanging over his head. While they gathered for a completely meaningless fixture, Hearts were surely going to win the Premier League because just a point was needed from Dundee.

But a stunted, socks-down scuttler ensured the dread inevitable didn't happen. His goals gifted the title to Celtic. Kidd wasn't just remembered, he was deified. Fans stuck for a pick from the dumplings in the Hibs team voted him their player of the year. If Kidd had turned up in Tamsons that day, or any Leith pub on any day, then, now and in the far-off future, there would be a fight to buy him a drink.

Which is kind of funny, considering he's equally revered by Celtic supporters, because he was not a prophet in his own land, or for his own team, barely scoring before that day and not at all after it, moving on and then moving away, right to the far side of the world.

Even funnier, in a story he tells against himself, is that when he was seeking Australian residency, immigration officials were underwhelmed by his application form's sizeable chunk of text promoting the footballing, instead urging him to expand on a couple of lines about a teenage apprenticeship in tool-making. 'I was responsible for two of the most important goals ever scored in Scotland and they just weren't interested,' he laughed. 'So I phoned my old man: "Dad, remember when you told me to get myself a trade? Top advice!"'

If that day in May up at Dens could have got any more joyful for Hibbies, ears burning pink from tuning in to the commentary on transistors, then it came from Kidd's uncanny resemblance to Bobby Ball, one half of hoary comedy troupers Cannon and Ball.

If that day in Tamsons could have got any more joyful for the assembled gathering then it came when our new favourite funster double act exited the pub for the walk up to the ground and once again some hurried positional rearrangement was required for the joke to succeed. It couldn't be 'Albert Kidd Remember' and these two were going to have to go through life being this particular, this precise, but it would be worth it.

123

'I ALWAYS KICK PETER'S HEADSTONE, FIVE GOOD DUNTS'

IT'S NOT essential by any means but still, maybe no bad thing if a stadium has a graveyard as a neighbour. Yes, football is important but here's a reminder just a lusty clearance away that some things matter more. There's one at Aberdeen, also Dunfermline Athletic and little Brechin City, too. And over the road from the Famous Five Stand, Eastern Cemetery which slopes like the pitch once did but being sacred ground will stay untouched. Every Euphemia and Wilhelmina, Bunty and Babs resident here is guaranteeing that.

Dan McMichael, the 1902 Scottish Cup-winning manager, is buried here and near the top of the slope and looking up at the stand is the grave of Peter Hughes, nestled in between his parents Michael and Prue. Peter, who died in 1992 aged 30, was the older brother of John 'Yogi' Hughes, former player, ex-manager, always and forever fan and, as often as his dodgy back was allowing him to cycle in from his home down the coast in Port Seton, an Eastern mourner with a long-established little ritual: 'I kick Peter's headstone, five good dunts.'

Of all the bosses who came and went quickly, and there have been far too many, I feel most sorry for Yogi. The docker's son who became a kind of Kirkgate cultural attaché, Desperate Dan chin jutting, lots of joking and japing and romanticising of Leith and Hibs, but deadly serious about sexy football only to have his star striker – Anthony Stokes 1.0 – snatched away just before midnight on transfer deadline day. Then for the board to hit the panic button.

He never failed to deliver a chortler or send the hacks away without a good line, but behind the banter lay a tragic family story and one that Yogi turned into inspiration. Peter was lost to drugs, a victim of the heroin scourge. 'He was two years older, a wonderful player, right foot and left foot and far better than me.

'Our dad would take him for a trial at Salvesen and he'd score a hat-trick but not go back the next week. Football could have saved him and he would still be here with us. But he just drifted and got in tow with the wrong crowd. What happened to him with the heroin killed our mum too. I remember how he struggled to go cold turkey. She just died of a broken heart.'

At the foot of the Walk there were close shaves for Yogi. Once, arrested for fighting, the Leith police did not dismisseth the Hughes brothers and when she was summoned to the station their mother suggested to the desk sergeant the pair be kept locked up to teach them a lesson. But football provided Yogi with purpose and passion and Peter was always on his shoulder. 'When I played and was competing for a high ball, or there was a situation on the ground where I knew the boots would be flying, I was aye thinking of him, aye trying to win the ball for him.'

Peter could not be saved although Yogi as a boss did his best to nurture wayward talents. Before Stokes and Leigh Griffiths became Hibees, he was their manager at Falkirk. 'I was tipped off about Sparky [Griffiths], this amazing kid at Leith Athletic, aged 15. I went down to watch him, saw him fight with a teammate, grab a corner flag and chase the laddie, get himself sent off. I thought: "He'll do me!"'

Stokes came from Sunderland where he'd driven Roy Keane mad, or madder. 'Football came easy to Stokesy. He was so talented he thought he didn't have to live his life properly. Roy could afford to chuck him out of the team but I needed him, even when he turned up late for the bus to Dunfermline, although I booted him off on the way back. Another flawed genius.'

These two owe their places in the Hibs hall of fame to Hughes, as indeed does everyone else. The walls in the corridors of East Mains were cold and bare until he instituted a gallery of notables from all the eras. Yogi is hugely proud of where he's from, as in Leith, and also where he's from regarding Hibee heritage. And, though he'd insist he's not worthy, his big grinning mug is right in amongst the tremendous tableau.

124

WHEN HIBS BECAME 'HYBERNIA', DISRUPTING THE BIAFRAN WAR

HIBS HAVE been adventurous travellers down the years, taking their football far and wide, as Pat Stanton and Jimmy O'Rourke acknowledged while out for a stroll in downtown Dallas in 1967. This was the year the club gave up their entire summer to play 12 games in a tournament designed to sell soccer to North America and, frazzled by the extreme heat, the constant criss-crossing of the continent on planes and the signs warning that jaywalkers would be fined, O'Rourke remarked: 'Christ, Pat, we're an awfie long way from the West Port.'*

But not all the touring worked out as planned and some of the excursions were madness, seemingly involving no planning whatsoever.

The organisers of that nascent US league handed out new identities to its guest teams and the Hibees were known as 'Toronto City'. Twelve months later, though, they'd gone from being missionaries to mercenaries, cast as 'Hybernia' for what was viewed as a callous, covert operation in a brutal civil war.

The conflict in Nigeria where the breakaway state of Biafra was being starved into submission shocked the whole world. Here, like in Vietnam, was a war playing out on TV, its audience being exposed for the first time to images of children who were no more than living skeletons. Broadcasting to an audience

* The heart of Edinburgh's Old Town where our story began.

of kids both well-fed and safe, *Blue Peter*'s Valerie Singleton leapt into action. She demanded our cottons and wools for an appeal to raise urgent funds for a hospital truck. 'You'll not be needing these,' said my mum, parcelling up my jammies in brown paper.

So when do Hibs come into this? Right now, in the urgent message from Dr Ifegwu Eke, Commissioner for Information for Biafra, reaching diplomats in New York in May '68: 'On Sunday, Britain dispatched 70 paratroopers who have now arrived in Lagos. To deceive the world, they are being disguised as footballers and given the name Hybernia . . .'

To deceive the world. Did they mean us? Apparently so. Just a few weeks after rounding off the domestic season with a draw against Kilmarnock (Irvine Welsh's Hibee awakening), Bob Shankly's team found themselves caught up, however innocently and daftly, in a humanitarian crisis.

On *Blue Peter*, Auntie Val said: 'We're not going to say which side is right and which side is wrong, except that all war is always wrong.' But Singleton and John Noakes and Peter Purves were collecting for Biafra; they were on the side of the little guys.

Harold Wilson's government, on the other hand, were backing Nigeria's blockade to attempt to starve Biafra into surrender. 'Truly disgusting,' wrote the great war reporter Frederick Forsyth years later. It was my jammies and others like them versus Wilson's bullets – fifty million tons of the latter in the latest shipment, according to *The Scotsman*, while Biafra, whose soldiers were so hungry they were reduced to catching and eating mice, was ordering 'this unusually large football team of 70 which includes T. Stevenson and C. Stein' to come clean.

It seems astonishing that Colin Stein and not T. but Eric Stevenson and the rest should have undertaken such an excursion when the Biafran War had been raging for a full year. Even if Hibs weren't geopolitically aware, shouldn't the Foreign Office have cautioned them about the trip?

The party were confronted at checkpoints, quizzed and searched. Their interrogators, armed with sub-machine guns, were sometimes as young as 14. One alarming journey by plane brushed the treetops. Those with a fear of flying – probably everyone that day – were informed by the pilot that the route he'd plotted was a necessity. 'Otherwise we'll be spotted by radar and shot down.'

Typical of footballers they carried on being footballers. Won three, drew one, lost one was Hybernia's record over the games in Nigeria and Ghana. Stevenson told me: 'The matches were great fun. I was playing keepy-uppy before the first one and the crowd loved it so I decided to show off the whole tour. Everywhere the locals got very excited, jumping up and down.' The desperate plight made an impression on Peter Marinello. 'We gave away lots of money to orphans,' he said. But for him there were a couple of dramatic experiences not usually part of games against Kilmarnock: losing his virginity and being kidnapped. Messing about in moored canoes upset the vessels' owners to the extent they tied him up and demanded reparation for alleged damage. And, having recently turned 18, his team-mates thought it would be a jolly good idea if they arranged for him to have an evening with a prostitute. Sitting round the bed they cheered him right to the end.

125

BACK FROM THE CONCENTRATION CAMP, EAGER FOR A GAME

SO YOUR striker was away on international duty and is not up to a full 90 minutes. Your midfielder who's running down his contract is unavailable once more. And have groin strains suddenly become contagious in the dressing room?

I get that football is faster now. More demanding. There are more games, increasing the risk of injury. And these days clubs are more attentive in the care of players. I get all that but still: read about Bobby Combe and marvel.

Combe served for Hibs splendidly over 17 seasons and also for his country. MIA – 'Missing in action' – trumps ACL and during a tense time for the fans in 1945 and what must have been an absolutely horrific one for his family there was no news of the soccer squaddie who'd play when the Second World War permitted.

Then this, just one line in the morning papers: 'Bobby Combe, the Hibernian inside forward who was previously reported missing, is now officially stated to be a prisoner of war.'

And then, on 7 May, the eve of VE Day, the 'Tron Kirk' column in Edinburgh's *Evening News* reported how Combe 'surprised Mr [Willie] McCartney by walking into the Hibernian manager's office this forenoon having arrived home at 4 a.m. in the morning after being flown back to Britain. He looks fit and feels it despite being in captivity and is eager for a first-class game . . .'

Combe's tank had come under attack and a fellow crewman became trapped. Accompanying tanks were forced to withdraw and when they returned, the Hibs man and his mates had rescued the wounded soldier. But Combe was seized by the Nazis and shunted round various locations before being incarcerated in Stalag X-B near Bremen.

This was a prisoner-of-war camp which, during his time there, according to testimonies, assumed the desperate state of a 'full-blown' concentration camp. There was a shortage of food, a typhus epidemic and the place was so overrun with vermin that the International Committee of the Red Cross recommended the barracks be burned to the ground.

As the Allies advanced further into Germany, prisoners from an official concentration camp nearby were dumped in Stalag X-B. In a hunger revolt, 300 were killed by guards. And when British soldiers liberated the hellhole they described it as a mini-Belsen.

Whatever horrors Combe witnessed, he seems to have kept them to himself, for obituaries when he died in 1991 make no mention of the fact he was a POW. Of course during and immediately after the Second World War, post-traumatic stress disorder wasn't recognised as such and no one talked about mental health. Now, the 'stiff upper lip' is almost regarded as an outdated character flaw, with 'Keep Calm and Carry On' a jokey slogan for a tea towel. With fortitude and stoicism, the war generation simply got on with it. And Combe wanted to get on with playing football again.

He was born within shouting distance of Easter Road, supported Hibs through the 1930s relegation years and made a scoring debut aged 17 in 1941 against Hearts alongside another new boy, Gordon Smith, who grabbed a hat-trick. If Smith overshadowed Combe, that was kind of the way it would be, no disrespect, and the little inside-forward was tenacious in his efforts to be mentioned in dispatches, ultimately claiming the accolade, absolutely no disgrace, of 'the sixth member of the Famous Five'.

In the 8–1 demolition of Rangers (see ch. 49) it was Combe, not Smith, who scored four. When the Five first teamed up and immediately became irresistible and unbudgeable, Combe was moved to half-back, found an extra £2 in his weekly wage packet as compensation for the switch minimising his international prospects and continued to be a key member of the triple title triumph.

Post-football he ran a grocer's shop on Leith Walk, but before then, and right after what the *Evening News* called the Nazis' 'great collapse', the conversation probably went something like this:

'Good to see you again, gaffer. When's the next game?'

'Well, VE Day's tomorrow and there's to be the Roseberry Charity Cup final against Hearts here the following day. Should be a marvellous atmosphere but a bit too soon for you, perhaps?'

'No, gaffer, count me in.'

The indefatigable, indestructible Combe captained Hibs, scored the first goal and would lift a trophy won 7–6 on corner kicks.

126

HIBS REJECT BEATS BLACK POWER, BECOMES WORLD'S FASTEST MAN

SUMMER 1972 and the fastest men on the planet are gathering in Munich for the Olympics. Actually, not quite all of them. There's no Tommie Smith, the reigning 200 metres champion, and there's no George McNeill, formerly of the Hibs left wing.

Both have been outlawed by athletics – Smith for his 'Black Power' salute on the podium at the previous Games in Mexico City and McNeill for what would be a one-match career at Easter Road, enough to debar him from running as an amateur. So instead these two – both world record holders – race against each other at a rugby league ground in Wakefield, West Yorkshire for the right to call themselves No. 1 in their near-ghettoised realm.

I've watched sports docs thinner on colour and incident than the story of McNeill, but Hibbies be warned: when our man re-enters football later there is a semi-tragic ending.

'I was quick – nickname Billy Whizz – with a not bad shot but my touch let me down,' he told me. 'My only game was against St Johnstone in 1965, a 3–0 win. I didn't score but hit the bar twice from corners. Then I was on the bench for the fantastic night when we beat Napoli 5–0 (see ch. 29). Eric Stevenson, the usual left-winger, got injured and could do no more than hobble about. Even then I couldn't make it two games. Napoli had had a man sent off so I think both clubs must have agreed to make it ten versus ten, rather than have me play!'

It was reckoned that the worst thing Jock Stein ever did for Scottish athletics was sign McNeill for Hibs. 'Well, Jock was a visionary. He tried me at left-back in the reserves, using my pace on the overlap, and I like to think I was a prototype for Tommy Gemmell. But when Bob Shankly let me go I was devastated. I was a Hibs fanatic and as a laddie must have collected Joe Baker's autograph 50 times. My dream had been shattered and I felt like such a failure.'

Then for a laugh a friend entered him in Edinburgh's Powderhall Sprint, a professional race for 99 years, the location taking its name from an old gunpowder factory. McNeill practised in borrowed spikes under street lamps with a toy gun which fired caps. He won the centenary event, and the following year set a world record for 120 yards which stands today.

His kind of running was secretive, almost sinister to outsiders, with sprinters training in balaclavas and using fake names to stay a few paces ahead of rivals and the gambling fraternity. And next to pulverising speedball sessions, Hibs workouts were 'like gentle exercises for old ladies'. McNeill was bettering Don Quarrie's times and matching anything Valeriy Borzov did and wanted to run in the Olympics. He offered to hand back his £1,000 prize but suffered from what he claims was hypocrisy and snobbery towards pro runners.

The fastest he ever ran was in a heat, the equivalent of ten seconds dead for 100 metres. Anticipating something momentous, ITN dispatched cameras to Edinburgh for the final, only for the race to disappear from the news schedules in the wake of the Ibrox Disaster on the same day.

McNeill would beat Smith to be crowned world pro-sprint champ. Then in the 1980s Hearts persuaded him to bring his speedball to Tynecastle as part of the coaching staff. This coincided with Jambo derby dominance, with Hibs presumably continuing to train like old dears. And he followed that with a stint at Livingston, his methods paying off with the 2004 League Cup triumph – over the Hibees.

127

IN BED WITH A DOLLY BIRD ACROSS HIS CHEST, SWIGGING CHAMPAGNE

FIVE FANS, 66 pints. No hang on, maybe it's 66 fans get to consume five pints during the course of a match as booze returns to the Scottish football scene. The detail is critical for this pilot scheme at an Ayr United cup tie, I agree, given that it's 45 years since we disgraced ourselves and a ban was introduced. But please understand: we're gasping. Facts can get lost in the rush to the bar.

The most notorious game involving Hibs and bevvy also involved Ayr United: a fourth round match in the Scottish Cup in 1980 when the problem wasn't pissed-up fans but a player who couldn't, or wouldn't, get out of bed.

It was that year's Old Firm final and the ensuing riot which did for drinking at games and it was George Best's second most outrageous moment of hotel dissoluteness which marked the beginning of the end for his Easter Road late-career interlude.

'George, where did it all go wrong?' That was the first of them, room service's reaction to discovering Bestie post-coital with Miss World on a quilt of banknotes. The second presented itself to John Lambie who led the search party dispatched to track down the wayward wingman one Sunday lunchtime with the clock ticking alarmingly close to kick-off.

Part of Eddie Turnbull's coaching staff, Lambie told me: 'The pre-match meal was at [Edinburgh's] North British Hotel where George stayed during his time at Hibs. Arthur Duncan was Corn Flakes and fruit as usual and the rest were steak and toast as usual but one seat was empty. Ned gave us the hard stare: "Fuckin' find him!" John Fraser and I went up to his room, knocked, no answer. Ned: "But you fuckin' had a look inside, aye?" "Sorry, no." "Get the fuckin' porter!"

'He was in bed with a dolly bird lying across his chest and swigging from a bottle of champagne, supersized. I said: "George, we're playing Ayr United. You need to get downstairs for your meal." He just smiled: "I'm having it here!"'

Hold the Corn Flakes – Best was glamorous women as usual. Later as a manager Lambie would coin one of Scottish football's all-time greatest quotes – on learning from his Partick Thistle physio that a player prostrate on the turf was concussed and didn't know he was: 'Quick, slap him with a sponge and tell him he's Pelé!' – but on this occasion, confronted by this horizontal footballer, couldn't find the words. Best, with a twinkle in his eyes if no longer quite so often in his toes, would have that effect.

In any case, that may have been George in his best fettle for four days. The Thursday – drinks after training with team-mates in the Jinglin' Geordie down an Old Town close – had produced the unfortunate photograph of him looking well refreshed at a table of drained pint glasses. The image was cropped to suggest they were all his although I prefer to believe the version of events involving just-departed journalists. During the 1980s I was a reporter on the *Evening News* across the close, when liquid lunches in the Jinglin' were the norm and Thursday was expenses day for distribution of the little brown envelopes of mostly fictional outgoings.

The Friday for Best had been a blur and during the Saturday he'd got in tow with France rugby captain Jean-Pierre Rives, in town for a Murrayfield international, and there was another gargantuan sesh. But despite the alluring mythology, this one did not involve a second striking blonde in Debbie Harry. With poor Willie Murray his much-booed stand-in against Ayr,

Blondie's song 'Rapture' and the line 'Barely breathing, almost comatose' might sum up Bestie that long weekend.

For his short stint as a Hibee, I prefer to borrow from a critique of the art of his drinking buddy when Rives turned to sculpture with French newspaper *La Dépêche* raving about 'a marvellous mixture of suffering, grace and beauty'.

But maybe Lambie should have the last word: 'George was the loveliest man, surprisingly shy, with no superstar airs. Often he'd go into the gym with the Hibs laddies and what a thrill that was for them. I put on his bets: three fifty quid doubles, one fifty quid treble every week. And here's something I'll never forget till my dying day: Ralph Callachan crossing balls at training and George turning his back and, 20 yards out, back-heeling them into the net. He never missed.'

128

EVERYBODY LOVES SUNSHINE

REMEMBER WHEN you had hardly any money and just a few singles (no LPs) to your name? There was no playback facility for Radio 1, the cassette recorder wasn't set up to tape and suddenly . . . what's that song? It sounds fantastic but who is it? The DJ will tell us when it's over and . . . ach, he doesn't. *Idiot.* Later you hear the song again, just the fade-out this time, but are still none the wiser.

There are other frustrating near misses in pursuit of it and you might say to yourself: I wish somebody would hurry up and invent a mobile phone and then invent a gizmo for the phone which identifies mystery choons. Until then, though, and for a good while, you might be chasing the bright elusive butterfly of love. And, yes, I suppose the song in question could well be 'Elusive Butterfly', a 1965 hit for American folkie Bob Lind.

No song is elusive any more but I kind of wish some were. 'Sunshine on Leith' by the Proclaimers, for example. I love it, it's my team's anthem. There's no chasing needed because I've touched it, I've claimed it. But I worry that some of the Reid twins' magic will disappear if it's heard too often so I've removed it from my iPod and am hoping that in the announcer's booth at Easter Road there's a warning notice pinned to the wall: 'You'll want to put this on every game. The power you can exert over the crowd will seem irresistible. But you are not Mussolini. Avoid.'

The rule should be limiting spins to important victories. Thankfully the team tend to keep their side of the bargain, leaving sizable gaps in between. What, you cry, cups etc. would be sacrificed in the belief this will preserve the potency of 5 mins 14 secs of cheap music? Am I a masochist? Do I believe Leith's motto should be changed from 'Persevered' to 'Perverse'? Yes. And? So? Less of the 'cheap' as well.

Nowadays, everyone's got access to everything instantly and 'Sunshine on Leith' is everywhere, available all of the time. There's ongoing chatter on X about it. A fan of another club will post: 'This is technically our "Sunshine on Leith"' . . . Or from Goodison, this: 'For ages Evertonians have been searching for their "Sunshine on Leith" . . .' The song has become the standard by which others are judged, the one supporters all wish was theirs. And every debate must come with clips of the Hibee Nation belting out their spiritual.

On a TV show called *The Assembly* where celebs are quizzed by a neurodivergent panel whose unvarnished, no-nonsense questions are like slide tackles, the actor David Tennant blubs when his interviewers pick up instruments and play out with their take of 'Sunshine on Leith'. Then, in another moment, the entire fan base collectively holds its breath: what appalling crimes against music are Coldplay about to visit upon 'Sunshine on Leith'? Or Robbie Williams, slotting it into his Murrayfield set list like Nigel Farage on the Scottish by-election campaign trail requesting a deep-fried Mars bar because it seems the done thing?

How did this all start? With the song's composition, Proclaimer Craig being moved by glimpsing Easter Road from his plane porthole. Then: UEFA Cup vs AEK Athens in 2001 just after 9/11, emotions boiling and Easter Road chanting 'USA! USA!' before the first, great stirring fan rendition. Then: the second, 'Sunshine on Leith' in the snow at Hampden, 2007 League Cup final. And after that there were three more in the delirium of great wins over Hearts.*

* All wins over Hearts are of course great.

But in 2016 when the Scottish Cup had been won, when the crossbar had been snapped, when the pitch had been dug up, when the paggering had stopped, when the polis on horseback had corralled the mad hordes from the east back into their corner, when no one was sure if the team would be allowed out of the dressing room to collect the trophy and maybe the victory would be declared null and void . . . it was then that 'Sunshine on Leith' went stratospheric.

This is the recital Sir Alex Ferguson raves about. The one with millions of YouTube hits. The one pined over by fans required to sing the non-specific 'Glad All Over' or the one-size-fits-all 'Hi Ho Silver Lining'. The one Liverpool Kop-ites acknowledge knocks 'You'll Never Walk Alone' out of the park. The one Jambos admit, dammit, that they can't help loving.

All of this is great but, similar to how exposure to too much sunshine is bad for you, what if the slow, tender, hymnal quality were to break, just like that crossbar? So I'm very happy to wait – and if needs be *wait* – for the next famous victory when it can be warbled by men and boys who never went to choir school but have elevated 'Sunshine on Leith' to the top of the charts as the most sacred and beautiful, the saddest and most uplifting song in all football.

129

AH! AH! AH! AH! COMIN' ALIVE!

BECAUSE OF its baseball-cap ubiquitousness you might think that Donald Trump or someone in his comms team came up with 'MAGA'. In fact it was back in 1980 that Ronald Reagan, bidding for the White House and with the US suffering from stagflation, urged voters to help him 'make America great again'.

The eighties was a fertile era for slogans. Reagan's wife Nancy had one of her own for anti-drugs campaigning: 'Just say no'. Nike doubtless paid marketing whizzes a huge sum for another three-word message not dispensing with 'just' – 'Just do it'. Back in politics, 'Where's the beef?' was pinched by Democrat hopeful Walter Mondale from a fast food chain.

And then there was 'Coming alive in '85'. What strange magic was this? A Saatchi & Saatchi confection? Another killer jingle from the brilliant mind of Margaret Thatcher's favourite ad man Tim Bell who'd already dreamed up 'Labour isn't working'?

Yes, you just knew it, 'Coming alive in '85' was Hibs. A statement of intent; also an admission of failure up until that moment. Following defeat at home to Dumbarton – attendance: a misbegotten 3,642 – manager Pat Stanton had resigned. What a quaint, old-fashioned term that is, belonging as it does to an age before compensation packages and pre-NDAs. A Leith legend had departed nobly and was replaced by another in John Blackley.

Early in 1985, a long winless run ended, of all places, at Ibrox, but as that season climaxed, Hibs were still deep in the relegation mire. This was a time of big hair, big shoulder pads, big disasters, small lunches ('For wimps,' said Maggie Thatcher) and even smaller points tallies for the Hibees. 'Coming alive in '85' makes me think of one of that decade's top fashionistas, Katharine Hamnett and her white T-shirts, voluminous and sloganed – also the Bee Gees. Dumbarton, again, would decide the Hibees' fate so imagine if the team had descended on Boghead for a demotion death match in the Gibb brothers' white suits, striding to a propulsive disco beat. A trick missed.

They could certainly have reverted to the white shirts of the club's beginnings to try and recapture some of the original spirit. Ralph Callachan, for possessing the bouffant barnet closest to Bee Gee Barry, would be right out front, with Paul Kane and Brian Rice shattering glass to reach those top notes and evoke another tagline of the period: 'Is it live or is it Memorex?'

All together now: 'Whether you're a brother or whether you're a mother we're comin' alive, comin' alive/Feel the city breakin' and everybody shakin' we're comin' alive, comin' alive. Ah! Ah! Ah! Ah! . . .'

Hibs, who laid on bargain-price bus travel for the grumbling rump, were able to save themselves but would continue teetering at the edge in the succeeding seasons. 'Where's the beef?' the long-suffering faithful would have wanted to know. Come to that: 'Where's the Keith?' Keith Wright would arrive eventually, but the rest of the eighties needed to be got out of the way first.

130

THE F-WORD (FLAIR, OF COURSE)

I'M NOT going to say that I'm as sick as a parrot because no one uses that phrase any more. But I will have to take a *long hard look at myself.* Seventy-six? Is that all? The number of times at my last newspaper that I put 'Hibs' and 'flair' together in the same sentence was only 76? I thought it would be more, *to be fair* (to be flair), many more.

I thought I gave *110 per cent* to the job of writing about football with unashamed partiality. The manager or editor – or to be accurate many editors because in papers, like football, *things change very quickly* – granted me that free role, the equivalent of a false nine, although some would probably say false journalist. But *at the end of the day* I feel I've *let myself down.*

It was an open goal. Football *isn't played on paper* but writing about football is. I was to be a fan with a typewriter, originally a term of mild abuse for Scots soccer scribblers coined by our English cousins, but in this case an upfront and unapologetic one.

So what went wrong? How did I – cue the great Hugh McIlvanney – *snatch defeat from the jaws of victory*? Did I in fact Hibs it?

Jambos, the westside frenemies, must be laughing. Laughing but also raging because they would argue that 76 is 76 too many. Flair is a great, big, walloping myth, they insist. 'Hoof!' they roar when a Hibs player in an Edinburgh derby rams the ball into a rocket launcher, presses the detonator and stands well back. But the local skirmish does not offer the optimum conditions – the pristine canvas, the hushed stage – for the kind of football we like to play, and the opportunity to boogaloo a rhapsody divine.

Oh yes, they snigger, and maybe rocket launcher is anachronistic. Maybe cannon, ignited from the touch hole with a long match, would be more accurate. For you Hibbies persist in using words to describe the kind of football you like to play which suggest romance, derring-do and valour. Words like 'buccaneering' from the 17th century and, for goodness' sake, 'cavalier' and 'swashbuckling' from the 16th. To this we say: 'Pray tell, your point is, caller?'

Still, only 76. *The table doesn't lie.* It's *a wake-up call.* I'm going to have to *dust myself down and go again . . .*

131

HE DIED OF A BROKEN HEART

ON CHRISTMAS Day 1909, the games didn't stop. Falkirk ruined the festivities for Rangers, Hearts sneaked a last-minute win over Queen's Park and Third Lanark vs Dundee attracted the biggest crowd. But at Firhill tragedy struck.

On an icebound pitch, Partick Thistle left-winger Frank Branscombe slipped and crashed into James Main, with Hibs' international right-back taking a heavy boot to the stomach. The match would never have been played today and modern medical care around football would never have allowed Main to head home to West Calder after the match with such deep indentations from the studs. That night, according to the *Dundee Courier*, 'alarming symptoms manifested themselves' and Main was admitted to Edinburgh Royal Infirmary where he was found to be suffering from a ruptured bowel. He died three days later, aged 24.

Hibs were Main's only club. He joined them at 18 and developed into one of the best defenders in the country. Earlier in 1909 he'd made his Scotland debut against Ireland, the 5–0 win following two matches against the English League. The tributes were glowing.

'A quiet, well-dispositioned young fellow . . . a splendid club player,' reflected Edinburgh's *Evening News*. 'Popular with all who came into contact with him,' attested the *Empire News*, while Dundee's *Evening Telegraph* put on record: 'Though strong and robust, Main never descended to any questionable tactics and was held in the highest esteem by all in Scottish football. His loss to the Hibernians cannot be properly estimated.'

Main was laid to rest at the cemetery in West Calder before a huge gathering of mourners. 'Seldom has the district been so moved as by this sudden and tragic extinction of a young life,' reported the *Midlothian Advertiser,* and the local paper did him proud by carrying the full text of the parish minister's tribute. Said the Reverend Dr Anderson: 'There are times when death almost seems to wear a friendly aspect: an old man full of years and honours falls quietly and peacefully asleep; or it may be that after long weeks of hopeless pain that rest comes to the sufferer. How different it is when a young man in the prime of his powers, before whom life is opening out with all the possibilities of success, is suddenly struck down by some terrible accident.'

There are a few things about Main's story and his short and tragic life which tell us that 1909 was a very different time and the Reverend Anderson revealed another: 'His suffering was at times acute but through it all the mind was ever clear and alert. His singing of that beautiful hymn "He Died of a Broken Heart" in ward 16 of the Royal Infirmary on the evening of his death will not soon be forgotten by any who was privileged to hear it. At its close there was a hush that could be felt. His testimony – "I have not been as decided for Christ as I ought but I am trusting him now" – will remain as a precious legacy . . .'

132

GONE IN 150 SECONDS

EASTER ROAD, a place where remarkable, astonishing and sometimes epoch-making things happen, welcomed Motherwell in August 1959 for a League Cup tie with the match programme anticipating a lively encounter against the Ancell Babes.

That proved to be an understatement. 'St John hat-trick shook the capital' gushed the *Motherwell Times*, but even this was underplaying things. The goals blurred past Hibs goalie Willie Wilson in the space of two and a half minutes – the speediest triple-deck sandwich in Scottish football and the quickest in top-flight Britain, beating that well-known slowcoach Sadio Mané for Southampton vs Aston Villa by 26 seconds.

The programme had remarked of Ian St John, the top goalscorer at Fir Park the previous season with 31 goals: 'Works in a Motherwell steel mill and the most consistent attack leader the club have had for many a long day.'

Well manager Bobby Ancell's young hotshots included two players who would end up at Hibs in Pat Quinn and Willie Hunter, but not before the inside-forwards had crafted the chances for their 21-year-old goal-grabber. The *Motherwell Times* credited St John with 'genius in opportunism' and 'a grand piece of imaginative football' – and that was just goal No. 1. The Hibees, the report on the 3–1 win said, were 'by no means a bad team' but Motherwell were 'devastating'. So much so that the home support 'could scarcely believe its eyes'.

They weren't the only ones, as St John told me when we met

long after he'd signed off as one half of the *Saint & Greavsie* TV double act: 'I was chuffed that a couple of pals from the steelworks came through to Easter Road to watch me play. But the buggers went up over the back of the high terracing for their Bovril and missed all three goals.'

133

'DID I HAVE A HIGH OPINION OF MYSELF? OF COURSE'

HOW LONG could he hover, two feet above the green, green grass of Easter Road or more often than not the heavily caked mud? How much time would pass while he was airborne at the back post, skulking menacingly?

As long as it took to recite 'Dave Dee, Dozy, Beaky, Mick & Tich' and list the band's first three hit singles. To tie your tie for school. To perform five, maybe six burpees (in black gym pumps, elasticated gussets). To list six, maybe seven cars from *Wacky Races*.

Peter Cormack made a sensational start at Hibs, volleying a goal in the victory over Real Madrid in 1964, and didn't hang about thereafter. Well, obviously he hung about for all those crosses without need of a jetpack, an outstanding feature of his game, and he stayed for nearly eight years, but it can seem like less when we realise how he was always in a hurry to get ahead, improve, succeed, how Hampden disappointments and Euro quarter-final exits frustrated him. 'I wanted to do better and to better myself,' he told me. 'After training the rest of the guys would drift uptown or head to the pub. I would stay behind and train some more.'

If he was different, he was still very much admired. Here's Jimmy O'Rourke: 'Peter was one of those fellows who was really good at everything: Scottish boys' snooker champ, rare singer, fantastic player of course, at least two times the emergency goalie when our keeper was injured and clean sheets as well – and on top of all that an annoyingly handsome bugger.' So are we ready for another Hibee first? Cormack reckoned no footballer had a girls-only fan club before him, with membership from as far afield as the United States.

We met in 2015 just after Hibs had scored four against Rangers. The last time that happened was the next game following Real, Cormack ghosting around Ibrox and grabbing two of them, an ambitious player espousing modernity who was coached by an ambitious manager espousing modernity. Unfortunately Jock Stein would leave for Celtic and Hibs' title bid in 1964–65 fizzled out, tiny consolation coming when Hibs again netted four at Parkhead with Neil Martin V-signing the old boss in celebration of his hat-trick.

After another 'What if . . . ?' season for Hibs, Cormack pushed himself more, running round Arthur's Seat and joining the Sparta boxing club where he was only beaten on points by a promising young fighter called Ken Buchanan. Cormack could float like a butterfly while waiting for a cross to come over. He was Peter the Prancer, lifting his knees as he ran. He could probably have done well at dressage, too, but craved football success in recognition of his talents. 'I always thought I was good,' insisted Cormack, who swapped Bob Shankly for Bill and the Cowshed for the Kop to win titles with Liverpool. 'Did I have a high opinion of myself? Yes, but if I hadn't I would not have reached the level I did. To get to the top a footballer needs to have that arrogance.'

Liverpool's caveman captain Tommy Smith reckoned that prancing confirmed him as a 'fuckin' poof', but he found a kindred spirit in Kevin Keegan, equally self-possessed and driven. Cormack, who had a shoe fetish, launched his own brand, putting his name to groovy polka-dot platforms. If he'd ever played in a pair, and still been able to propel himself for a soaring header, no one would have been the least bit surprised.

134

DID A HIBEE CREATE THE MONSTER BECKHAM?

TELL ME you did this, too. Not having any money for bubblegum but craving a fix, you'd scour the school playground for discarded blobs. A quick run under the tap to remove the grit and you were ready to join the cool gang, popping and swapping cards.

First the American Civil War. Then Sad Sack, the klutzy cartoon grunt. And at last football, not just the glamour boys from England but wild Scotsmen, hair all over the place and teeth missing, shot from awkward angles so that floodlight pylons sprouted from their heads against a backdrop of empty, crumbling terraces and the glowering close-season summer skies.

I had a doubler of Tony Higgins but couldn't move it on. And before very long a trebler. I didn't tell Higgins this when we met, but in any case he had a better story for me involving bubblegum, which turned into yet another tiny triumph for Hibs as a force of good in the game.

Higgins had muscled his way into Turnbull's Tornadoes, no mean feat. Now, a real tornado can lift a cow a hundred feet into the air, if disaster movies like *Twisters* are to be believed, but I'd like to have seen one knock big Tony even slightly off course as the corn-fed utility man thundered around the park. His impact was noted by card kings A&BC who wanted to sign him up for their gum giveaways.

'This was the deal – £5 for the use of my ugly mug,' he told me. 'It was a one-off payment and the contract would cover five years.' Was it binding? Did A&BC hold exclusive image rights? Acknowledging he wasn't a superstar of the game – or a hunky, immaculately groomed member of Italy's Azzurri, rather a peely-wally plodder of the Scottish scene – wasn't the fee a bit of a swizz?

Higgins asked these questions because even as a teenage prodigy he was interested in politics and workers' rights. With his six Highers from school he'd contemplated an undergraduate life. 'So when Eddie Turnbull used to yell at us, "Lazy bastards – you could all be down the mines!", I was able to respond: "Actually no, boss, it would be second year, Glasgow Uni for me."' He showed the contract to Easter Road's established stars. 'They probably thought I was this impetuous upstart. Stick in, was the advice, and I could earn a fiver a year.'

If that was top whack for pix then football's shop steward needed to know about it. 'Alex Ferguson, when he was at Falkirk, got on my train every morning. It may sound funny now, us two having an intense discussion about bubblegum, but given the sums involved I suggested it might be better if they came to PFA Scotland, the players' union. Later, when I took over from Fergie as chairman, and Panini took over the card contract, that's what happened and we put the money into education programmes.'

They probably seem like trifling things, but these two and a half inch by three and a half inch depictions of the fitba panoply would propel Higgins into a long and successful career looking after player welfare in Scotland and throughout the world. He was 'Tony, Mr Africa' to the woefully under-represented of that continent and helped to unionise them.

But something else: in his own small way he alerted football to the significance of image. Now imagine a blob of bubblegum rolling down a hill, everything sticking to it, as a metaphor for said image and how its commercial potential has ballooned. Did Higgins have a hand in creating the monster that is David Beckham?

135

THE SCOREBOARD WAS A 'SON ET GLOOMIERE' DISPLAY

ACH, NOT every innovation comes off, changes the world, eclipses the momentous pan loaf cut into same-sized segments. Just ask Thomas Edison and just ask Hibs. In 1879 Edison invented the light bulb but rather less epoch-making were his electric pen and talking doll. Rebutting his critics he declared: 'I have not failed 10,000 times – I've successfully found 10,000 ways that will not work.'

If the American whizz basked too long in the afterglow of his literal light-bulb moment then perhaps Hibs did the same following their trailblazing floodlights (see ch. 29). For the electronic scoreboard which came later flickered and fizzled and eventually went phutt.

Unveiled in 1985, magisterially positioned on the Cowshed roof, the contraption was billed as yet another first. 'Stop it, Hibs, you're spoiling us!' must have been the reaction from the terraces, exhausted by all the innovation.

This was going to be like What the Butler Saw superseded by Roadrunner. More specifically, the letters and numbers which relayed the most modest of match data – half-time scores from around the country – usurped by nothing less than a hurtling information revolution. Game commentary, cheerleading, birthday messages from Auntie Bessie. The potential seemed limitless.

We were ready to be bedazzled by our state-of-the-art scoreboard, the envy of the land – we really were. Like little kids or hicks from the sticks. Sadly it didn't always work properly, or fully, announcing 'GO. . .L!' or alternatively 'GOA. . .!' (Wait, did Hibs ever tour Goa? In 150 years they seem to have played just about everywhere else.)

The messaging would have benefited from some humour. 'Well done, George McCluskey' greeted a goal from the striker,* the joy of the moment not really captured on the wheezing tickertape. Couldn't he at least have been called by his nickname, Beastie?

We hoped for cartoon caricatures of the players or jokey symbols – a half-shut knife for sleeper-keeper Alan Rough, say, sticks of TNT for the alarmingly combustible Bobby Thomson and maybe rock group Boston's spaceship insignia for Willie Jamieson (think hair: Willie boasted an almost similarly ginormous afro to the singing drummer). Unfortunately a pair of clapping hands was just about the full extent of the graphics.

All too quickly the scoreboard evoked sniggersome memories of an earlier, ill-fated Leith *son et gloomiere* display. In 1973 the promise of an 80-foot piece of public art was that whichever way the wind blew, it would respond in vibrant colours. The kinetic sculpture was made up of neon strip bulbs in a wonky design which Edinburgh MP and future Secretary of State for Scotland, Malcolm Rifkind, presumed was the work of a 'drunken scaffolder'. Its timing was terrible with Ted Heath's three-day week almost immediately restricting usage. But, free from the need for electricity to be conserved in the face of miners' strikes, it rarely glowed.

* Beastie's trademark finish was hard and low, pranging one of the stanchions much like Alfredo Di Stéfano's sixth for Real Madrid against Eintracht Frankfurt in the 1960 European Cup final at Hampden. Unlike the scoreboard his strikes were never indecisive, never stuttering.

The tower being dismantled coincided with the scoreboard going up. When Hibbies reel off those firsts, this is the one requiring tongues to be lodged firmly in cheeks. They might try and point across to Tynecastle, so dank in its dreary municipal maroon livery, but will be forced to admit their gizmo was rubbish.

And yet the current Easter Road regime, blissfully unaware of the scoreboard's short-circuiting shortcomings, have pounced on it as inspiration for one of the new stadium restaurants. The eaterie is called Pioneers in recognition of the club 'leading the way in many aspects of football' and the scoreboard is the first one listed in the promotional bumf.

Maybe in a junkyard somewhere a bashed screen will be crackling with electronically contrived applause.

136

TRAUMATISED BY THE THREE-HEADED MONSTER

OF ALL Hibs' great gifts to the game, there must surely be gratitude from the rest of Scottish football that they'll never have to suffer like we did in 1979.

That was the year of the three-headed monster of a Scottish Cup final, the longest in the competition's history. Rangers suffered, too, but after five and a half hours ranging across more than two weeks which proved too much for some 20,000 fans who went missing between the first and third instalments, along with the original referee, victory was theirs.

Exhaustion, cramp, boredom, ruined summer holidays, familiarity breeding contempt, early onset madness from having to perform the same tasks again and again (and again) – these can all magically disappear with the trophy cradled in sweaty arms at last.

It was the *War and Peace* final although you might also have called it the *Peyton Place* final. Leo Tolstoy's novel, first edition, ran to 1,225 pages. The American soap opera lasted 514 episodes. Anyone who's read the book, though, must feel a sense of quiet triumph at reaching the end – just as fans of the serial would have experienced a profound sense of loss as favourite characters walked off into the sunset. Did Derek Johnstone and Alex MacDonald feel like part of the family at the final's conclusion? Hmm, not really. But then nor did Jackie McNamara or Ally McLeod or George Stewart and I loved all of these guys (still do).

The problem was that as we trudged back to Hampden for the third game, the final seemed like punishment. As if we were bound for the police station at Mount Florida instead, reporting for regular monitoring of consistently erratic behaviour likely to cause alarm.

Or this alternative scenario: the cops hadn't caught up with us and it wasn't football we were going to watch but an underground, illegal activity, e.g. dog fighting, with the evening's heavy downpour battering off the corrugated roof adding to the air of dark desperation.

You shouldn't feel furtive about attending a showpiece like the Scottish Cup final, but second replays can do that. The FA Cup final has never had one while our final's previous three-gamer was in 1910 when Dundee eventually overcame Clyde. There will never be another, indeed even single replays are history now. The 1981 final needed one of those but there surely can be no doubt it was the spectre of a repeat of the Hibs–Rangers slugathon which frightened the beaks into introducing on-the-day verdicts.

Margaret Thatcher and Ayatollah Khomeini altered the course of world events when they came to power in 1979, but a bigger question from that year was posed by Arthur Duncan: if he hadn't put through his own goal with a fantastic diving header, would there have been a fourth game?

That isn't something which seemed to concern anyone beyond those who stood on Hampden's slopes and endured. Not then and certainly not now. Rev up Wikipedia and you'll find a blank space where the story of the final should be. Switch on YouTube for highlights – the first game was screened live by both BBC and STV – and there's a fuzzy, pathetic 54 seconds, that's all.

It's the final time has forgotten except that while Rangers were claiming yet another trophy, their 23rd Scottish Cup, Hibs fans couldn't forget. The team might have won all three matches and oh what a fate to have befallen poor Arthur, second only to Gordon Smith on the appearances roll of honour.

One aspect I had forgotten: the pre-match entertainment. The bill in the match programme lists the Kilward Alsatians Dog Display Team, the British Airways Rommettes and, 'direct from *Top of the Pops*', Legs & Co. It says something about the sensory deprivation caused by the final that I have no memory of the one they called Sue, the dancer most fancied, and the erotic shapes she carved on the back of a coal lorry. Just 30,602 of us were left at the end, all zombies.

In *Peyton Place* the schoolteacher Elsie Thornton says: 'A person doesn't always get what they deserve.' That was true of Hibs in 1979 but, regarding the Scottish Cup, as we staggered away from Hampden for the last time, we were less inclined to believe this from *War and Peace*: 'Everything comes in time to him who knows how to wait.'

137

'MON THE CABBAGE!

NAT KING Cole, Jeremy Hunt, J. Arthur Rank, our own Shereen Nanjiani and Gary Glitter, just some of the famous folk who've had their names taken in vain for the purposes of rhyming slang. (Well, you can't take Glitter's name any more in vain than he's taken it himself, but you get my drift. It's the Glitter Band I feel sorry for. Not every pop group sounded great coming out of the tinny first-gen Easter Road public address, but these double-drumming blow-dried tassel-armed thugs always did.)

Previously there was an innocence to the rhymes. Many came from the world wars and periods of privation. There was a gentle humour to them while reflecting the modesty of people's lives. Presumably it was during such a period that cabbage and ribs enjoyed popularity as a dish and presumably it was around the same time that Hibs acquired their nickname.

''Mon the Cabbage!' I first heard the shout when my father and I moved from Easter Road's old centre stand to the main terracing directly across the pitch. It was the regular exhortation of a man, older than Dad, whom we stood alongside for years. Dad would chat to him about this and that but mostly football and I don't think we ever knew his name. Then one Saturday he wasn't in his usual spot and we never saw him again.

Formalised as Cabbage & Ribs, the nickname is obviously a handy rhyme, but you can make it suit the club. In those poverty-stricken early days in Little Ireland there may only have been the leafy green veg plus some scraggy cuts of meat secreted underneath. Dessert? No, you'd have to sneak across town and hope that a jam tart had fallen from the table of a member of the Hearts-supporting boss class.

Unfortunately, though, this may not be the optimum moment to be shouting about leafy green veg. Liz Truss spoiled it for all varieties during her disastrous premiership when the *Daily Star* predicted a lettuce would outlast her, that she'd be booted from No. 10 before mould set it, and the paper called it right.

138

UP PERISCOPE TO TORPEDO THE CHAMPIONS LEAGUE SUPREMACISTS

EVERY NOW and again my children will stop Snapchatting and TikToking and Instagramming and watching other people watching other people play Minecraft and they'll say to me:

'Daddy-o, put down your newspaper and turn off your record player and tell us a story about media in olden times.'

'How far back do you want to go?'

'Further than tin cans on strings!' yells one. Another: 'No, further than bonfires on hillsides! Daddy-o, what was Periscope?'

Actually, kids, Periscope dated from the twenty-tens. Jargon-wise it was a 'mobile teleportation service'. Hibbies didn't invent it but they exploited it to the fullest, at the same time sticking two fingers to 'The Man', in football's case Gianni Infantino of UEFA who was attempting to dictate which games we watched.

Hibs had been relegated but were far from diminished. They drew big crowds, claimed international caps and knocked top-flight teams out of the League Cup. In 2016 a Scottish Cup tie against Hearts went to an Easter Road replay. I queued for three hours on a cold and frosty morning to buy one of the last tickets and there were many turned away disappointed. Never mind, TV will show it. Oh no they won't, declared UEFA. There would be no other matches screened which could potentially lure armchair fans away from – all praise! – the Champions League. On this particular evening the competition featured Chelsea, Paris Saint-Germain and Zenit Saint Petersburg in a private contest over who possessed the least amount of heritage but the most amount of money.

Periscope was founded by an enterprising American called Kayvon Beykpour. He got the idea for a live video screening app after a visit to Istanbul when the city was suddenly hit by civic unrest. He could read about the demos on Twitter but not see footage, despite being pretty certain that countless camera phones at the location would have been recording the protests.

What a great name for his gizmo which for Hibbies of a certain age would have evoked memories of Sunday afternoons gripped by wartime movies on TV, one of which was actually called *Up Periscope*.

It would have been a younger generation who filmed the tie that night. They might have lacked the unshakable calm and grace under pressure of, say, Kenneth More or John Mills in the midst of crisis on the high seas as they struggled to stay focused on the play during the constant pie runs. But the interruptions, noises off and general tumult captured with shoogly lens work made for the visceral excitement of a punk rock gig compared with the bombastic blah-blah of most TV coverage of football.

The Easter Road periscopers attracted 10,000 viewers, half the size of the crowd in the stadium, but when Hibs and Hearts reconvened there in the same competition 12 months later, for another replay blacked out by the big, bad, bullying Champions League, there was a tenfold increase in the audience – enraptured like first time round by a stirring victory.

139

LIKE SMASHING THROUGH ICE FOR A PENGUIN DINNER

FROM THE pitcher's mound 60ft 6ins away, a baseball hurtling at 90mph takes 0.4 seconds to reach the home plate. The hitter only has half of that tiny, tiny moment to check the arrangement of the throwing fingers – to register whether he's facing a cutter, a curveball, a slider or a change-up – and decide if he's going for the shot. And the other half of that tiny, tiny moment to swing his bat.

I'm listening to the New York Mets' first baseman Pete Alonso describe the day job on Netflix's hunting reality show *MeatEater*. He's a keen outdoorsman and presumably the mule deer he goes after in Colorado must liken their confrontations to baseball when the intended prey scrutinise Alonso's trigger action in a similarly microscopic way.

My interest in Alonso is his nickname – The Polar Bear. I'm sure he's brilliant at his chosen sport, but the moniker doesn't really fit. Not when compared to Conrad Logan.

Alonso's hair is blond but Logan's is almost snowy white. Alonso is a sizable unit but Hibs' Scottish Cup hero blots out the sun. And the clincher is Logan's day job – he's a goalkeeper. You don't see too many polar bears wielding lumber – the slang term for a baseball bat – but the way the Irishman plunged to scoop up a shot with his giant paws was just like one of these magnificent creatures smashing through a layer of ice for dinner, either penguin or baby seal.

The number of times I've been properly awestruck at a game probably amounts to just three. The first would have been 1972 in the Scottish Cup, the semi-final replay, showing we could beat the big, bad bogeymen of Rangers, in Glasgow, in a meaningful game, actually playing them off the park. It was a sensational football insurrection and surely the beaks were never going to allow us to get away with it. But they did.

The second was being relegated by Hamilton Accies in 2014 when a two-nil lead from the play-off's away leg turned to dust or more specifically mud as apocalyptic rain hammered on to the West Stand roof and the thunder cracks spooked the players before the manager, Terry Butcher, was swept away and right out of Easter Road.

And then there was Conrad. For the semi-final in 2016, Hibs needed an emergency goalie, the regular one having been suspended following a search for a contact lens which went on far too long for the ref's liking. Where do a club find these guys? In the Yellow Pages next to emergency joiners? An emergency joiner will board up a great gaping hole in the side of your house. Against Dundee United, Logan battened down his goal and rendered it watertight without the need for MDF; he simply used his sheer bulk.

I'll never forget my first glimpse of him, fielding cross balls in the warm-up. It was exactly the same as everyone else's first glimpse because to the Hampden crowd he was a complete unknown beyond the sparsest of career detail, the most grabby of which was that he hadn't played a game for 16 months.

What a fine figure of a man. Okay, so screaming fluorescent yellow perhaps wasn't the most flattering attire and, yes, there seemed to be some activity ongoing in the moob area. But it didn't matter that he could have been – back to joinery – carrying timber. That, as the opposition fans' chanting intimated, in Tayside-ese, he was chief suspect for having eaten all the *pehs*.

Dundee United fired cutters, curveballs, sliders and change-ups at Logan. The good ship *Discovery* was recommissioned and fitted with cannons to aim broadsides. Oor Wullie mustered a catapult army and Desperate Dan converted the dustbin he used to smoke through a drainpipe into a bazooka for a last, desperate assault, all to no avail. What a performance by the Polar Bear, right up there as one of the greatest individual displays in our 150-year history.

140

A TRADITIONAL SCOTTISH SPONGE CAKE

FOR THOSE too young to have seen the Famous Five play, Willie Ormond was probably the most conspicuous in later life. Certainly among the wider football public. While Eddie Turnbull was 15 years a leading club boss, most of the time he would only be glimpsed in the dugout, back when the manager's berth really was hewn from the earth. The telly cameras rarely cut to halfway for the reaction shots which are so familiar now and there were no fly-in-the-linament docs following every team talk and capturing every swearie word, which in Ned's case was probably just as well.

No, it would be Wee Willie in charge of Scotland with the benefit of internationals being shown live and him sat watching the play as if parked for the evening in his favourite wheezing armchair: Brylcreemed hair, suit of RAF blue or crackly nylon sports fatigues with his little pot belly protruding, gnomic and not moving, not crouched on haunches like today's coaching maestros demonstrating Zen contemplativeness and gluteal muscle control, nor running along touchlines or booting water bottles or smashing seats.

Oh, Wee Willie, we can't quite imagine you with a ball at your feet, Hibs' left flank your 'hood for the glory years, but thankfully your good friend Ned will help. In his memoir Turnbull compares and contrasts the Five's wide men, Gordon Smith's poise, elegance and artistry with Ormond as 'a different kind of winger altogether. He would run straight at a defence, his direct approach unsettling opponents. He was clever, but he only had one way to beat a man. Everybody in the game knew that but still couldn't do anything about it, which was to charge up to the full-back and lift the ball over his outstretched leg and skip away, leaving the defender floundering. And Willie was such a lovely crosser of the ball.'

In another way, Turnbull could have been detailing a cake recipe – traditional-seeming Scottish sponge but made up of elusive ingredients with a wow factor topping – although maybe that could apply to other members of the Five as well.

The skill set was developed at Stenhousemuir and brought to Easter Road in November 1946. 'A few minutes before midnight,' reported the next day's edition of Edinburgh's *Evening News*, 'Mr Harry Swan, chairman, and Mr Willie McCartney, manager, left Ochilview with the signature of the clever outside left, W. Ormond.' He was the only member of the quintet to cost money – £1,200.

Ormond scored on his debut at Queen of the South and the following week in his first game at Easter Road a last-minute equaliser against Rangers in front of 41,378. In all, and despite three leg breaks, there would be 133 goals with Ormond remaining a Hibee after the others had stopped. He also contributed countless assists – almost fetishised nowadays, not tallied back then. His left foot in modern football parlance would be described as a 'wand', but the man himself would probably deem that much too pretentious.

He was Wee Willie from Fisherrow who would lead a great Scotland side to the World Cup and come back unbeaten. Before the tournament, to gain an insight into the workings of this modest, couthie fellow, the *Sunday Times* treated him to lunch at an expensive restaurant. 'Crivvens,' he remarked, 'here's me eating fish on a Monday.'

141

SCOTTISH CUP FINAL, 2012 (AAGH!)

OKAY, IT'S a cheap trick. Instead of talking about something you don't want to talk about, talk round it. As a stalling tactic, bring up another thing completely unrelated, beyond the fact it happened on the same day and at the same time.

Yes, I know: hackneyed, desperate and rather childish. Like sticking your fingers in your ears and going: 'La la la la la . . .' But come on, where's the compassion? This was the derby of derbies and results-wise the worst of the worst. After the 47th minute when Hearts scored their third goal – or for the insanely optimistic the 50th when they scored their fourth – no Hibs fan wanted to be at Hampden any more. So where could they have gone instead?

This may seem a bit of a stretch, even for aesthetes, but how about the Hayward Gallery in London and an exhibition billed as the first in Britain to 'explore emptiness'. The show was previewed in newspapers on the day of the final. Hibbies over breakfast who read about the picture frames with nothing inside would probably have laughed. Later, though, they might have wished to be standing in front of them, desperately trying to lose themselves in the void.

Being a day they so desperately wanted erased from the calendar, the shell-shocked could have found succour in another exhibit, the movie shot without any film in the camera. Oh that all the Hampden cameras were similarly disabled, ruining the commemorative DVD souvenir market for Jambos.

'It is not a joke,' stressed the Hayward's director, Ralph Rugoff, of *Invisible: Art about the Unseen*. Hailing it as 'conceptual' and 'sublime', he added: 'This is the best exhibition you will never see.'

Maybe on any other day the show would seem like modern art at its most ludicrous, but not on 19 May 2012. I can imagine Hibbies rushing to self-lobotomise by squinting into the great, arid blankness. Anything would be better than being forced to watch the procession – no, cortège – of Hearts goals. Even nothing.

Maybe eyes would have turned bloodshot and veins in foreheads would have burst open as the Leith contingent struggled to pinpoint even the merest hint of a curvy outline in Tom Friedman's work 'Erased Playboy Centrefold'. Maybe a title like that was piling cruelty on top of torture. Still, infinitely preferable to the horrors of Hampden.

All of Gianni Motti's 'paintings' in the exhibition were created with invisible ink which is typical of this Italian artist who delights in the subversive. Not only does he blow up preconceptions, Motti has claimed responsibility for earthquakes. He's commemorated his own funeral which, in the wake of post-traumatic derby disorder, might have sparked a trend. He's also masqueraded as a professional footballer and on 19 May 2012 that was definitely a stunt much copied.

142

A DREAM GOAL, MYTHICAL AND SMITHICAL

IN A club wrapped in so many folk tales, we almost need VAR to draw the lines and sort out fact from fiction, the dream-like from the dream on. There's a goal scored by Hibs' greatest-ever player that's mythical, indeed Smithical. Gordon Smith when he went sensationally solo. The ball never touching the ground from halfway line to opposition box, head, shoulders, knees and toes, knees and toes, before being thrashed high into the net.

Down the slope, down the right wing, the crowd following the bouncing ball like it was tapping out the rhythm for an old movie singalong. My father witnessed the goal, recreated it for me using the kitchen condiments umpteen times, always adding another bounce. I'd think to myself: 'Come on, Dad. I know that besides having the same name you looked a bit like Gordon Smith. I know that's why you added the W. to your name to avoid any confusion. I know too that you really enjoyed the confusion. But by profession you're a teller of tales. That scar on your neck didn't really come in a sword fight because these weren't a thing in the Second World War.' So did that goal really happen? 'Oh yes,' he said. 'And I'm pretty sure it was against Airdrie.'

Later in life my father got to know Jim Souness who had the most thankless task in football as Smith's deputy for when the celestial being was injured and he remembered a goal like this, perhaps not with as many bounces and with the ball not staying airborne throughout, but couldn't be sure of the opposition. Clyde perhaps? The history books record a Smith slalom begun on halfway against the Bully Wee in October 1953, finishing with a shot from an impossible angle. And in December 1955, in a 6–3 win over Dundee, another wonder goal.

By then the Famous Five had started to break up but their peak years had featured foreign tours and challenge matches in England, treating others to Smith's transcendental talents. In April 1949 in a friendly at Tottenham Hotspur, for one of the strikes in a 5–3 win, he left three defenders with twisted blood and probably intestines arranged to spell 'G.S.' Spurs immediately tried to buy him. The bid was £35,000 – big money for the era – but as with the avid interest from Manchester United, Arsenal and Newcastle United it was rebuffed.

Only *three* men? Had Smith agreed to play hopping on one leg or something? Against Motherwell in November 1947 he scored what he rated his best-ever goal. 'My team-mates told me I beat seven of their guys,' he said. 'I couldn't do anything wrong that day.'

Sadly there were no cameras present and precious little footage of Smith exists. So fans' memories, rather than lie dormant, can ferment and bubble, causing light-headedness, tampering with veracity. Ball juggling like that is the preserve of comic strip footballers, half-time interlude jesters and Sly *'Escape to Victory'* Stallone massively overdramatising what's physically possible in football for a Hollywood ending. Did Dad really see that goal?

Another who worshipped Smith was Douglas Cromb. As a boy he stalked his idol in Edinburgh's Saughton Park – 'Me and my pals would follow him so we could say we'd walked in his footsteps.' Cromb became Hibs chairman and the obsession didn't dim. He told me: 'I was lucky enough to get to know Gordon. We had lunch not long before he died and I said to him: "There's something I need to know." "Ask me," he said. "Was there a game when you dribbled right down the slope, playing keepy-uppy all the way – or did I imagine it?" "No, that happened," he said. "Then I popped the ball into the air for a header only for the goalie to punch it away."'

This was probably the week after the Motherwell game when Third Lanark were crushed 8–0. So was Smith mortal after all? Maybe not. In this match he netted five – a Scottish record for a winger never bettered.

143

CAN YOU PLAY ANOTHER WAY? STOP THIS BUNKER-BUSTING?

IT SEEMS more than coincidence that Hibs have had not one but two former England B caps as managers who'd been commanding Celtic centre-backs but in the dugout were almost invisible.

That's not a criticism, far from it. I revelled in the time of Tony Mowbray and the time of Alan Stubbs. These were quiet, soulful characters, though that's just about every boss there's been at Easter Road compared with Neil Lennon (big fan of him, too). These guys did not love the sound of their own voice, or David Brent's voice, like Lee Johnson. They did not start spats, and when others tried to start spats with them, Craig Levein in Mowbray's case and Mark Warburton in Stubbs's case, they were shocked.

My favourite Mowbray moment actually came from his time in charge of Celtic later. It was his first Old Firm game as a boss and, interviewing him before kick-off, one of that fixture's meeja fluffers tried to get him to talk up, praise to the heavens, consecrate Celtic vs Rangers as the key to the meaning of life. Oh I don't know, he said, isn't it just another game?

Some fans need to see jumping up and down on the touchline, the managerial equivalent of kissing the badge. There are bosses who will show off, unable to resist trapping a misdirected pass hurtling towards them. There are managers who, when a goal is scored, gather their assistants for bouncy hugging like schoolgirls on exam results day. This pair weren't willing to do any of this, it just wasn't their style, Stubbs preferring to keep his own counsel in the dugout, sipping tea.

But they both got Hibs, got the need for flair. Mowbray inherited a clutch of excitable, exciting kids and let them loose. Stubbs had the harder job: relegation turned supporters grumpy as hell and almost mutinous and, after the disaster of a supposed sure thing in Terry Butcher, this was his first gig. Oh, and by the way: complete rebuild required.

'Desperate' – that was how Stubbs summed up the mood of Easter Road when we met in August 2014, just after his first game in charge. 'I encountered a club at its lowest ebb.' Eyes were fixed on the floor, voices were monotone murmurs. Though they accepted some culpability for Hibs' downfall, the players did not like the football Butcher made them play. It was – euphemism alert – direct. The ball was regularly booted so high above the cloud line it must have come back down with bunker-busting force. Could they play another way? Yes please. In that first game away to Rangers, the passing was quick, slick, bold – and low-level. Stubbs told me this would be his style for as long as he remained in management.

He recruited well and in some areas, like midfield, brilliantly. He couldn't quite get the team out of the Championship and maybe, if 21/5/16 hadn't happened, he wouldn't have been allowed a third go. He failed at his next two clubs where maybe more prosaic methods were needed. But – and what a qualifying statement, few coming as close over these 150 years – he won Hibs the Scottish Cup.

As a player Stubbs had to battle testicular cancer. The first game in his Celtic comeback was at Easter Road. Hibbies sang his name that night and he's never forgotten it. The chant of 'Stubbsy, Stubbsy' will echo round Leith whenever he returns.

144

THE PROTOTYPE HEAVY LIFTER, DISCOVERED BY JIMMY SHAND

SCOTLAND AS depicted on a shortbread tin lid, there's a corny old movie called *Geordie* about a Highland laddie, skinny-malink at first, who enrols in a Charles Atlas-type bodybuilding correspondence course and after many tartan-flecked trials and tribulations, throws the hammer for Olympic gold. It always makes me think of Des Bremner.

The stories of Geordie MacTaggart and Bremner, the Highland laddie who shot furthest from Hibs and became a European Cup winner, are not completely identical. Bremner wasn't a weakling as a kid and indeed aged ten was fast-tracked into his school's under-15s team.

But Bremner's yarn is, if anything, more couthie than the film, more romantic. His Aberdeenshire village is Aberchirder. 'Just three streets, nickname Foggieloan, which everyone shortens to Foggie so I'm a Foggie loon,' he told me. The headmaster who spotted his talent was – like the heedrum-hodrum godhead – called Jimmy Shand.

And best of all, no mail order chest expanders here, Bremner built up his strength and stamina on his dad Sandy's farm with a back-story the film missed. 'I've got three brothers and we all had to help out Father, evenings and weekends. It was hard, hard work and I don't think any of us fancied taking over the farm from him. With hill cattle you have to do a heck of a lot of chasing. And in wintertime the tractor pulling their hay would only get so far up the road and we'd have to strap the bales to our backs and climb through the deep snow to feed them.'

After Foggie, Edinburgh for Bremner was a great, steaming metropolis with – oh the decadence – discotheques lurking beyond the city centre and in one of them he would meet his wife. After just a handful of reserve games he was suddenly the ten-year-old playing with the big boys again: John Brownlie had broken his leg and right at the start of 1973, Turnbull's Tornadoes urgently needed a replacement full-back.

He pretty much stayed in the team after that but would be moved up into the midfield where his incredible energy was vital alongside the creatives, Ally MacLeod and Ralph Callachan. And he must have felt like he'd never left Foggie: still climbing hills, still feeding languid creatures.

Bremner was heavy lifting before the term ever came into football usage. When he left at the decade's end – for Euro glory with Aston Villa – my father remarked how Hibs would need three men to cover for him and all his thankless tasks. Relegation immediately followed.

145

THE *TRAINSPOTTING* TEAM HAD THEIR OWN EXCLUSIVE-USE STATION

IT WAS the end of the line for trains serving Loch Lomond in 1950 when a number of Highland routes also closed. In more upbeat news for the railways, that was the year Hibs opened their very own station.

Honestly, if you're tired of Hibee innovation you're tired of life. The Famous Five era represented peak ambition and imagination. Everyone wanted to see Britain's most exciting team and this was a gesture to smooth the passage of away fans. Far better than shoving them into a 'restricted view' corner of the stadium, vulnerable to bombardment with half-eaten pies and worse.

Easter Road Park Station was situated behind the main terracing. A short walk up some less than bonnie, bonnie banking and you were watching your favourites being ripped apart, as happened to Clyde on 8 April of that year, right after the ceremonial cutting of the ribbon.

There was no station as such. In railway parlance this was a halt. But it was the thought that counted, with the line opening up every other Saturday to siphon football specials from the main network.

Being Edinburgh, though, away supporters were informed: 'You'll have had your return journey.' The service was only one way. Getting home required a walk to Leith Central or other stations where at least there was the opportunity to buy a cup of tea or something stronger.

Still, that Clyde game was notable on the pitch as well as off it. The Bully Wee were hit for six on what was one of those treasured occasions when the Famous Five all scored. The service ran until 1967 but sadly for trainspotters the station has disappeared under new housing.

146

WRONGED WOMAN GETS REVENGE, HELPS SAVE HIBS

IT WAS tense in the boardroom. The oak-panelled walls were sweating as terrifying Tynie telekinesis caused the prizes in the trophy cabinet to shoogle on their plinths. Which way would Sheila Rowland vote?

The first woman to sit on a Scottish football board – more ground broken and another flag planted – Rowland was the ex-wife of the man who'd loaned Thatcherite yuppie David Duff the money to buy Hibs, but in 1990 was promising his 29.9 per cent stake in the embattled club to Wallace Mercer.

In the eyes of the most innocent Hibbies, David Rowland had swapped sides, but he was no football man and business doesn't work like that. Did he think, though, that installing Sheila on the board would help his cause beyond the £1 million he'd reportedly already made from involvement in Easter Road?

Rowland had fathered a child with hairdresser Linda Christy, five years before leaving Sheila to marry his mistress. To outside eyes – and regarding the highly secretive tycoon that's almost everyone – Sheila continuing to have anything to do with him will seem odd. Well, she didn't have anything to do with Hearts' takeover bid.

A successful solicitor specialising in probate, she wasn't ready for Hibs to be declared deceased. 'Sheila fell in love with the club,' Duff remarked later. 'She went to games, travelled on the bus and was in boardrooms around the land.' (Where women were allowed at least; that didn't include Tynecastle.)

There are photographs of the Hibs' pioneering lady director in a green and white shirt – the P&D Windows one – standing with her foot on a ball in front of the Cowshed of blessed memory. Maybe she no longer – cliché alert – looks for our results every Saturday. Most likely she missed the Humphrey Rudge years (actually eight games). But when it came to the crunch on 6 June she defied her ex-husband to side with the campaign repelling Mercer.

An estranged couple at war in a boardroom like this, with the woman refusing to fall into line behind the man who at one time was worth £650 million, seems to be in the spirit of classic Greek drama. Actually, better than that: an episode of 1970s road haulage telly saga *The Brothers* where Jenny votes against Ted on continental expansion, changing axle suppliers or some such gripping issue.

All together now: 'One Sheila Rowland, there's only one Sheila Rowland . . .'

147

CAN ANYONE HERE TONIGHT PLAY CENTRE-FORWARD?

ALAN SHARP, Scotland's greatest screenwriter, penned tough words for tough actors like Burt Lancaster, Gene Hackman and George C. Scott during the 1970s when Hollywood was still making movies for grown-ups. But there was one role he created for himself which never came to pass.

For Scotland internationals he always wore a dark blue shirt underneath his jumper – just in case the Tannoy broadcast the plaintive cry to Hampden's slopes: 'Can anyone here tonight play centre-forward?'

Sharp revealed this to my father when Dad profiled him for TV on a film set in Portugal. During a break in shooting *The Last Run*, there was a five-a-side game among the crew with the wordsmith smashing a goal from far out. He first-footed us one New Year and we took him along to the derby at Easter Road – an appalling nil-nil draw which seemed like further Edinburgh punishment for the man, having had his debut novel banned from the capital's libraries for being too filthy. Really, Sharp missed his time. If he'd been around during Hibs' early struggles he'd have definitely got a game.

In that very first match in 1875 it was Hearts who began three men short. Many clubs, feeling their way in football, functioned seat-of-the-pants. Airdrie turned up at Easter Road a man missing, Rangers cancelled on Hibs after being unable to raise an eleven, but when newly formed Celtic lured away half the team in 1888, secretary Tom Nolan was forced to wade into the crowd and find emergency replacements.

Three honorary Hibees were needed for a home match against Leith Athletic, a pair of proxies made up the numbers at Albion Rovers and then away to Glasgow's Linthouse, could Hibs muster four A.N. Others? A Linthouse reserve volunteered, joined by two from other local clubs, spectators for the day and so presumably dressed in suits and ties. But the best that could be said for James Kerr was that he was willing. The game proved too hectic and, thoroughly knackered, he had to be carted off the field.

But he served. We would all be James Kerr if we could, do what he did if the call came, as it sounded around Scotland during the First World War when the regular guys were away fighting. For how many times, even as grown men, have we fantasised about even just a ten-minute cameo? And how many times, when an open goal has been missed most horribly, have we groaned: 'I could have scored that!'?

Just to be out there, before a full house – what must that feel like? I'm not sure the fan behind the most thrilling terracing intervention I've ever witnessed could tell us, but he had the whole crowd rooting for him. It was another New Year derby at Easter Road, 35,393 present and I reckon, 35,391 minus my little brother and me, still under the influence from the night before. The most stocious hadn't been summoned by a desperate manager and indeed it was half-time; the teams were back in the dressing rooms. But a slaloming stagger-run from halfway, *sans* ball, was greeted with chortling and cheers until from 20 yards out the fellow drew back his foot and let fly with an imaginary shot. Everyone followed the trajectory of the 'ball', everyone was convinced the net bulged, everyone wanted to be that hero.

So let's hear it for James Kerr, the honorary half-hour Hibee.

148

YOU'LL NEVER GUESS MY SECOND TEAM

SOME HIBS fans would claim that water torture wouldn't make them comply, not even if it was to be Bovril instead when the pain would be intensified by the wastefulness. They'd insist they wouldn't crack, not even if they were being interrogated by *Line of Duty*'s Ted Hastings. Not even if they were strapped down like James Bond in *Goldfinger* and a laser was about to slice them in half, starting at the testicles.

Acknowledge Hearts. Go on, do it. Accept their right to be. Dare you. Admit you'd miss them if they were gone. 'No, no!' would be the Hibby wail, and if they remember their George Orwell from school and *Nineteen Eighty-Four*: 'There's this pressure to submit to a modern, touchy-feely, antiseptic, anodyne, woke ideal of football rivalry, otherwise . . . what? I'm going to have my face eaten by rats?

'Do it to Julia!'

Or: do it to Julien Brellier! He was Hearts' psycho enforcer once upon a time, the kind of player opposing fans love to hate. Hibs down the years have had players Jambos loved to hate (though not as many skin graft while-u-wait types). No one really means for there to be rodent-themed demises, but football rivalry has come a long way, or maybe I mean dropped a long way. I am, though, that curious beast: one who started out going to Tynecastle as often as Easter Road.

I was the last of the weekabout generation, a quaint, noble and – yes, these days – laughable tradition. My teenaged son cannot conceive of such a thing. My father, though, was weekabout and while the custom would have been established by the previous generation, it properly took hold for him in the 1950s when it was the Famous Five one Saturday and the Terrible Trio the next. A carnival of football, an orgy, enjoyed by men who never removed their ties.

Post-war privations impacted on the rest of life but not those sensational forward lines. A bunneted cognoscenti was founded and moved carefreely between Leith and Gorgie on trams to pack out the terraces. They will have had a feeling for one team or the other and maybe a passion, but no one was interested in declaring it, or demonstrating a division. After the Second World War, the country had had enough of fighting. Everyone just wanted to get along and enjoy themselves.

For as long as weekabout lasted, I enjoyed Tynecastle. Donald Ford was an active presence in my life, the statue-like Alan Anderson a less active one. Ernie Winchester had a great name, melding Benny Hill with Wyatt Earp though he wasn't the sharpest shot. Eric Carruthers had great hair, making up for Wilson Wood who didn't have much. To adopt a popular Gorgie phrase, I will remember them.

Maybe I didn't enjoy the honk from the nearby breweries – a shock to the nasal passages when you're more accustomed to the smells of Bazooka Joe bubblegum, Airfix glue and Scalextric after an afternoon's high-speed cornering – but even though we're obviously Sydney Sweeney – sexy – and they're *The Sweeney*, and even though we're obviously *Oppenheimer* – grandiose, challenging, deep – and they're *Barbie*, I have no problem saying this: Hearts are my second team.

That might seem a hippie thing to say, a Fotherington-Thomas thing to say (he was the drip in the *Molesworth* books who skipped around chirruping 'Hello clouds, hello sky!'). Straight up, though, it's true. I may love Hibs but, ergo, I don't hate Hearts and certainly didn't hate Ergo Winchester when he ballooned another easy chance over the School End, usually always feeling sorry for him. Admittedly there was no polarising social media back then, but more recently, unlike some, I did not cheer during those moments when Hearts' livelihood was under threat and was not getting ready to dance on their grave.

Hibs need Hearts. Should this state of affairs feel like a bittersweet existence, as if your only vital organ match is with the school bully, then tough. The dung beetle's survival depends on it pushing shit more than 200 times its own body weight. The ring-tailed lemur's conflict-resolution tactic is a stink fight. The defence mechanism of the sea cucumber involves ejecting intestines and other organs out of its anus.

Hearts and all their anuses need Hibs and all theirs just as much so it remains absolutely astonishing that Wallace Mercer ever attempted that takeover which, if successful, would have seen the Hibees disappear. Not everything in life can be parcelled up into a slick business deal. I mean, you wouldn't get the leader of the free world behaving in such a manner, would you? America's president examining one godforsaken hellhole of a warzone and thinking how he could turn it into a beach resort? Or examining another godforsaken hellhole of a warzone and thinking how he could plunder the essential minerals?

149

HE SHOOTS FROM INSIDE A CROWDED BOX, FROM THE ROOF OF THE WILD WEST SALOON

I'VE HIBSED it. Though I wasn't actually on the pitch – just in case Police Scotland haven't quite closed the file on Hampden Park, 21 May 2016 – it is the case that later that night some of the pitch came into my possession.

Not having a garden in which to plant my turf souvenir I popped it in an empty jam jar – damson plum conserve, and yes I know: *so* middle class – screwed the lid tight and . . . of course for the clump of grass there would be *untended* consequences. Nine years of neglect means the soil has long since lost its consistency and turned to dust. This will be the fate of us all, of just about everything connected with the greatest day. Maybe the only thing left will be Anthony Stokes's hair weave, abandoned on the ground, forlorn as roadkill, so clasp those memories tight, Hibbies. It's not clear when the next lot will arrive.

Every 21 May I rewatch the Scottish Cup final, dressed in what I wore that day. The jeans have gone at the crotch and the desert boots have split, but because of the unfortunate divot incident I cannot bring myself to throw them out.

And even though I pretty much know the game off by heart, it still surprises, still terrifies. When Stokes scores in the third minute I still think it's too soon and there's no way we're winning after that kind of senseless provocation. Indeed, when he runs into the fug of red, white and blue smoke I'm still worried he won't come back. That as the "Your defence is terrified" chant rings out, he's actually on fire.

Then, right after Rangers' inevitable equaliser, when Stokesy from far, far away – the Asda car park behind the East Stand at least – fires that rocket which thuds off a post, I still think that's it, that's our tragedy right there, the absolute quintessence of Hibbydom, shoot me now.

Then, right after Rangers' inevitable muscling into the lead, and even after Hibs equalise, when David Gray goes down and doesn't get up, I still think that's the captain's final over and he's not going to be around for, say, a 90+2-minute hoodoo-smashing header or anything of that order.

Then, with Hibs in such a tearing hurry, I still think there's something weirdly wrong about this game, that it's almost as if Rangers are about to let us win, and obviously when that's discovered later, the scandal will be huge.

Then, when the fans rush from the stands, and seem intent on wrecking the joint, I still think that down in the bowels of Hampden the SFA engraver, requiring an extra-strong microscopic eyepiece to etch the improbable sequence of letters beginning 'Hib . . .' will feel a firm hand on his shoulder and be told: 'Scrub that. Just put an asterisk.'

After all these reruns the final should be familiar – over-familiar. Because of that the pace of the game must slow, yes? So why does it seem even faster with every Hibee continually chasing, harassing, niggling, snapping, lunging, haka-ing or who knows maybe haiku-ing in the pinched faces of the Rangers men and winning 30/70 challenges?

And why aren't the entire team drug-tested, alongside somnolent chairman Rod Petrie, who explains away the behaviour of the fans at the final whistle in one word – 'Exuberance' – which no one can remember him ever using before and certainly not in relation to himself?

Why, because for once, in a radical break with tradition, everything is perfect. Perfect backstory of seasonal failure until this moment. Perfect number of PTSD cases from previous

Hampden disasters (Paul Hanlon, Lewis Stevenson). Perfect number of Scots – ten are used on the day – with at least one of them fond of the 'YLT' street-gang greeting whose mum flies a Hibs flag in her front garden guarded by an Alsatian in a green and white neckerchief (Darren McGregor). And, notwithstanding all that, perfect poignancy of this being the first and last time the starting line-up will take the field together.

Also, the perfect loan players combo. The club got the policy hideously wrong in the 2012 final, but Liam Henderson is the most committed, passionate, unloaniest loanee there has ever been. Conrad Logan is only there for eight games but has learned the words to 'Sunshine on Leith'. Let's not forget Niklas Gunnarsson who almost knocked Hibs out of the cup at Tynecastle with what would have been the OG of this or any other season and is poised for the winner if Gray doesn't score. And then there's Stokes.

He's like a western's classically corny anti-hero, the enigmatic gunslinger operating just inside the law who's hired by a fearful town for a perilous mission which will rid it of an old curse. Thus far he's been erratic and seemingly disinterested with conversation not extending much beyond Gary Cooper's 'Yup' and 'Nope', but on the momentous day he shoots at Rangers from absolutely everywhere. From inside a crowded box, from out wide and impossible angles, from the roof of the saloon, from the back of a covered wagon parked up at the general store. They cannot handle him. It is a sensational individual performance, one of the greatest ever in a cup final. Who is this dead-eyed desperado? No one really knows for sure. Then he leaves the town, moseys back, leaves again, this time in mild disgrace.

How very Hibs? Yes, but 21 May 2016 turns out differently. It is epically stressful sitting through the final as if for the first time every year in my knackered old clothes – plus the hair shirt and the head crusher concealed in the bobble hat – but I am a fan, no, an aficionado, of Hibernian FC, and wouldn't have it any other way.

150

TO BE CONTINUED . . .